Making Sense of Motherhood

Becoming a mother changes lives in many ways and this original and accessible book explores how women try to make sense of and narrate their experiences of first-time motherhood in the Western world. Tina Miller pays close attention to women's own accounts, over time, of their experiences of transition to motherhood and shows how myths of motherhood continue because women do not feel able to voice their early (often difficult) experiences of mothering. The book charts the social, cultural and moral contours of contemporary motherhood and engages with sociological and feminist debates on how selves are constituted, maintained and narrated. Drawing on original research and narrative theory, the book also explores the disjuncture that often exists between personal experience and public discourse and the cultural dimensions of expert knowledge.

TINA MILLER is Senior Lecturer in Sociology at Oxford Brookes University. Her publications include journal articles and book chapters on mothering, reproductive health, narratives and methodological issues in qualitative research. She is co-editor of *Ethics in Qualitative Research* (with M. Mauthner, M. Birch and J. Jessop, 2002).

Making Sense of Motherhood

A Narrative Approach

Tina Miller

CAMBRIDGE
UNIVERSITY PRESS

PUBLISHED BY THE PRESS SYNDICATE OF THE UNIVERSITY OF CAMBRIDGE
The Pitt Building, Trumpington Street, Cambridge, United Kingdom

CAMBRIDGE UNIVERSITY PRESS
The Edinburgh Building, Cambridge, CB2 2RU, UK
40 West 20th Street, New York, NY 10011–4211, USA
477 Williamstown Road, Port Melbourne, VIC 3207, Australia
Ruiz de Alarcón 13, 28014 Madrid, Spain
Dock House, The Waterfront, Cape Town 8001, South Africa

http://www.cambridge.org

First published 2005

Printed in the United Kingdom at the University Press, Cambridge

Typeset in 10/12pt Plantin   [PND]

A catalogue record for this book is available from the British Library

Library of Congress Cataloging-in-Publication Data

Miller, Tina, 1957–
    Making sense of motherhood : a narrative approach / Tina Miller.
        p.   cm.
    Includes bibliographical references and index.
    ISBN 0 521 83572 0 (hb : alk. paper) – ISBN 0 521 54364 9 (pb : alk. paper)
    1. Motherhood.   2. Mothers.   I. Title.

    HQ759.M59 2005
    306.874′3–dc22   2004054238

ISBN 0 521 83572 0 hardback
ISBN 0 521 54364 9 paperback

Contents

Dedication

This book is dedicated to my mother and my three beautiful daughters, Hannah, Freya and Lydia. Their lives so full of promise and potential stretch before them; my hope is that in this uncertain world their journeys will be peaceful.

Acknowledgements

In many ways this book echoes my own personal and academic journey to date, and there are many people to thank from along the way. Living in the Solomon Islands provided a rare opportunity to explore different cultural practices and become friends with the warm and friendly people of Munda. Other friendships were later forged in the contrasting circumstances of profound poverty and inspiring determination in Bangladesh, another beautiful country but so often, and unfairly, ravaged by disaster. The people met during these years of living and working in different countries and cultures taught me many lessons and have enabled me to see, and to respect, how other lives are lived. More recently and closer to home, colleagues at Oxford Brookes University have generously supported my research and writing endeavours and I am very grateful for this. Particular thanks are due to Abbey Halcli and John Carter, who read and commented on this book as it took shape. Friends and colleagues in other institutions and other countries have also contributed in a variety of ways, providing critical comment, friendship, encouragement and support. These have included fellow members of the Women's Workshop on Qualitative Research in London, and others in Switzerland, Italy and the USA. Thanks also go to Jane Ribbens-McCarthy and Maxine Birch for years of friendship interspersed with the occasional discussion of weighty, academic matters! Also to Frank for travelling with me and continually providing support and love. But the final thanks go to all the women who shared with me their journeys into motherhood. Without them this book would not have been possible.

Introduction

Becoming a mother changes lives in all sorts of ways and this book explores how a group of women make sense of their journeys into motherhood. The seeds for this book were sown many years ago: probably around the time I left school and spent a year in Canada employed as a 'mother's help' and had my first taste of doing mothering work. University and a degree in sociology were followed by a number of years living and working in different places – the Solomon Islands and Bangladesh – and observing different practices around pregnancy, birth and childrearing. More recently, university posts have involved my teaching sociology to a range of students from different disciplines, including midwives and other health professionals, and somewhere along the line I became a mother myself to three very lovely daughters. This book then emerges from the criss-crossing of threads that have run through my academic and personal life.

The context in which I became a mother is different from that of my mother, or her mother, but many features have also remained constant. For example, even though fertility rates are declining in many countries in the West, a majority of women will still at some point in their lives become mothers and take primary responsibility for the rearing of their children. To this extent little has changed for women over the centuries. But in other ways there have been significant changes. In the UK and the USA the average age of all mothers at childbirth has risen, but is highest for those who are married. Whilst women are increasingly delaying childbirth, in the UK teenage pregnancy is also a feature of patterns of reproduction. For those who delay childbearing – a group who are largely represented in this book – becoming a mother is increasingly a planned event in lives where choice and control are more dominant features. At the same time shifts in family formations and different ways of living mean that informal sources of knowledge and support may no longer be readily available, or as relevant, as families are geographically dispersed and many more women work outside the home. Average family size has also decreased and women have much less opportunity to learn first hand about mothering. In the West, for most women, childbirth is safer than at any time before and yet perceptions of risk lead us to seek out and rely on expert guidance throughout transition to motherhood. This changing context raises questions about the ways in which motherhood experiences are shaped and maternal responsibilities configured in contemporary society.

This book is written with the intention and hope of reaching a wide audience. Although it is written from the discipline of sociology with a broader social science and health professional readership in mind, the kernel of the book interweaves women's own accounts of their multi-faceted journeys into first-time motherhood with contemporary debates. The intention is that the book should engage the academic, the practitioner and, importantly, those for whom being a mother is perhaps a desire, an experience or even a fear: women. At different levels and in different chapters the book both theorises what it means to become a mother in late modernity and explores the experiences of a group of women as they become mothers. This is achieved through the inclusion of their profound, personal accounts produced as their experiences of transition unfolded, and gathered through longitudinal research. The theoretical and empirical threads of the book are prioritised in different ways in different chapters – the theoretical stage is set across the first three chapters and then illustrated with empirical data in the central three chapters and finally returned to in the concluding chapter. Your interests may lie across all the areas covered in the book, but the following sign-posts are provided for those who may have more specific interests and limited time.

As noted above, chapter 1 provides the theoretical, conceptual and methodological framework for the book. It engages with contemporary debates on how human life is storied, reflexivity practised and selves constituted and maintained. The research which provides the materials for the core chapters in the book is also outlined. In chapter 2 the cultural dimensions of birth practices and different constructions of 'authoritative knowledge' are explored. Fieldwork observations from the Solomon Islands and Bangladesh provide a backdrop to this chapter. The focus returns to the West in chapter 3, which charts the medicalisation of reproduction and childbearing, engaging with contemporary feminist debates around mothering and motherhood. In the following three chapters the women's own accounts move centre stage. Chapter 4 focuses on women's experiences of the antenatal (prenatal) period, chapter 5 on the birth and early postnatal period and chapter 6 on the later postnatal period, as their children reach nine months of age. These core chapters focus on how women make sense of their transition to motherhood and the ways in which they narrate their experiences: what can and cannot be said in relation to mothering and motherhood. The theoretical and methodological questions raised across the chapters are drawn together and addressed in chapter 7.

In some chapters you will find key terms used and definitions of these now follow. The book is set within the context of 'late modernity' and this refers to a period that has followed the modern era and is characterised by rapid changes and uncertainty. 'Cultural scripts' refers to 'a specific cultural set of ideas about how events should take place' (Willard, 1988:226). The term 'discourse' is used to mean 'a bounded body of knowledge and associated practices' (Lupton, 1999:15). 'Knowledges' is also used to describe different ways of knowing – non-expert and expert, horizontal and hierarchical (see chapter 2) – and associated practices. Different ways of knowing are underpinned and shaped by different discourses, which can dominate in powerful ways. Similarly, the term 'meta-narrative' (Somers, 1994) is used to describe the traditions in which we are embedded as actors in the social world, these again are shaped by dominant and powerful discourses especially in relation to mothering and motherhood and they will in turn shape the 'ontological narratives' – the personal, individual stories – that we produce. The terms 'mothering' and 'motherhood' are also of course used liberally through-out the book. 'Mothering' refers to the personal, individual experiences that women have in meeting the needs of and being responsible for their dependent children. 'Motherhood' on the other hand refers to the con-text in which mothering takes place and is experienced. The institution of motherhood in the Western world is, then, historically, socially, cultu-rally, politically and, importantly, *morally*, shaped. In turn, it powerfully shapes our experiences as women, whether or not we become mothers, because of the cultural assumptions related to women's desire to be mothers. It also makes it hard to talk about unexpected and/or difficult aspects of new mothering, leading us to conceal what are normal experi-ences and reactions, and so perpetuates the old myths of motherhood.

My own experiences of becoming a mother are also included here because they touch on many of the themes raised in the book. They also range across different countries and cultures. I found out I was pregnant with my first child on a short holiday in the UK whilst living and working in Bangladesh. My pregnancy was confirmed shortly after I had received confirmation that I had also contracted hepatitis A – probably picked up on a trip I had made to Darjeeling shortly before the trip to the UK. The doctor in England who confirmed the diagnosis of hepatitis A prescribed medicine that was contra-indicated for pregnant women, asking as he did so whether I felt pregnant. I replied that having never been pregnant I didn't know what it felt like, but that as I had been trying to conceive there was a possibility that I could be pregnant. This was brushed aside, no pregnancy test offered and the prescription made out. Back in my home town, I revisited my own general practitioner (GP), who two weeks earlier I had seen because of my concern that I was taking some time to conceive. I relayed to him my diagnosis of hepatitis A, and the fact that I was also pregnant. He immediately and without hesitation recommended that the pregnancy be terminated. As far as he was concerned there was no other course of action and he made no attempt to soften the blow, to suggest any alternatives, or to offer any support. I left the surgery numbed and confused. I clearly remember the twisted irony and emotion of telling my mother the news she had long hoped for – that I was pregnant with her first grandchild – and in the next sentence that I couldn't actually have the baby. Deciding to seek a second opinion, I was told that my liver would be in such a bad state from the hepatitis that I would not be able to withstand a general anaesthetic even if I wanted to terminate the pregnancy. I then set about trying to find out as much as I could about hepatitis and pregnancy, writing to the world-renowned London School of Hygiene and Tropical Medicine. I received a very polite reply but I was told that any detailed information could only be given to me via my GP. I returned to Bangladesh to join my partner, pregnant and worried. Four months into the pregnancy, I flew to Bangkok, Thailand for a scan, as part of an arrangement made for British employees in Bangladesh. The state-of-the-art hospital had all the latest equipment but hard as we tried, we could not understand either the fuzzy images on the monitor or the explanations of the doctor; we left feeling even more confused and uncertain. Back in Bangladesh, the American doctor said that because I had hepatitis so early on in my pregnancy the most likely outcome would be that the baby would be born with a limb missing. At just over seven months' pregnant I returned to the UK to await the birth of my baby and during one antenatal (prenatal) visit met an Indian trained obstetrician working in the local National Health Service. He told me that his experience in India suggested that hepatitis was much more of a problem in later pregnancy. The birth was not as I had expected. I soon realised the taped music ('Relax don't do it' by Frankie Goes to Hollywood, cheerfully recorded by my sixteen-year-old sister) would be completely redundant and the Evian spray for my face incredibly annoying! I gratefully accepted a large dose of pethidine (routinely offered at that time) and thought ruefully that none of the books, or anyone else, had described the pain of birth in any ways that came close to what I was feeling. Imagine then my absolute relief when Hannah was finally born with all her limbs, a perfect, pink, warm, wrinkly baby. When she was brought to me from the nursery the next morning (a practice that now seems archaic), it felt like the best Christmas present ever as I cradled the little warm body – something I don't think I had allowed myself to envisage through the months of my pregnancy.

Mothering is of course diverse; it is not a universal experience and yet many mothers (and fathers) will share similar 'struggles, joys, and hopes and dreams for their children' (Chase and Rogers, 2001:xiv). Whilst researching and writing this book I have watched my own daughters grow and sisters and friends become mothers and grandmothers, whilst other friends have made decisions not to become parents. I have witnessed their fears, as births have not gone as planned and new babies have given cause for concern, and their hopes for their children as they have grown. I have watched other friends comfort their children through the loss of a parent, and shared the sadness with my own children at the loss of their grandparents. Even the loss of family pets can require disproportionate amounts of comforting and love. I have celebrated their achievements and commiserated on failures: the highs and the lows, demands and rewards of mothering. Being a mother is clearly filled with mixed emotions and feelings – and hopefully large amounts of love. If we ever doubt the deep and all-encompassing dimensions of this relationship we come to have with our children, we need only imagine the almost unimaginable experience of the loss of a child to confirm its profound, poignant and enduring dimensions.

There are so many caveats that I want to place around what follows in the book. I am aware that the majority of the women whose stories unfold identify themselves as middle-class; they are white and partnered, and live in circumstances that afford them possibilities and choices denied to others. They had mostly planned their pregnancies and all the births went to term and resulted in the births of healthy children. But this allows us to see both similarities and differences in women's lives and experiences of mothering and motherhood. Similarly, when I have presented the findings from the research at academic, practitioner and service user conferences in the UK, mainland Europe and North America, I am always surprised and gratified by the resonance they have for so many different women. Somewhere in the accounts I have presented at these conferences, women in the audience find their own experiences – often tucked away and long unspoken – being voiced. Most importantly then, what lies at the heart of this book are women's personal and profound accounts of their journeys into motherhood.

1 The storied human life: a narrative approach

> I'm doing all the practical things of a mother. But it hasn't actually sunk in, it's like I'm living this part in a play and in fact I'm going through all of the motions, but is it actually reality and is this what motherhood is all about? (Abigail, interviewed eight weeks after the birth of her first child)

This book explores women's journeys into motherhood in late modernity. It brings together research carried out in the UK and fieldwork observations from Bangladesh and the Solomon Islands in order to illuminate women's experiences of becoming mothers and motherhood. In many Western societies patterns of reproduction discernible in previous generations, and practices associated with childbearing, have changed. Increasingly, if women choose to become mothers at all, they come to motherhood either much earlier in their lives as teenage mothers, or later once careers have been established, in partnerships or alone. These changes in timing and frequency of childbearing have been mirrored by changes in the meanings ascribed to, and women's experiences of, motherhood. Becoming a mother changes lives in all sorts of ways. It has major significance for individual biographies, yet expectations and experiences will be shaped by the social and cultural contexts in which women live their lives. Indeed there is some irony that women becoming mothers can experience their transition as confusingly uncertain and risky at a time when biomedical, expert knowledge has apparently provided greater scientific certainty than at any time before. By focusing on women's experiences of transition to motherhood in contemporary society we can see the ways in which the biological is overlaid by the social and cultural in the Western world: and how motherhood is differently patterned and shaped in different contexts. In addition, by taking a narrative approach, the ways in which women make sense of and narrate their experiences of transition to motherhood in late modern society can also be explored. The particular social, cultural and, importantly, moral contexts which underpin contemporary motherhood simultaneously shape what can and cannot be voiced in relation to experiences of being a mother and associated responsibilities. This chapter will provide the theoretical, conceptual and methodological framework for the book. This will involve engaging with contemporary debates on how human life is storied and selves constituted and maintained. In relation to mothering and motherhood this requires us to tread a tricky path that on the one hand engages with 'fleshy, sensate bodies' and at the same time avoids the ever-present risk of falling 'back into essentialism' (Jackson and Scott, 2001:9).

Researching women's lives

This book is written as debates continue about the relevance of feminisms to women's lives in the early twenty-first century. The topic of mothering and motherhood is an area of social research that has greatly benefited from a range of feminist contributions, not least identifying it as an area worthy of scrutiny. Most importantly, it was earlier feminist research, debate and argument that led to the mapping out of the contested terrain of mothering and motherhood (Firestone, 1971; Rich, 1977; Chodorow, 1978; Oakley, 1979, 1980; Ruddick, 1980; Davis-Floyd, 1992; Ribbens, 1994). These writers questioned the social processes that framed motherhood in particular ways and challenged assumptions of biological determinism and essentialist readings of the self. More recently others have charted the contours of continuing scholarly work on theorising motherhood and women's experiences of mothering (Arendell, 2000; Chase and Rogers, 2001), whilst others have critically explored new reproductive technologies and the ways in which scientific 'advancements' and their management continue to produce new challenges for women and their bodies (Stanworth, 1987; Rapp, 2000). The invidious ways in which women continue to be defined and labelled according to different types of mothers – 'good', 'bad', 'single', 'lesbian' – has also been recently noted (Garcia Coll *et al.*, 1998). Given this context, I believe there is no question about the continued relevance of feminisms to women (and men's) lives today. Gendered assumptions and stereotypes continue to shape experiences and knowledge claims, for example in relation to parenting, whilst structural and material inequalities prevail. In view of this, the question is not about whether feminisms are relevant in the twenty-first century, but rather how they can fail to be relevant. This book then is written as a result of my work as a feminist researcher. I position myself in this way because of my concern, noted elsewhere, 'with conducting research about neglected aspects of women's lives, grounded in their own experiences and from a particular theoretical and methodological perspective' (Birch *et al.*, 2002:3). I acknowledge that there is breadth in the term 'feminist' but share with other feminists an 'interest in the interplay between public, social knowledge and private and personal lived experiences' (Birch *et al.*, 2002:3). In this book, I explore the ways in which the constructions and reconstructions of individual narrative trajectories of transition to motherhood are contingent on the societal framing of contemporary motherhood. This approach brings into focus new mothers' everyday experiences of becoming mothers and motherhood, and enables us to see the gaps between expectations and experiences: how things should be and how they are currently configured and experienced. For as Chase and Rogers have recently noted 'it is only when we pay close attention to mothers' everyday experiences are we [*sic*] informed enough to contribute to discussions about how motherhood *should be* socially constructed' (2001:xx, emphasis added). In the following sections current debates concerning narrative, selves and approaches to collecting ontological self-narratives are explored.

Narrative

I became increasingly interested in the function that narratives were perceived to serve as my research interests unfolded. A key interest centred on how women strategically constructed and voiced narratives, drawing on the cultural and social knowledges that constitute 'meta narratives' (Somers, 1994). This was particularly apparent in relation to women presenting a particular version of their selves for example as a 'good' or 'coping' new mother, and the ways in which this was culturally patterned. Traditionally, narrative has been a concern more readily associated with philosophy, literary and linguistic traditions. However, a turn to narrative is now clearly discernible within the social sciences (Plummer, 1995). This interest, in part, can be attributed to the increased interest within the social sciences in subjectivity and the meanings attributed by individuals to their actions. The study of narrative is one attempt at coming to terms with how social identity and, in turn, social action, are constituted and guided. This linking of identity and action, the ontological condition of social life, has challenged earlier thinking around narrative as merely textual, non-theoretical representation. It has also contributed to the considerable debates on how selves are constituted and maintained in late modernity. The focus then has shifted to take account of the way in which human life is storied. As Lieblich *et al.* (1998) have observed, 'we know or discover ourselves, and reveal ourselves to others, by the stories we tell' (1998:7). Narrative then can help us to understand social life and social practices. This is achieved by bringing together dimensions of narrative, for example social action, historicity, temporality and relationality, which in the past have been often overlooked and which a focus on transition to motherhood enables us to explore. Through the construction and reconstruction of narrative accounts, using devices such as emplotment (Corradi, 1991; Somers, 1994), events are brought together as episodes and a life is given unity and coherence. In practice, of course, unity and coherence may give way to (usually) temporary 'bafflement' as people struggle with 'chaos' in their lives (Frank, 1995). But the important point is that as individuals we are 'not only the actor, but also the author' (MacIntyre, 1981:198) as we travel through and make sense of our lives.

Past philosophical debates around narrative have been concerned with how human life is storied. Contributing to these debates, Alasdair MacIntyre comments that 'human life is composed of discrete actions which lead nowhere, which have no order; the storyteller imposes on human events retrospectively an order which they did not have while they were lived' (MacIntyre, 1981:199). Life then is not lived as a neat, chronologically ordered series of events. Rather, as actors we are able, through narrative construction and reconstruction, actively to impose some order, some intelligibility on events, retrospectively. Devices such as plot enable the individual to weave accounts into continuous and intelligible stories (Ricoeur, cited in Valdes, 1991). Clearly, then, being able to produce intelligible and culturally recognisable and acceptable accounts of events is an important feature of the storied human life. We use these accounts both to make sense of our own experiences and to present ourselves in particular and strategic ways to others. Yet some life events and life transitions may challenge our ability to do so: becoming a mother and early experiences of motherhood are such events.

The more recent claims that narrativity is more than a method of representation lead us to consider further the links between individuals and their actions. To talk in terms of the construction and reconstruction of narrative accounts implies a distancing of individuals from their actions and does not sufficiently address the notions of an individual's intention and accountability. Yet intention refers to the individual as a competent social actor with ideas and aspirations, who possesses the ability to 'move purposively in the world' (Stephenson, 1999:114). If we are to understand an individual's behaviour and the narratives he/she construct then these need to be considered within the context of longer- and shorter-term intentions and ordered both causally and temporally. Accountability for action is also linked to intention. For example, MacIntyre has argued that we can ask an individual 'to give an intelligible narrative account enabling us to understand how he [*sic*] could at different times and different places be one and the same person and yet be so differently characterised'

(1981:202). We can understand narrative history and 'narrative truth' (Lieblich *et al.*, 1998:8), then, through an understanding of intention and context. Yet human life is both fragile and unpredictable. The potential for the discontinuity of a narrative account, both in terms of making sense of experiences to oneself, and producing accounts for others, is ever present. For example, when experiences do not match predicted expectations or marry with intentions, an individual's ability to produce and sustain a coherent, culturally recognisable and socially acceptable narrative may be challenged. It is through the device of narrative *re*construction – the revisiting and reordering of past experiences – that long-term 'bafflement', or narrative lapse can usually be avoided and continuity be maintained/regained. Yet self-reflexivity is key here, for as Frank has pointed out, 'those who are truly living the chaos cannot tell in words. To turn the chaos into a verbal story is to have some reflexive grasp' (1995:98). We will return to explore the contours of reflexivity later in this chapter and in chapter 7.

In seeking to understand how individuals make sense of disruptive or transitional events in their lives, the role of narrative retelling has been recognised as an important enterprise in which 'individuals actively shape and account for biographical disruption' (Reissman, 1990:1196). Yet we are not isolated actors but make sense of events and construct narrative accounts in relation to past experiences and future expectations, and importantly in relation to other social actors. Narratives are, then, interpersonally and interactionally constructed. As individuals we are guided in our storytelling by reference to multi-faceted cultural scripts, which provide the contours of particular ways of knowing (see chapter 2). Actors, then, are limited in their narrative construction and reconstruction and make sense of their experiences from, and within, particular locations in the social world. Somers points to the important interplay between meta-narratives, which shape our actions, and the stories that we produce individually. She points out that 'stories guide action' and the social and cultural contexts in which we live will offer us 'an ultimately limited repertoire of available social, public and cultural narratives' (1994:614). The implications of this are that particular ways of knowing may be privileged over others. These may be 'contested politically and will depend in large part on the distribution of power' (*ibid.*:629). In the case of reproduction and motherhood the shifts that have occurred in the management and place of birth and the role of biomedicine in many Western societies show how particular stories can come to dominate and shape practices and expectations. Where biological 'facts' are also a facet of the stories that shape practices, as in the example of childbearing, the power of particular ways of knowing can appear incontrovertible.

Narratives, then, exist at different levels. They are individual stories emanating from personal experience and reinterpreted and reconstructed over time and in different contexts. They are also collective stories of discernible groups in wider society, which provide the contours of the available and, importantly, acceptable cultural scripts. It is important then to note the cultural dimensions of narratives. The cultural embedding of narrative accounts has been emphasised in the work of such theorists as MacIntyre (1981), Ricoeur (1981) and Barthes (1977), and is explored further in the next chapter. In his work on illness narratives, Kleinman (1988) too has emphasised the importance of cultural belief systems that are reflected in narrative accounts and the need to be sensitive to these.

It is argued, then, that as human beings we are storytelling animals. We act with intention and purpose and make sense of past experiences, present and future hopes and expectations, in relation to particular historical, cultural and social contexts. And it is this ability that 'provides us with an identity – a sense of existing through time and of acting purposively in the world' (Stephenson, 1999:114). Taking a narrative approach in the study of subjective experience, then, enables the researcher to access and explore individual identities: the ways in which social actors *actively* produce narrative accounts and present their selves to others. This approach, however, raises further questions about, and throws light on, the ways in which identities and 'the self' are constituted and maintained, situated and narrated. Theoretical positions in relation to debates on the self have ranged across contested terrain, from those grounded in essentialist arguments of a pre-existent, core self, through liberal humanist arguments of a disembodied and disembedded self, to postmodernist positions and the 'death of the subject' (Butler, 1990, 1993; Griffiths, 1995; Evans, 2003). Feminist contributions have noted the tenuous, changing and fragmented dimensions of the self and emphasised the importance of situating the self (Benhabib, 1992; Stanley, 1993). Life events, such as the onset of chronic illness or becoming a mother, provide opportunities to explore the ways in which selves are constituted and maintained. These enable us to see how individuals make sense of periods of biographical disruption and personal transition. A focus on the constituents of a life, narrative, identity and the self, reveals the complex interplay, fluidity and ultimately precarious nature of these components.

Selves

Debates concerning the self and social interactions have provided an enduring area of interest in the social sciences. The relationship between language and the self was first explored in the classic work of Mead (1934). Mead argued that the mind and self were not pre-existent, but emerged through language and in relation to interactions with others. Goffman, too, made a major contribution to debates on the self. His detailed analysis of social interactions enabled him to make claims about the ways in which the self is socially constructed (Goffman, 1969). In his work, Goffman revealed the ways in which we are able to present a particular self in particular settings using 'impression management' to manage performances. He drew attention to the 'all-too-human' task of staging a performance and concluded that the self 'is a *product* of a scene that comes off, and is not a *cause* of it' (Goffman, 1969:245). A more recent reading of this work draws attention to a duality of self that is implicit in Goffman's distinction between an 'all-too-human self' and a 'socialised self' (Branaman, 1997). Branaman argues that 'the all-too-human self is the human being as a psychobiological organism with impulses, moods and variable energies, but also is the self which engages in the all-too-human task of staging a performance' (1997:xlviii). Goffman, then, is concerned with performance and management in terms of bodily action rather than engaging with the potential messiness of 'the sensual, visceral' embodied social actor (Jackson and Scott, 2001:11).

The notion of 'true' selves and 'false' selves is found in Hochschild's work and moves beyond the performative self found in Goffman's work. Hochschild focuses on our ability to carry out 'emotion work' through 'surface displays of the right feeling' and 'deep' work (1983). More recent contributions to debates on the self have importantly noted the gendered and embodied nature of identity, that 'in our society we are never simply selves, but gendered selves' (Coole, 1995:123; Brook, 1999; Evans, 2003). The connections between agency and women were of course made much earlier in the works of Simone de Beauvoir (Evans, 2003). All this has implications for our reading of Goffman's work, for as Jackson and Scott point out, 'while embodied actors are ever present on Goffman's social stage, he was always concerned more with bodily action and performance than with the sensual, visceral body' (2001:11). Indeed, the lack of attention to 'emotional needs' more generally in sociologies of the self has also recently been noted (Elliott, 2001:44). Clearly, taking account of the embodied, gendered dimensions of the self is important. This is especially so when focusing on women's experiences in relation to their bodies and perceived biological and social roles, together with conventional expectations of 'being there for others' (Bailey, 2001; Adkins, 2002).Yet not all theorists would accept such a reading of gender. The positions, according to Evans, divide according to 'those who accept the givens of biology' and 'those (and most influentially Judith Butler) who argue that all gendered behaviour is a matter of the internalisation of social expectations' (2003:57). Indeed, for Butler it is the performative self that is emphasised, there being 'no doers behind the deed', where 'the production of self and gender (are) a discursive effect' (Elliott, 2001:117). But social expectations and experiences around reproduction and motherhood sit precariously within both camps. For me it is necessary in any analysis of aspects of the social world to take account of the ways in which material circumstances and embodiment shape expectations and experiences. The notion of a clearly gendered self, which draws on the differences in bodily matters between men and women, is, then, an important consideration here (Almond, 1988; Jackson and Scott, 2001; Evans, 2003). Almond 'argues that the physical facts of menstruation, conception, pregnancy, childbirth and menopause generate a series of moral problems related to identity and self concept for women which are different to those experienced by men who do not go through such changes' (cited in Griffiths, 1995:78). So, as we actively make sense of experiences and produce and sustain (and reconstruct) narrative accounts we do so from embodied, gendered and unequal positions within the social world. These gendered positions are also closely bound up with (apparent) choices in a life. Commenting on the actuality of choices in a life and the ways in which these are linked to identity, Benhabib poses the question, 'how does this finite embodied creature constitute into a coherent narrative those episodes of choice and limitation, agency and suffering, initiative and dependence?' (1992:161). The focus on transition to motherhood taken in this book provides an opportunity to explore the complexities inherent in selves, agency and the production and maintenance of coherent narratives.

In recent years feminist debates and other theoretically grounded discussions have also emphasised the importance of contextualising experiences and situating the self (Benhabib, 1992; Stanley, 1993; Griffiths, 1995; Brook, 1999). For example, our experiences can vary significantly from expectations that have been shaped by available cultural scripts and particular ways of knowing. In relation to mothering and motherhood our ideas will be culturally and socially shaped and, importantly, morally grounded. This is a powerful context in which the biological, although overlaid with social and cultural meanings, continues to shape expectations, modes of authoritative knowledge and professional practices. For women who need time to develop their mothering skills and who do not necessarily feel able 'instinctively' to mother, even though they may feel they should instinctively know, this can raise concerns. As will be seen in later chapters, it may lead to self-silencing and social isolation as women try to make sense of their early experiences of mothering. The gendered self then is not simply constituted through 'modern discourses and disciplinary techniques' (Coole, 1995). Rather, it is constituted in the context of particular historical, social, moral, political and material circumstances and embodied activities. Caring for and having responsibility for our young, dependent children are also highly gendered practices, which are also linked to the gendering of public and private (Ribbens McCarthy and Edwards, 2002). All these – gendered selves, practices and spaces – clearly have implications for the ways in which agency is operationalised and motherhood experienced and narrated. Debates on the 'freeing of agency from structure' have largely failed to take account of the embedded and embodied dimensions of agency and the ways in which this is played out in different material circumstances and differentially experienced (Adkins, 2002:3).

The moral dimensions of motherhood, childrearing and associated practices are hard to escape in any analysis of recent literature and research (Glenn *et al.*, 1994; Arendell, 2000; Chase and Rogers, 2001; Ribbens-McCarthy *at al.*, 2000, 2003). The 'moral minefield' in which motherhood is experienced clearly shapes the types of accounts of motherhood we feel able to construct and how we present ourselves (Murphy, 1999:187). Indeed, in contrast to Goffman's claims that our activity 'is largely concerned with moral matters, but as performers we do not have a moral concern with them' (1969:243), it will be argued throughout this book that it is the moral context in which women give birth and become mothers in Western societies that has crucial implications for both a sense of self and presentation of self as a mother. Although it is noteworthy that debate continues as to whether or not there is 'a moral sensibility' at the core of Goffman's work, it is clear that his 'theory of self says surprisingly little about the emotional or psychosexual dynamics of personal life and social relationships' (Elliott, 2001:35–6).

Clearly, becoming a mother provides new opportunities for presentation of self. However, the biological fact of giving birth and the expectations that surround mothering can render early experiences as ultimately precarious, overshadowed by concerns that 'performances' will be discredited. Because becoming a mother involves a biological act, even though the context in which mothering is then experienced is socially located and culturally embedded, being a mother is always more than 'playing a part' (Goffman, 1969:28). It involves an embodied experience, culturally located feelings of responsibility and being able to meet a baby's needs. At the same time, it has profound implications for a woman's sense of self. As data in subsequent chapters will show, although women might have all the 'props' (Goffman, 1969) apparently necessary to be able to give a convincing performance as a mother – a baby, pram etc. – at times this is not enough. Women claim that they do not *feel* like mothers and can express concerns that they are fearful they will be 'found out'. Such worries are deeply rooted in perceptions of the moral context in which mothering occurs. They go beyond concerns with impression management and highlight the embodied and embedded dimensions of being a mother. This is not to subscribe to essentialist arguments of there being a core self, although women coming to motherhood may themselves have quite essentialist expectations and can experience confusion when these are found to be misplaced. Rather, my argument is that the practised, recognisable gendered and embodied self, which makes up our identity, is challenged by the experiences of first time motherhood: over time, a new social self as mother has to be learned.

In her recent work 'Mothering the Self', Lawler usefully captures contemporary notions of selfhood which go beyond the static and unchanging self. She notes that 'most Euroamericans incorporate various forms of understanding of the self into an overall schema of self-understanding' (2000:57–8). As data presented in subsequent chapters will show, a prime concern for new mothers is regaining a sense of a recognisable and practised (pre-baby) self, which is described in relation to 'getting back to normal'. This involves the women, over time, coming to make sense of the embodied and other changes that accompany transition to motherhood. It also involves developing and incorporating an understanding of self-as-mother into their broader schema of self-understanding. That mothering continues to be regarded by many as biologically determined only serves to complicate the context in which women must make sense of their experiences. Not only can it be a moral minefield, but women are also expected *instinctively* to know how to mother. Indeed, their 'femaleness' may be questioned if they experience normal difficulties. Yet any examination of the cultural practices and ways of knowing about mothering shows the variations that exist: mothering is not a universally standard experience. Many of the skills associated with mothering, fathering and parenting are only gradually acquired. So, whilst the performative nature of self is emphasised in Goffman's work, the complexities of putting on and maintaining a performance clearly need further scrutiny in relation to becoming and being a mother. For example, different settings can provide different challenges. The home may be felt to be a safer environment in which to manage early mothering experiences whilst public settings may be seen as too risky a stage. Performances are, I suggest, also grounded in an underlying, recognisable sense of a pre-motherhood self, a self which encompasses emotions and feelings and perceptions of particular ways of being in particular circumstances: characteristics which are hard to escape in relation to mothering.

What all this means is that selves are complex, changing and, at times, fragile, embodied constructs. Yet a sense of self that can be reflexively sustained and maintained, by making sense of experiences is, it is argued, necessary for ontological well-being (Giddens, 1991; Holstein and Gubrium, 2000). This is perhaps especially so in the face of greater uncertainties thrown up by the transformations that characterise late modern societies. According to Holstein and Gubrium 'the self is an increasingly complex project of daily living' (2000:x). Similarly, the importance of being able to 'make sense' in daily life has been noted by Giddens. He observes that 'how far normal appearances can be carried on in ways consistent with the individual's biographical narrative is of vital importance for feelings of ontological security' (1991:58). Reflexivity in this context concerns self-reflexivity and moves beyond being 'a defining characteristic of all human action' (Giddens, 1994:89), referring to a deeper and more engaged inner form of self-practice. It becomes an active, individual response to modernity: a changed context in which the move to a post-traditional order apparently necessitates greater self-monitoring in order to maintain ontological security. Yet this begs the question of how far striving for, and sustaining, a sense of ontological security in this format is a Western- or class-, or 'race'-bound phenomenon. Clearly, the ways in which we experience individual agency are contingent on multiple factors including material and structural circumstances and our sense of self. In turn, our experiences and expectations of 'ontological security' or well-being will be shaped in relation to these wider factors. For example, when living and working in Bangladesh (see chapter 2) it was apparent to me that the main concern for the majority of urban and rural poor was securing enough rice to feed their families. This was a daily concern for many and could literally mean the difference between survival and premature death. In such a context the idea that people were reflexive practitioners, in the way the concept is understood in the West, maintaining ontological security through reflexivity, is unsupportable. Yet this is not to say that reflexivity is not a characteristic of all human action at some intrinsic level, or that certain groups lack the capacity to be reflexive, but rather to urge caution in the claims we make in relation to its practice (see for example Adkins, 2002 for an excellent overview of recent debates on reflexivity). As the example from Bangladesh shows, although individuals had a clear *understanding* of the consequences of the material circumstances in which they lived their lives – they must generate enough income to buy food in order to survive – the opportunity and relevance of individual reflection in relation to ontological well-being would not have been either a major concern, or relevant in the context in which their lives were lived. Lash has also pointed to the need to consider the structural conditions of reflexivity (Lash, 1994). Yet in stark contrast, in the USA and more recently the UK, the cultural acceptance and dependence on therapy and counselling indicates a growing need amongst some groups in more affluent societies actively to work on their selves (McLeod, 1997; Birch and Miller, 2000). The recognition of the growth of these practices is not to privilege particular ways of being in the world. Rather it is to acknowledge that in some (Western) societies, such practices are discernible and have developed alongside, and apparently in response to, the rapid transformations that have occurred in these societies (see chapter 3). What ontological security is perceived to be, and the work on the self that might be necessary to achieve and maintain particular ways of being in the different worlds we inhabit, clearly differs in different contexts. It is also important to note here the gendered and embodied dimensions of reflexivity and ontological security. Reflexivity comes from the experiences of real bodies; it does not just exist in, and emanate from, the mind. Indeed, Giddens' conceptualisation of reflexivity has been criticised for neglecting the 'fleshy and sensual aspects of the body in favour of a more cognitively and reflexively managed body' (Jackson and Scott, 2001:12). Similarly, both Giddens and Beck have been criticised for producing 'overly cognitive or rationalistic understanding of the late modern self and human action' and failure to take account of issues related to gender identity in relation to reflexivity (Adkins, 2002:36). As will be seen in subsequent chapters, it is the 'fleshy body' that plays a key part in women's reflexivity and their constructions of social selves in relation to their experiences of their bodies and becoming mothers.

Reflexivity as a component of agency is, then, experienced and practised in different ways in different contexts. In relation to childbearing and motherhood, women's experiences are diverse and fragmented: mediated by socio-cultural factors such as class and race and whether partnered or alone (Hill Collins, 1994; Duncan and Edwards, 1999). And the same observations can be made in relation to experiences of choice, reflexivity and agency (Lazarus, 1997). For some reflexivity may be an important device in helping to make sense of experiences, especially those that do not resonate with expectations. For others, lives may be lived in contexts where individual, active reflexivity is not a major component of daily life. Clearly, all sorts of factors mediate the ways in which we operate in the social world. For example, the ways in which women engage with, or reject, scientific or medical discourses, that is, exercise an aspect of agency, has been explored in the work of anthropologist Emily

Martin (1990). In her work, Martin considers the ways in which class and race impact on women's use of medical discourses to explain menstruation. She found that middle-class American women's explanations of menstruation 'incline toward the medical view', whilst, in stark contrast, 'all other working-class women interviewed, black and white – share an absolute reluctance to give the medical view of menstruation' (1990:78). Martin considers her findings within the context of differing 'material forces in society'. She argues that whilst agreeing 'that science should not be privileged as a description of "reality"… this does not mean that the discourse of science (indeed any discourse) may not in fact be socially privileged by its relation to structures of power' (1990:79). Martin's work, then, emphasises the different ways in which agency is operationalised. It illuminates the differences that might be expected in the narratives produced by women whose lives are shaped by different material and structural circumstances. Where reflexivity is a feature of everyday life, accounting for and making sense of periods of biographical disruption can become an important device, as will be shown in subsequent chapters.

Taking a narrative approach

The more recent resurgence of interest in biographical, or self-narrative and narrative approaches, in qualitative research mirrors other changes in late modern society. In contexts where individuals are faced with greater uncertainty and more choice, reflexivity can become an important aspect of making sense of experiences. A focus on narrative helps the social scientist better to understand the social world of such lives. A quick leaf through the abstract list of any social science conference in the Western world will confirm the interest now being paid to narrative. 'Narrative methodologies have become a significant part of the repertoire of the social sciences' (Lieblich et al., 1998:1) and their applications have ranged from exploring individual, subjective experiences to group and organisational dynamics. Yet claims to be taking a narrative approach often appear based on widely varying understandings of the philosophical and/or theoretical roots from which the tradition emanates. An understanding of these as outlined above is important in adopting an appropriate methodological approach. Whilst most qualitative research may be seen to produce narrative accounts in some form, for example transcribed texts generated from the interview encounter, such studies do not all frame themselves in terms of a narrative approach. Even when a narrative approach is claimed, the work may actually only be regarded as narrative in that it emanates from a biographical account given by a respondent.

In this way most, if not all, qualitative research has some narrative elements. Yet the use of narrative as a method through which to explore how individuals account for, and make sense of, their actions requires more rigorous application: its wide use and variable interpretation has 'sometimes led to a lack of clarity and precision' (Polkinghorne, 1995:5). Crucially, a narrative approach should encapsulate and emphasise the 'temporal ordering of events that are associated with change of some kind' (Hyden, 1997:50). This facilitates a way of understanding the meanings individuals give to actions and identities, or indeed the lack of these. The ways in which narratives are constructed, configured and contextualised (through 'emplotment', see Ricoeur (1981) for further discussion of 'emplotment') then become key defining features of narrative inquiry. So too are the (apparent) omissions, incoherent or chaotic dimensions of narratives.

This narrower definition of a narrative approach attends to how people make sense of potentially disruptive life events which can lead to biographical disruption, for example the onset of chronic illness or divorce (Bury, 1982; Williams, 1984; Reissman, 1989; Frank, 1995). In such an approach, 'plot is the narrative structure through which people understand and describe the relationship among the events and choices of their lives' (Polkinghorne, 1995:7). Such an approach is facilitated by a longitudinal component. In their work on cancer narratives, Mathieson and Stam (1995) draw a distinction between conversations and narratives that goes some way to explain how a focus on narrative construction differs from some other qualitative approaches. They argue that conversations become narratives when they are used to construct a personal identity, so that 'of the many stories we tell it is those which are ours, not only about us but by us, that have the most meaning to who we are, where we have been and where we intend to go' (1995:284). Narrative approaches, then, look at how individuals *actively* construct and reconstruct narratives in the process of making sense of their experiences and presenting their self/selves. As such, it may indeed be the case that narratives are much more available to the middle classes as a means of talking about their lives and selves: or that some groups in society are more rehearsed and practised as 'storytellers'. But importantly, whoever the narrator is, 'stories, as dialogue, do not present a self formed before the story is told'; rather it is through the constructing, linking and telling of a series of events, a story, that 'the process of becoming for the first time' is revealed in the research encounter (Frank, 2002:15). The search, then, for the researcher is not for any objective, measurable 'truth'. Rather it is to understand how individuals make sense of, and ascribe meanings to, periods of biographical disruption or transition: how they narrate their experiences 'in the context of passionate beliefs and partisan stands' (The Personal Narratives Group, 1989:263). As Frank has noted, 'authenticity is created in the process of storytelling' (2002:1). The value, then, of narrative is that it provides the researcher with 'a vehicle for confronting the contradictions between an individual's experience' and constructions of self, 'and expectations based on shared cultural models' (Mattingly and Garro, 1994:771).

Yet such an approach has not gone uncriticised. A research approach that focuses on individual experiences and pays close attention to individual constructions of events and contexts always runs the risk of being accused of relativism. Further, the privileging of 'certain ways of experiencing over others' is, according to Paul Atkinson, a potentially dangerous endeavour. This is because such an approach can be seen to emphasise the 'therapeutic rather than analytic', leading to a new variant of social actor, 'the isolated actor who experiences and narrates as a matter of private and priviledged experience' (1997:335). Indeed, as researchers we should be ever vigilant about how and where the boundaries are drawn in our research, and the potential impact of different approaches. For example, Ribbens-McCarthy and Edwards (2000) have argued that in-depth interviews may require people to produce reflexive narratives that they otherwise would not do. Others have commented on the relationship between doing social science research and doing therapy work (Birch and Miller, 2000). However, the fear that the outcomes of such an approach will necessarily or even probably lead to 'a new variant of social actor', is pessimistic and, I think, misplaced. This is because whilst narratives may be collected as individual accounts and analysed as such, this does not preclude a search for meaningful subsets of experience. This can be undertaken across and between accounts and lead to the building of theory based on shared (or different) experiences. As Frank has recently noted, 'rather than bemoan the low condition of storytelling in the "interview Society", researchers can lead the process of storytelling toward something better. People are not going to stop telling stories; moral life, for better or worse, takes place in storytelling. Narrative analysis can be a significant model for a society that will continue to work out its moral dilemmas in story form' (2002:17).

Clearly, then, the narrative enterprise sits in stark contrast to universalistic notions of instrumental rationality, although at some level a characteristic of narratives is that they *are* produced as rational responses to particular circumstances. The increasing recognition of the complexity and diversity of human experience, and the shift away from universal notions of agency, has led us to consider other ways of knowing and experiencing the social world. Doing narrative research does not have to entail adopting a totally relativist stance. But it does demand high levels of researcher reflexivity, whilst avoiding the trap of falling into auto-therapy. Indeed, in describing how they go about the analysis and interpretation of narratives, Lieblich (1998) and colleagues simultaneously allude to the complexity of human lives and the research enterprise. They state 'we do not advocate total relativism that treats all narratives as texts of fiction. On the other hand, we do not take narratives at face value, as complete and accurate representations of reality. We believe that stories are usually constructed around a core of facts or life events, yet allow a wide periphery for the freedom of individuality and creativity in selection, addition to, emphasis on, and interpretation of these "remembered facts" ' (Lieblich *et al.*, 1998:8). Collecting and analysing narratives of private experience and placing them in a public arena can, then, provide a means of making 'visible a different, alternative social and cultural order within which to define our identity and subjectivity' (Edwards and Ribbens, 1998:13).

A narrative approach is, then, one of a subset of qualitative research methods in which, just as in other types of qualitative research, different approaches to analysis are utilised. Methods of analysis will vary according to the type of narrative inquiry undertaken. Different approaches have involved different strategies, from intensive analysis of linguistic codes to the identification of 'meaning units' (Mishler, 1986), and 'narrative genres' (Reissman, 1990) to 'frameworks' that can help to 'disentangle types of narrative' (Frank, 1995). In her work, Reissman has drawn a distinction between the analysis more commonly undertaken in traditional, code-based qualitative research and that of narrative analysis. This, according to Reissman, 'does not fragment the text into discrete content categories for coding purposes but, instead, identifies longer stretches of talk that take the form of narrative – a discourse organised around time and consequential events in a "world" created by the narrator' (1990:1195). This is a helpful observation but it is also important to note the role of both the narrator and the interviewer in the data that is generated in an interview setting. The interview encounter is influenced by many factors including, importantly, the questions that are posed by the researcher. These will help to shape the data generated. As such, the text that results from an interview is a co-production in which the researcher 'becomes a constituent of his or her own object of study' (Corradi, 1991:108). High standards of reflexivity throughout the research process, together with openness about the choices that are made as research unfolds, should be key features of all qualitative research. It is only through paying close attention to decisions taken as part of the research process, and making them transparent, that the value and contribution of any piece of qualitative work can be assessed. The demands of qualitative research require that we are continually sensitive to, and able to account for, the intricacies of the process of researching people's lives in ways that are not usually asked of those involved in large-scale questionnaires and randomised control trials.

The data and findings that are generated by adopting a narrative approach are open to the same questions concerning 'validity' or 'credibility' as any other qualitative approach. The arguments about how far it is appropriate or desirable to use positivist terminology to make judgements about qualitative research – which is grounded in different epistemological positions – have been widely discussed elsewhere (Lincoln and Guba, 1985; Atkinson, 1998; Cresswell, 1999). The adoption of terminology which more accurately reflects the naturalistic dimensions of qualitative research is recommended by Lincoln and Guba (1985; Guba and Lincoln, 1994). They propose that the 'trustworthiness' of a study can be assessed through consideration of the following: 'credibility', 'transferability', 'dependability' and 'confirmability', and recommend techniques for operationalising these 'measures'. More recently, growing recognition by policy-makers and others of the value of findings generated by qualitative research has led to the production of appraisal and assessment tools (Spencer *et al.*, 2003; Dixon *et al.*, 2004). These are intended to enable the credibility of research findings to be assessed.

Within the narrative genre there are then different research approaches and types of analysis. The overarching aim in the ways in which a narrative approach is employed in this book is to understand and account for periods of transition and resulting biographical disruption. Such an approach enables us to understand the ways in which individuals construct and communicate meaning (Chase, 1995). It has also been observed that collecting and listening to 'women's personal narratives provide immediate, diverse and rich sources of feminist revisions of knowledge' (The Personal Narratives Group, 1989:263). This approach therefore lends itself to longitudinal research during which changes and transitions can be observed, interpreted and theorised. Proponents have emphasised different aspects of narrative research including most recently a call to 'rethink the concepts we use by refining further the notions of narratives of location and positionality' (Anthias, 2002:493). Although written in relation to work on identity, which is an implicit or explicit dimension of most narrative research, this call reinforces the importance of both situating narratives and paying attention to the ways in which situations are narrated. It also raises the question of what happens when people feel that their experiences cannot be accommodated within available repertoires of socially and culturally shaped narratives. In her work, which calls for a reframing of narrative, Somers (1994) argues that when people find their experiences do not fit with existing narratives they produce 'counter-narratives'. This then becomes 'a crucial strategy when one's identity is not expressed in the dominant public ones' (1994:631). The construction of counter-narratives in response to experiences of first-time motherhood will be returned to in later chapters.

Clearly, narratives concern experiences that are lived within particular historical, social, cultural and moral circumstances, which in turn shape the narratives that can be constructed. Narratives, then, can be used strategically, not only as sense-making devices in terms of individual experiences, but importantly as a means of positioning and presenting oneself as a competent social actor in the social world. Through the construction of recognisable and culturally acceptable narratives, social actors place their experiences, their selves, within the context of wider social groupings and cultural settings. As noted earlier, changing patterns associated with women's lives and reproduction have produced new challenges for those experiencing contemporary motherhood. As a result of exploring how women experience first-time motherhood in this changing context, my work has led me to focus on the interconnections between experiences, narratives and the ways in which selves are constructed, maintained and narrated in late modern society. The rich accounts produced by women coming to motherhood provide the core of this book, underpinned by fieldwork observations and exploratory research focusing on women's experiences of motherhood in different cultural contexts (see chapter 2).

Methodology used in main study

The data which contribute to the observations, arguments and reflections developed in this book were generated by following seventeen women through a year in their lives in which they became mothers (see appendix for sample characteristics). This detailed, iterative research process involved women being interviewed on three separate occasions, contact by telephone and an end-of-study questionnaire, which was used to collect data on the participants' experiences of being researched. The first interview was timed to take place antenatally, between seven and eight months, once the pregnancy was well established. The second interview was scheduled to take place between six and eight weeks postnatally, following what in the UK is a routine six week postnatal health check with a health professional (usually a general practitioner). The final interview was scheduled to occur between eight and nine months postnatally. In effect, the research was largely defined by reference to the public events in the childbirth process. Similarly, descriptions of the different phases of childbirth have relied on public (usually medically defined) language.

The decision was taken to access potential participants through the technique of snowballing, using mothers at my local school as potential gatekeepers. Although access through more formal channels such as antenatal clinics or health professional contacts would probably have been quicker, these means of access were rejected. I wished to capture women's own accounts of their experiences and did not want the women accessed to feel obliged to present their experiences in a way that mirrored public accounts given by health and medical professionals. One result of using my own social networks to access a sample was that the women who finally participated in the study were from backgrounds which most described as professional or middle class and married or partnered. The sample were all white heterosexuals and the mean age of the participants was 30 years at the time of the first antenatal interview; ages ranged from 21 years to 36 years. This was slightly above the national average age for first birth in Britain which at the time was 28.6 years (Social Trends 28, 1998). However, it is typical of the trend among professional women who delay decisions about reproduction until a later stage of their lives, usually once their careers are established. In many ways this sample conforms to stereotypes that are held in wider society about those who are positioned as 'good mothers'. These women were white, predominately middle class and either married or in partnerships. Yet the data reveals how diverse and complex their experiences of becoming mothers were. Even for this apparently homogeneous group, presenting a (convincing) self as a mother, especially in the public sphere, could be problematic. This led some of the women to confine themselves to the home in the early weeks following the birth of their child. The relationship between narrative construction and social action will be explored in later chapters.

Separate interview schedules were compiled for the antenatal and postnatal interviews. Interviews were carried out in the home of the participant or a location of their choosing (one interview was carried out in my office and another in the home of a relative). The longitudinal component of the research mirrored the period of transition, giving the data collection period a fluidity not achieved in one-off interviews. Access was renegotiated before each of the interviews. Before returning to carry out the postnatal interviews, extracts from the respondent's previous interview were incorporated into the interview schedule. In this way participants were reminded of the ways in which they had previously constructed their accounts. This process also enabled developing concepts to be further explored. All interviews were tape-recorded with permission and at the end of the study the tapes were returned to the participants who wanted them. The tapes were transcribed verbatim. During analysis, the complexity of the narrative enterprise soon became clear as the data revealed the ways in which 'individuals react to pressures to conform to dominant social narratives which are available to them' (Andrews 2000:1). At one level, asking women to speak about their experiences of becoming mothers, listening to their accounts, and analysing and interpreting these accounts, seems straightforward. Yet it is because the event of childbirth and becoming a mother are both highly significant for private lives and personal biographies, and simultaneously a very publicly defined affair, that difficulties are encountered and narratives produced shaped and regulated in particular ways. In the data analysed over the course of forty-nine interviews, the ways in which different, multi-layered narratives are produced to serve different purposes was explored. These multi-layered narratives comprised public, private and sometimes personal threads, drawing on a range of public knowledges and private experiences. The components of a shifting sense of self were highlighted through the analysis of these rich accounts. As the women in the study attempted to make sense of their shifting sense of self, they used different strategies to construct what they perceived to be acceptable accounts of becoming a mother and new motherhood. The complexities of producing culturally recognisable and acceptable accounts of early mothering were revealed through the longitudinal dimensions of the research. Over the course of the research the women embarked on what can be seen as narrative trajectories. During this time the types of accounts produced changed as confidence in their own mothering enabled the women to retract and revise, retrospectively, the accounts they had given. So, whilst other research has contributed much needed broad-brushstroke pictures of mothering and motherhood, this contribution takes a more detailed approach, focusing on the complexities, coherences and contradictions in individual narratives constructed through a period of significant transition: becoming a mother in late modernity.

Conclusion

Becoming a mother is, then, potentially disruptive to a sense of self. Making sense of the event is complicated by the interplay of dominant biological, social and moral discourses. This is because becoming a mother involves physical, embodied, emotional experiences that for most result in the birth of a baby for whom some sense of responsibility will come to be felt. However, increasingly the ways in which we live in late modernity mean that women come to motherhood with little, if any, first-hand experience of babies. Similarly, their expectations often do not match the everyday experiences of mothering. Although our sense of confusion and uncertainty may be short-lived, or experienced over a longer period, because of the moral context in which we mother it is still hard to voice experiences that we do not think are 'normal' (Mauthner, 1995; 2002). Ironically, by silencing ourselves and only retrospectively voicing accounts of normal difficulties and uncertainties, we help to perpetuate and reproduce the myth that mothering is instinctive and natural. Any attempt, then, to tease out the ways in which childbearing and motherhood are framed, to explore the context in which women construct particular narratives in particular circumstances or indeed remain silent, raises questions about the ways in which 'selves' are conceptualised and presented, and a sense of self re/defined over time. It is the moral context in which women give birth and become mothers in Western societies that has crucial implications for both a sense of self and presentation of self as a mother. Being a mother is always more than 'playing a part'. Women's experiences of transition to motherhood reveal the tenuous and precarious, as well as the recognised and practised, dimensions of embodied selves. In the following chapters the complex story of how selves are experienced, made sense of and narrated in late modernity will be unravelled: for 'somewhere behind all this story telling there are real active, embodied, impassioned lives' (Plummer, 1995:170).

2   Making sense of motherhood: cultural scripts

> I've heard people talking, like you know they are embarrassed and feel
> shamed the way they check out you especially with your first baby ... it's
> because they're so different they've never seen these sorts of things
> before. (Munia, commenting on the experiences of recently immigrated
> Bangladeshi women receiving antenatal care in the UK)

The different and sometimes competing cultural scripts that shape
ways of knowing about reproduction and childbirth in different cultural
contexts were powerfully demonstrated to me at the time of the birth
of my first daughter. During the 1980s I had lived in Dhaka, the capital
of Bangladesh, for two and a half years. I worked at a children's hospital
and spent time in the 'bustees', the urban slums. My job involved tracing
former inpatients of the hospital in order to assess their nutritional status.
Following an eventful pregnancy (see Introduction) I returned home to
England for the birth of my first child. The morning after my daughter
was born in the local National Health Service hospital, I was aware of
a commotion in the next bed. The new mother, by coincidence a young
Bangladeshi woman, was in a state of bewilderment. The two auxiliary
nurses she was appealing to had failed with sign language and were
looking slightly bemused. I was able to interpret for her; she was in
pain and thirsty. The sense of her bewilderment at being in hospital to
give birth with no means of communication and no family members there
to provide support has remained with me. The young mother had only
recently arrived in the UK. Her expectations around childbirth did not
resonate with the medicalised mode of birth widely practised in the
Western world. I knew from living in Bangladesh that in her culture
very different ways of knowing shaped expectations, and experiences, in
relation to pregnancy and childbirth. For the vast majority of women
there was no system of formalised, professional antenatal (prenatal) care.
Delivery for most women occurred at home, sometimes in a specially
built room because of associations with 'pollution'. The event took
place either alone or with the assistance of female relatives or women
experienced, but not formally trained, in delivering babies, known as

'dais' or 'dhorunis' (Islam, 1980). Clearly, the cultural scripts that were dominant in Bangladesh stood in stark contrast to those that shaped childbirth in the UK.

The contexts in which women live their lives as mothers are, then, socially constructed, historically specific and culturally varied. As noted earlier, motherhood is often considered to be a universal experience and yet becoming a mother is everywhere socially and culturally marked and shaped (Jordan, 1993). For example, the new mother in Bangladesh will have different expectations and experiences from the new mother in the UK – and some aspects may be shared by both women. Becoming a mother, then, is always more than a biological event. The ways in which 'a society's core values and organisational principles' structure reproductive behaviours and practices has been noted in recent years by anthropologists and sociologists (Oakley, 1980; Rothman, 1989; Davis-Floyd, 1992; Jordan, 1993; Davis-Floyd and Sargent, 1997). Women's expectations and experiences around reproduction and childbirth are produced through interactions with others, and shaped by reference to dominant forms of 'authoritative knowledge' (Jordan, 1997). As a result, there may be little 'cultural space' available for alternative ways of thinking or knowing about reproduction and childbirth (Davis-Floyd and Sargent, 1997). In this chapter, the interplay between different ways of knowing in relation to cultural scripts will be explored in the context of making sense of motherhood and narrative construction.

As noted in the previous chapter, narrative construction is a means by which we can make sense of, and reconcile, past and present expectations and experiences and future hopes. A focus on transition to motherhood provides a rich backdrop against which to see how expectations and experiences are culturally located and shaped: to explore the cultural contexts in which narrative accounts are constructed. Cultures, according to Willard (1988), 'provide a script or rather a specific cultural set of ideas about how events should take place so that members of that culture can be guided through major life events and changes' (1988:226). In the same cultures the different scripts available to guide people through an array of life events may contain inherently contradictory messages, for example, those which exist in the West in relation to mothers with young children and working outside the home. Yet this does not diminish their power, but rather helps to shape the complex context in which experiences are lived out. In relation to pregnancy and childbearing dominant cultural scripts are discernible, but these shift over time, and have dimensions to them which may fit with and/or contradict individual experiences. Whatever the particular dimensions of the cultural scripts available in any culture, they will shape individual expectations in various ways. For example, where dominant cultural scripts are underpinned by social structures and practices which serve to reinforce and legitimise them, they become accepted as the 'normal' or 'natural' way to do things and, as a result, may be difficult to resist.

Authoritative knowledge

The contours of the cultural scripts available to women in different cultures are premised on forms of 'authoritative knowledge' (Jordan, 1997). In different cultures the forms of authoritative knowledge that count in relation to pregnancy and childbearing, whether hierarchical as in the UK and North America, or more horizontal as in Bangladesh, will shape individuals' expectations and experiences and ultimately how sense is made of them. The concept of 'authoritative knowledge' derives from Brigitte Jordan's innovative work from the 1970s in which she took a biosocial approach in order to explore birth practices in four different cultures (1993). Up until this time, and reflecting a wider lack of academic interest in the private sphere and women's lives, reproduction and childbirth had largely remained outside the scope of many research agendas. In her work, Jordan explored the ways in which authoritative knowledge contextualised and shaped women's expectations and experiences of birth. According to Jordan, 'the power of authoritative knowledge is not that it is correct but that it counts' (1997:58) and so in different cultures, different forms of authoritative knowledge are discernible. In much of the Western world the medicalisation of reproduction and childbearing has led to highly technological practices around childbirth. In contrast, much more low-tech or no-tech practices contribute to authoritative knowledge in many developing countries. Authoritative knowledge is not, then, premised on 'highly developed technology' but rather on recognisable and accepted practices that are continually reinforced, and through their practice given legitimacy (Sargent and Bascope, 1997:203). In some contexts authoritative knowledge is consensual and shared, based on a horizontal model of knowing and practices. In others one kind of authoritative knowledge dominates, is hierarchically organised and regarded as most powerful. Most importantly, authoritative knowledge is 'socially sanctioned' and requires that 'people actively engage in (its) production and reproduction ... thus continually reinforcing its validity' (Sargent and Bascope, 1997:183).

The ways in which authoritative knowledge is produced, reinforced and maintained will differ from culture to culture. The determinants and display of authoritative knowledge will also be varied. But clearly they relate to the ways in which women and their bodies are viewed within a society and, in turn, the practices that exist around childbearing. In the following section these areas will be explored. Examples from research and personal observations from the field in Bangladesh and the Solomon Islands, where I lived and worked during the 1980s and, latterly the UK, will be used (Miller, 1995). In considering cultural constructions of women and their bodies, Szurek has made the observation that 'the ways in which a society defines women and values their reproductive capability are reflected and displayed in the cultural treatment of birth' (1997:287). In the UK, pregnancy and birth are largely regarded as medicalised processes that require expert management and supervision. As Ussher has commented, 'pregnancy, childbirth and the postnatal period have been pathologised ... positioning women's experiences as an illness in need of intervention' (1992:47). As a result, the vast majority of births take place in hospital (98 per cent), which has become regarded by many as the 'natural' place to give birth. In most cases women do not resist this highly technological and medicalised approach to birth, but rather collaborate in its maintenance and perpetuation: although retrospectively they may come to resist and challenge aspects of it (Miller, 2003). Feminists and others have regarded the medicalisation of childbirth as indicative of the wider social structures that differentially shape women's lives in patriarchal societies. In a Western context, the shifts that have occurred around reproduction and childbearing can be explored and explained through an analysis of the interwoven themes of knowledge production, power, medicalisation and patriarchy (see chapter 3).

In the UK, authoritative knowledge in relation to reproduction and childbearing is based on biomedicine and technology, in the context of heightened perceptions of risks, which are themselves cultural constructions (Lupton, 1999; see chapter 3 in this volume). The result of this is that 'cultural authority' is seen to reside in the medical and health professionals who manage pregnancy and childbirth (Sargent and Bascope, 1997:183). The ways in which this authoritative knowledge translates into practices and in turn shapes women's expectations and experiences is displayed through the development of highly formalised services around pregnancy and childbirth. Regular monitoring and screening form part of the process of antenatal preparation for childbirth in the UK. Women are expected to make routine visits to either a midwife, general practitioner (GP), and/or obstetrician during their pregnancy. As already mentioned, for the vast majority of women, childbirth takes place in hospital and is professionally managed by highly trained health professionals. Following the birth of a baby, postnatal care in the UK is less structured. It is based on home visits made by midwives and health visitors, with the number of visits made related to professional perceptions of coping and need (Miller, 2002). The models of practice that exist around childbearing in the UK, as in many Western societies, are based on one form of authoritative knowledge being more powerful than other ways of knowing. This is also the case in the USA, where Jordan notes that 'medical knowledge supersedes and delegitimizes other potentially relevant sources of knowledge such as women's prior experience and the knowledge she has of the state of her body' (1997:73). Such dominance leaves little opportunity for other ways of thinking about pregnancy and childbirth, whilst at the same time reinforcing 'pre-existing patterns of authority' (Sargent and Bascope, 1997:192).

In many Western contexts, then, authoritative ways of knowing are hierarchical and have led to distinctions being made between those who are regarded as 'expert' – the medical and health professionals, and those who are not – childbearing women (Miller, 2000, 2003). Authoritative knowledge is displayed through constructions of expert knowledge. Yet these are rarely resisted but instead interactionally constructed 'in such a way that all participants come to see the current social order as a natural order, that is, the way things (obviously) are' (Davis-Floyd and Sargent, 1997:56). The findings from research focusing on women's experiences of transition to first-time motherhood, which is detailed in the previous chapter, demonstrate this. They show the ways in which the dominance of expert knowledge is not rejected or even particularly resisted, but rather engaged with and thereby reinforced. An overarching theme in the interviews with women during the antenatal period was that there were culturally appropriate, morally underpinned and socially acceptable ways of preparing for childbirth and motherhood. Antenatal preparation involved engaging with or, in some cases, wanting to hand over to, others who were perceived to be 'experts', those who were perceived to possess authoritative knowledge and cultural authority and were located within the medical and health services (see chapter 4). This appears in stark contrast to the findings from other research that both supports a critique of medicalised childbirth (Oakley, 1979, 1980; Rothman, 1989) and has shown the ways in which individuals have resisted and challenged medical discourses (Cornwell, 1984; Martin, 1990; Blaxter, 1990). However, such findings may be a feature of women's shifting relationships with ways of knowing, especially in relation to reproduction and childbirth in late modern Western societies. It may also be a feature of their age, social class and status as first-time mothers. Certainly the findings are supported by more recent research from North America, which claims that 'although some women are alienated by their experience of medicalised birth, many women across social classes welcome medical intervention, if not management, and are quite satisfied with hospital deliveries' (Fox and Worts, 1999:328). These findings also point to the dynamic nature of cultural scripts which are not static but rather shift over time (see chapter 7).

Bangladesh: authoritative knowledge and associated practices

Notions of authoritative knowledge and associated practices that shape women's expectations and experiences of pregnancy and childbirth in the UK stand in sharp contrast to those in Bangladesh and the Solomon Islands. The cultural patterning of pregnancy and childbirth practices in these different contexts once again demonstrates the variation in acceptable ways of knowing about birth, and the different ways in which what counts as authoritative knowledge is constructed and practiced (Sargent and Bascope, 1997; Jordan, 1997). Bangladesh is a beautiful and largely rural country, which is frequently tested by the ravages of natural (and man-made) disasters. It has a population of 126 million and a per capita income of US $370 per annum, which means that many families live in acute poverty. Most girls marry by the age of 18 years and begin to have children whilst still in their teens (Yasmin *et al.*, 2001). In the 1980s fewer than 2 per cent of women gave birth in a hospital (McConville, 1988). This figure has now risen and figures for 1997 record that 5 per cent of all births took place in an institution (Unicef, 1997). As noted earlier, I lived in Bangladesh in the 1980s and worked in a children's hospital carrying out a follow-up study of malnourished children in the urban slum areas of Dhaka (Miller *et al.*, 1983). During my time at the hospital my work brought me into close contact with women and their (often critically ill) children. The tenuous nature of lives lived in profound poverty was brought home to me on a daily basis. Children brought to the hospital regularly died, from poverty-induced malnutrition, in their mothers' arms before admission could be arranged. The death of a child was always accompanied by painful, heartfelt wailing, mixed with a stoical resolve that it was Allah's will: 'inshala'. The cultural and religious practices that existed around death and bereavement again were in stark contrast to the practices I was familiar with in the West.

Bangladesh is a highly patriarchal society in which a woman's status is inextricably linked to her fertility and the birth of a healthy (male) child is highly prized (McConville, 1988). The practices around pregnancy and childbirth are shaped in and by this context, together with the pervasive beliefs in pollution that exist around women's bodies, particularly during menstruation and childbirth. Pregnancy and childbirth in Bangladesh have 'for centuries been shrouded in the mystery of the women in "purdah"' (McConville, 1988:135). Similarly, 'the associated concepts of "pollution"' and shame, and in many rural areas 'the belief in evil spirits or 'bhuts"' have been a defining feature of folklore and childbirth in Bangladesh (McConville, 1988:135; Islam, 1980). These spirits and *bhuts* are believed to be particularly attracted to pregnant and breastfeeding women. In this culture, pregnancy and childbearing continue to be considered as part of a natural, non-medicalised process, and men are largely excluded from all matters relating to it. Indeed, it is one area of women's lives over which they can exercise some control. Any knowledge a woman may possess about childbearing will usually have been gained in the private domain, passed on to her from her mother, mother-in-law or by another female relative. The activities and diet that characterise the pre- and postnatal periods continue to be shaped by traditional practices and religious beliefs. During the birth, which for most women takes place in the home, the vast majority of women will either be alone or attended by female relatives and/or other women experienced in helping during labour and childbirth (Islam, 1980). McConville has described a hierarchy of those who attend women during birth in the following way: doctors, nurse-midwives, family welfare visitors, traditional birth attendants, *dai*s, and then the relatives of the women in labour (1988:141). More recently there have been concerted efforts by aid organisations to train traditional birth attendants in an attempt to reduce high maternal mortality rates (see chapter 7). The village *dai* has traditionally been of low-status and uneducated, present at a birth in order to perform menial tasks specifically related to the removal of pollution, rather than as someone with expert knowledge or skills. Interestingly, and in a very different context, the concerns with risks of pollution that Okley found amongst the gypsy society she studied in the UK in the 1970s have resonance with those in Bangladesh (Callaway, 1983).

The different practices, both positive and harmful, that surround birth in Bangladesh have been documented by anthropologist Thérèse Blanchet (1984) and midwife Frances McConville (1988). They show the ways in which overriding concerns with pollution and, importantly, the removal of pollution, together with perceptions of 'shame', underpin many traditional practices and reinforce particular cultural constructions of women's bodies. It is also important to note that there is rich cultural variation within areas of Bangladesh. Whilst for Hindu women (who form a minority in a country that is predominately Muslim) the attendance of a *dai* at a birth has been an essential practice as she will transfer the pollution to herself (Blanchet, 1984), some Muslim women continue to give birth unattended because of the 'shame' associated with childbirth

(McConville, 1988). Birth, then, is considered a dirty event, surrounded by superstitions and concerns over 'pollution' and the 'shame' that would result should others become polluted. For up to forty days following the birth of a baby, a woman is considered to be in a polluted state.

The practices that surround pregnancy and childbirth in Bangladesh clearly shape expectations and experiences and, as subsequent chapters show, are different from those in the Western world. Whilst working in the Children's Nutrition Unit in Dhaka, I helped to put together 'maternity kits' to sell to the pregnant women who came to the hospital. This was undertaken in a bid to try to reduce the infection that could accompany the delivery of a baby, particularly in the *bustee* (slum) areas. The kits consisted of a small square of plastic sheet (as many women give birth onto earth floors), some clean cord, half a razor blade (such were the levels of poverty that a complete, new razor blade may be sold at market and not used for the intended purpose) and some antiseptic cream. I only later came to fully appreciate the basic nature of these kits, and the different cultural constructions of the 'tools' necessary for the management of birth. This realisation dawned when I returned to Bangladesh following the birth of my first child in a UK hospital; the contrast was profound. The ways in which authoritative knowledge around childbearing operates in Bangladesh is, then, as in other cultures, complex and varied. The exclusion of men from matters related to pregnancy and childbirth points to contrasting patterns of power and authoritative knowledge when compared to those that exist in the West. For example, in the UK the processes of medicalisation have led to men's increased professional participation in all aspects of reproduction and childbirth. However, the powerful associations of pollution and evil spirits, noted above, may help to explain why men in Bangladesh have not sought to intervene in, or control, this particular aspect of women's lives. Reproduction and childbearing continue to be areas of female expertise in which more horizontal forms of authoritative knowledge dominate.

The Solomon Islands

The Solomon Islands form a chain of islands in the south-west Pacific. The population of less than half a million (447,900) is composed of 93 per cent Melanesian, 4 per cent Polynesian and 1.5 per cent Micronesian, and has a significantly higher per capita income than Bangladesh ($926 in 1997). During the 1980s, a few weeks after graduating with a degree in sociology from a British university, I went to live on one of the larger of the Solomon Islands, New Georgia. During the two years I spent there I travelled amongst the main islands and, amongst other things, assisted my husband – a tropical forester – in data collection. I also used my recently acquired 'sociological lenses' to observe the rich and diverse cultures, languages and customs that characterised the Solomon Islands. We lived in a village called Munda; our house, built on stilts, sat at the edge of a lagoon and coconut and banana palms formed a natural boundary to the garden. We lived without electricity and like our Solomon Island neighbours benefited from the abundant natural resources of fish from the sea and produce from the rich garden areas behind the village. I was welcomed by the local women and invited to join in many of their activities. These involved such things as weaving baskets and mats, which were produced on a regular basis in order to raise money for the local Methodist church. The church provided a key focus for many of the villagers and missionaries had set up a hospital in Kekengala and a college on a nearby island. The *wontok* system was also a feature of Solomon Island life. This involved reciprocal obligations that spread out from direct family members to friends, neighbours and fellow villagers and beyond, all of whom were considered to be each other's *wontoks*. Solomon Islanders could travel within and between the different islands and call upon *wontok* ties for hospitality and help. In many ways the *wontok* system provided an informal support network, particularly for those in need. However, it was also open to abuse. *Wontok* ties could be exploited and individual families drained of resources as they felt obligated to help others. For the most part, however, like so much of Solomon Island life it was accepted with benign good grace – after all, as a Solomon Islander you never knew when you might need to call upon and make use of *wontok* ties.

As noted earlier, the ways in which women and their bodies are viewed within a culture can provide important markers for how authoritative knowledge in relation to childbirth is constructed. At the outset, I was struck by the freedoms that, from a Western perspective, were enjoyed by women in relation to their bodies and their apparent ease with their different sizes and shapes. There were not the same invidious pressures that are perpetuated and reinforced in the West, that compel many women to try to achieve unnaturally thin body forms. Of course, some twenty years later, with the enormous changes that have resulted from globalisation, these freedoms may now no longer be so easily enjoyed. However, whilst living in the Solomon Islands, I noticed that larger bodies were celebrated. Indeed, I listened with intrigue to stories about the butcher's shop on the island of Gizo selling large quantities of pork fat to the Gilbertese women, amongst whom a substantial body and ample backside were highly prized and considered to be symbols of beauty. Pregnancy outside marriage was also regarded with a similarly relaxed attitude. The state of pregnancy was described in the lingua franca, pidgin English, as being 'bubbly'. Although the earlier arrival of missionary hospitals on some of the main islands had led increasingly to women giving birth in hospitals, hospital facilities remained basic. Apart from the hospital in Honiara, the capital of the main island of Guadalcanal, most hospitals were very low-tech, consisting of no more than a few rooms. The hospital provided a place in which to give birth, but only for those who could walk to the hospital or who did not live too far from the hospital to make the journey by canoe. This shift for some in place of birth, from village house to hospital, had not at the time led to widespread, formalised antenatal care, although basic advice on diet might be given should the woman find herself at the hospital. Pethidine was available as a form of pain relief, but apart from this, the birth was just as likely to be attended by hens scratching around the floor as the hospital doctor.

At the time, men and women shared many of the tasks involved with daily living, tending the vegetable garden areas and fishing. Members of the extended family, particularly older siblings, shared in the care of younger family members. The society was arranged according to ways of living that were not so hierarchical or divided according to gender as those in the West: patriarchy was not a dominant, organising feature. In more recent times the Solomon Islands have been recorded as having amongst the highest population growth and fertility levels in the Pacific. In 1995 fertility levels stood at 5.7 births per woman aged 15–49 years. High maternal and infant mortality rates have also been recorded. These have been explained in terms of pregnancy-related complications, reproductive tract diseases and cancers (http://www.spc.int. 27/10/03). Sadly, as I write this chapter the Solomon Islands is experiencing a period of continued civil unrest. Ethnic rivalries between inhabitants of the main island, Guadalcanal, and the neighbouring island of Malaita, erupted in 1998, leading to considerable loss of life. Australian troops have recently been recruited in to try to restore law and order, but this period of unrest has had serious consequences for the infrastructure of the islands, including health services, which at best were already rudimentary and fragmented. Similarly, the crippling nature of the *wontok* system described earlier has also recently been noted. The Chairman of the National Peace Council, Mr Paul Tovua, has claimed that the *wontok* system is 'inconsistent with democracy' because loyalty to *wontoks* is greater than loyalty to the law or parliamentary democracy (ABC News Online, March 2004). But dismantling deeply culturally embedded practices such as those associated with *wontok* obligations will not be easy. Concerns have also been expressed by various aid organisations about both the growing maternal mortality rates and the increase in unprotected sexual activity among young people and corresponding high teenage birth rate, behaviour which has been compounded by increased alcohol and drug abuse amongst teenagers. It seems that patterns of behaviour common in the West now shape practices in these once remote islands (see chapter 7).

Shifting cultures

In these different and shifting contexts, the available cultural knowledges and practices that shape pregnancy and childbirth ensure that birth is always more than a biological event. As noted earlier, cultural scripts provide individuals with the ideas and practices of a particular culture so that members of a culture can be 'guided' through life events and transitions (Willard, 1988). Yet confusion may be experienced if women physically move between cultures and find that their ways of knowing, and related practices, do not resonate with the expectations of the culture in which they come to reside. On my return from living and working in Bangladesh I carried out a small piece of research. This explored the influence of cultural traditions and religious beliefs on British Bangladeshi women and their use of antenatal services (Miller, 1995). The rationale for this piece of exploratory research was that 'Asian' women living in Britain had been found to have higher perinatal mortality rates than other mothers. One explanation for this had focused on their (lack of) use of antenatal services. The research findings brought into relief the ways in which different cultural ways of knowing exist in relation to childbirth. It also showed that what counts (and who says what counts), varies greatly between different cultures, and as societies become more culturally diverse, *within* cultures. Women becoming mothers in cultures into which they have moved can find that their expectations and experiences are not easily accommodated or recognised within the dominant culture. The form of authoritative knowledge that underpins expectations and practices may also be differently constructed. My own decision to return to the UK from Bangladesh for the birth of my first daughter is an example of this. According to my own culturally inscribed ways of knowing about childbirth, I had at that time accepted (or at least did not question) that hospital was the safest place to give birth, especially for a first birth.

My research on Bangladeshi women living in England was carried out in a city in the south of the country. Whilst hierarchical forms of authoritative knowledge dominate in the West, the findings from this research showed that some aspects of authoritative knowledge that did not fit with other, culturally inscribed ways of knowing, could be resisted. Resistance, however, could lead to those in whom cultural authority had been vested, the health and medical professionals, to be critical of cultural practices they saw as different. A dominant theme in the qualitative interviews revolved around the difficulty of maintaining cultural and religious practices, for those who had moved from Bangladesh to live in England. As Munia commented:

> Actually when we are living in England we can't keep everything like we would in Bangladesh ... when you step out from your home everything is different.

The women interviewed in the study had all attended antenatal clinics during their pregnancies in Britain. However, those who had also had children in Bangladesh had not previously had any *formalised* antenatal care. The women spoke of having attended antenatal classes in Britain because they thought they had to. This suggests a partial acceptance of the dominant culture, an acceptance of one aspect of pregnancy and child-bearing which has traditionally been located within the private sphere shifting into the public sphere. However, an area in which resistance was discernible was in relation to parent-craft classes. At the time the research was carried out (the early 1990s) there were attempts by various health authorities across England to encourage Asian mothers (including Bangladeshi women) to attend parent-craft classes (Jain, 1985; Munro, 1988). But the women in the study had resisted these attempts and said they could not see the relevance of 'practising'. Munia spoke passionately on the subject of attendance at parent-craft classes:

> That is what most mothers-in-law doesn't like, they said 'why so much bothering ... you have to go and practice?' ... I think that's not necessary because our culture is so different, we do learn so much from our Mum. A lot of like English girls they're away from their Mum, and I think for them it's good. But for us it's not because we do listen to our Mum ... our culture is totally different.

The ways in which cultural differences play out in relation to the expectations and practices that surround and shape preparation for childbearing are clear in the above extract. Cultural authority was traditionally seen to reside in Bangladeshi women's mothers, mother-in-laws and other female relatives, and in relation to preparing for motherhood traditional practices were maintained. However, to be seen to resist aspects of antenatal care could lead to women being perceived as not preparing 'appropriately' by the medical and health professionals in whom cultural authority has been vested by the dominant culture. Another of the Bangladeshi mothers in the study spoke of cultural assumptions being made by the health professionals with whom she had contact:

> Well, I think I give the image of being an Asian woman and people have their barriers ... it's difficult to be assertive even when you have the language, I feel

I was bossed around and I feel quite resentful about that . . . and then the health visitor who came to see me before my child was born was making all sorts of wild assumptions too. She was all right once she got to know me, but she was being patronising at first.

Cultural practices may also be further challenged for those who do not 'have the language'. Language difficulties, combined in some cases with the break-up of extended family units, have led to changes in traditional practices amongst some British Bangladeshis. Because many women do not speak English they must take a relative with them to the antenatal clinic to translate for them. As seen earlier, in Bangladesh matters relating to pregnancy and childbirth are the domain of women alone; mothers, mother-in-laws or other female relatives, give any advice thought necessary. The break-up of large extended family units brought about by migration to Britain means that in many cases there is no mother or mother-in-law living in Britain. Increasingly, husbands are becoming involved in this traditionally female area, acting as interpreters for their wives when they make clinic and hospital visits. As Munia commented:

The husband goes because they [the women] feel scared to death, they don't speak the language and everything is so strange. For a woman from the village they feel strange.

Problems of access to, and/or any potential for sharing of, authoritative knowledge may be heightened, then, where the dominant language is also a second language. Sargent and Bascope have observed that 'the production, possession and display of knowledge of any sort is a product of the capacity to participate in interactions with doctors and nursing staff' (1997:197). In the Bangladeshi study it was found that language difficulties had increasingly led to men becoming chaperones and interpreters for their wives. In so doing, this new practice further distanced the women from the cultural processes they associated with childbearing. In turn, this practice led to complaints from doctors to the local Bangladeshi language group that husbands and wives never seemed to have discussed anything before they went to the clinic. Clearly, the doctors were making assumptions based on particular cultural understandings of marital relationships which were not appropriate in this context. But this observation also shows that whilst men may have become involved in one area of childbearing, chaperoning and translating for their wives in the public sphere, in the private sphere of the home matters relating to pregnancy and childbirth remained within the control of women and were not openly discussed with male partners.

The interplay between different ways of knowing and cultural scripts was demonstrated in this piece of research. The findings illustrate the ways in which script-based knowledge can be challenged in different cultural contexts. They also show the power of hierarchical models of authoritative knowledge that dominate in the West. There is little 'cultural space' available for alternative ways of knowing. Practices that do not appear to fit with the dominant cultural model may be dismissed as inappropriate, or worse, 'feckless' (Miller, 1995; Davis-Floyd and Sargent, 1997). As Jordan has observed, the 'consequence of the legitimation of one kind of knowing as authoritative is the devaluation, often the dismissal, of all other kinds of knowing' and associated practices (1997:56). Resistance to different, alien cultural practices may offer the possibility for women to retain some control in their journeys into motherhood, but simultaneously risks condemnation from those in positions of power. For example, other research carried out during this period showed the ways in which Asian mothers living in the UK were stereotyped and labelled as poor mothers. This was because those in whom cultural authority was invested, the health professionals, thought the mothers lacked 'normal maternal instinct and feelings' (Bowler, 1993:13).

The ways in which cultural contexts shape expectations and practices has implications for how we make sense of life events and transitions through narrative construction. Yet, as in the previous chapter, we must once again consider how far the need to actively make sense of these events is a Western phenomenon and what part different models of authoritative knowledge play in the process. As noted earlier, in the context of the UK and America hierarchical forms of knowledge permeate and shape notions of reproduction and childbearing. Little space is left for other ways of knowing. Legitimacy is given to medical knowledge, and health and medical professionals and many women accept this as normal and (ironically) natural. In contrast, in Bangladesh and the Solomon Islands different, more horizontal forms of authoritative knowledge have shaped the practices that surround childbearing. In these different cultural contexts the interplay between knowledges, practices and the contours of the available cultural scripts reflect pre-existing patterns of authority. They serve to demonstrate 'the extreme cross cultural variation in the kinds of care available to pregnant and birthing women' (Davis-Floyd and Sargent, 1997:14).

Yet the contours of cultural scripts can and do shift over time. Also, some aspects of ways of thinking about reproduction and childbearing may be shared across seemingly very different cultures, but result in different practices. An example of this is apparent in relation to the accounts of childbearing collected from new mothers in the UK and the cultural beliefs that underpin practices in Bangladesh (Miller, 2000). As we have seen, in Bangladesh women's bodies are closely associated with pollution whether during menstruation, childbirth, or whilst breastfeeding. Cultural practices exist which serve to protect those around these women from contamination, which is thought to accompany these aspects of women's lives. In the very different cultural context of the UK, the accounts of women collected in a study of transition to motherhood (see previous chapter) also included references to cleanliness and smell in relation to childbirth. In these accounts, decisions to give birth in a hospital were partly justified on the grounds that birth was both smelly and messy and something to be contained and kept away from the home. The comments from Felicity and Philippa below illustrate this:

The one thing about birth that really worries me is the mess. The mess and the smell ... (Felicity)

I mean, partly because I don't know what to expect. I think I'd rather have everything on tap at the hospital if necessary because you don't really know the shape ... or anything, so I just think I'd rather, especially for a first baby, I'd rather have the care on hand if I need it ... I do think I'd rather come back to my house as something that is kind of sorted out, to some extent quite clean and what have you, rather than where this kind of event takes place ... I can't see the benefit of having it at home. I just think I'd rather go away, do it somewhere else and then come back. (Philippa)

Although smell and mess are associated with childbirth in both cultures, the ways and places in which these dimensions of childbirth are managed differ according to the form of authoritative knowledge that shape cultural practices. In Bangladesh 'pollution' following childbirth is eliminated through 'the cleansing of the woman, her clothes, the environment and all the equipment' following delivery (McConville, 1988:183). Clothes worn by the labouring mother together with the placenta will usually be burned or buried in order to avoid contaminating anyone or anything around the childbearing woman. The 'dirty event' of birth for most women takes place on either the earth floor or on a mat in the home (McConville, 1988). In the UK a clear distinction is made between the hospital in which 'this kind of event takes place' and the home, which for the majority of women is no longer regarded as the normal or natural place to give birth. The mess is also regarded as 'worrying' in a society where practices around both birth and death are in place to sanitise and depersonalise these events. For example, for the most part, these events have been removed from the home and placed in other settings where they can be controlled, managed and contained. In societies where individual control is highly prized, the risk of losing control, especially control of our sometimes leaky bodies, is particularly worrying (Douglas, 1966; Jackson and Scott, 2001).

Authoritative knowledge: collaboration and consensus?

The similarities and differences in meanings and practices that exist in relation to the management and experience of childbearing emphasise the complexities inherent in drawing distinctions between different forms of authoritative knowledge. Over time, ways of knowing and what counts as authoritative knowledge shift. Similarly, boundaries around and between cultural scripts cannot be rigidly defined and should not be tightly drawn. But clearly some key differences are discernible and these do help to shape the forms of authoritative knowledge and associated practices that dominate in different cultural contexts. For example, using their work in Jamaica, Sargent and Bascope (1997) have shown that highly developed technology need not be a prerequisite for the possession of authoritative knowledge, or for perceptions of who holds authoritative knowledge. In contrast, however, technology has become an important feature of authoritative knowledge in the USA and UK. In these countries technology increasingly plays a part in constructions of 'expert' and perceptions of 'expertise' in relation to pregnancy and childbirth and associated normative practices. Professional expertise is premised on hierarchies of knowledge developed through often lengthy training, which in turn is related to positions of power. The development and use of technological interventions in reproduction and childbirth also has a gendered history. It is interesting to note that men first became involved in assisting at births when forceps were introduced (Tew, 1990). Of course, modern technologies can be both liberating and oppressive. But as tools which require expert management, they can be seen to further contribute to hierarchical forms of authoritative knowledge, distancing women further from knowing their own bodies (see chapter 3). Yet, as earlier noted, because of the processes by which practices and knowledges become normalised and accepted over time, many women actively collaborate with those they regard as experts. In the West these are the health and medical professionals (Davis-Floyd, 1992; Fox and Worts, 1999). This may be especially pronounced in those who are becoming mothers for the first time when particular 'expert' ways of knowing are prioritised and regular interaction with professionals sought (see chapter 4). But as journeys into motherhood unfold, or as subsequent births are experienced, perceptions of who is the expert, what constitutes authoritative knowledge and the ways in which cultural scripts shape narrations, may shift.

As we have seen in this chapter, in some contexts authoritative knowledge is consensual and shared. In others, one kind of knowledge is regarded as most authoritative and more powerful, reflecting pre-exisiting power structures. The important point is that 'the power of authoritative knowledge is not that it is correct but that it counts' (Jordan, 1997:58). A shared characteristic of cultural scripts that shape reproduction and childbearing in the UK and USA is that any knowledge a woman may have about her own body is regarded as less accurate or relevant when placed alongside biomedical ways of knowing (Graham and Oakley, 1986; Davis-Floyd, 1992). As childbirth becomes increasingly medicalised there is a pressing need to take account of lay knowledge, which is not 'simply diluted versions of medical knowledge', but rather ways of knowing grounded in subjective, embodied experiences (Nettleton, 1995:37). In turn, biomedical knowledge resides within professional groups who occupy positions of power and in the West this hierarchy shapes 'the way interactions take place', although historically this has not always been the case (Sargent and Bascope, 1997:192). One aspect of this changing context is 'the current revolution in reproductive technologies' which has led to new ways of thinking about 'social definitions of motherhood and fatherhood' (Scheper-Hughes and Sargent, 1998:16). Contexts, meanings and associated practices, then, shift over time. So, how can we move towards a more collaborative, consensual model of authoritative knowledge in which different types of knowledge can be accommodated and shared? A model that does not reinforce pre-existing forms of gendered authority and power? It is this quest which Jordan regards as being 'the challenge for the future of childbirth in the technologized western world, as well as in the developing countries of the third world' (1997:73).

Yet the complexities and challenges in moving to more consensual, collaborative constructions of authoritative knowledge, not just in those contexts currently characterised by high-tech, are considerable. This is because of the complex interplay between technology, development, perceptions of progress and different ways of knowing: all of which are set within an increasingly globalised world. As Scheper-Hughes and Sargent have pointed out, 'local societies and cultures are as much influenced today by what goes on outside their borders as within them' (1998:10). However, these changes and transformations continue to be differentially experienced, intersected as they are by class or caste position, gender and other structural inequalities. As we have seen, whilst technology is not a necessary prerequisite for constructions of authoritative knowledge, and there are very real dangers in confusing development with technology, nonetheless many developing countries aspire to patterns of development seen in the West. For example, the increase from 2 per cent to 5 per cent of women in Bangladesh giving birth in hospitals will be widely welcomed as progress. And if perinatal and maternal mortality rates fall as a result, it is a form of progress. Is there greater opportunity now, as a result of increased global communication, for convergence between different ways of knowing, and is this desirable? Certainly, in those societies characterised by more horizontal forms of authoritative knowledge and where technology has not largely replaced more embodied, experiential ways of knowing, there remains the opportunity to build more collaborative and inclusive models of authoritative knowledge. However, in the USA and UK, transformations and changes in how we live mean that individuals continue to look to experts for guidance, even though some theorists claim trust in expert bodies of knowledge is increasingly regarded as less relevant (Beck, 1992). In the case of childbearing, many women prioritise information from professionals. They seek out and value particular 'expert' forms of authoritative knowledge, which they have come to accept as the natural and normal way to prepare for motherhood. Moving to a more consensual and collaborative construction of authoritative knowledge in this context will be much harder to achieve, so accepted and normalised are current practices. The themes raised here: perceptions of development, technology and ways of knowing in the context of differentially experienced transformations, bring together important questions, which will be revisited in chapter 7.

The path to achieving more consensual, collaborative models of authoritative knowledge is a difficult one to negotiate. The challenge is how to retain the best practices of the collaborative models that currently exist in different cultures, at the same time, making available to all women the means by which pregnancy and childbearing can be made safer and ultimately more personally fulfilling. This raises questions about the relevance of cultural scripts in an increasingly globalised world, where cultural boundaries are becoming less distinct. A more individualised focus is called for by Willard, who argues that it is 'necessary to turn our focus away from those cultural scripts that are increasingly unconnected to the realities of women's lives and turn towards the experience of women themselves as they make decisions about their lives in relation to cultural expectations and realities' (Willard, 1988:231). Yet there remains much to be learned from observing and exploring the different (and similar) cultural practices that exist around childbearing. They help to remind us of the shifts that have occurred in how we think and practice reproduction and childbearing. They enable us to question and challenge taken for granted practices such as the liberating and oppressive dimensions of development. But most crucially, they remain important because individual lives are lived out in particular cultural contexts. In all societies, then, transition to first-time motherhood involves women in journeys that are both culturally scripted and personally uncertain.

Conclusion

The concept of cultural scripts and the ways in which these translate into types of authoritative knowledge and related practices provide us with the means to map the different cultural terrains of childbirth and motherhood. In so doing, they highlight cultural reference points that become even more important as boundaries are increasingly blurred by the processes of globalisation. Exploring different cultural practices around reproduction and motherhood lead us to a position where we can acknowledge the diversity of cultural practices. It also enables us to be cautious and questioning of developments that are closely associated with technology in relation to women's bodies, and to celebrate those practices that are inclusive and fulfilling for all women becoming mothers. And of course there is still much to be learned. Over subsequent chapters the ways in which culturally located knowledges shape women's accounts will be illustrated. In the following chapter we turn to focus on the ways in which women's expectations and experiences of motherhood are shaped in a Western context. By charting the medicalisation of reproduction and childbearing and associated normative practices, we can begin to see how confusing and complex journeys into motherhood have become.

3 Setting the Western context: mothering in late-modern society

As was noted previously, childbirth is always more than a biological event. Within Western cultures this position has provided a powerful, shifting and contested context in which women come to understand and make sense of their experiences of becoming mothers and motherhood. Experiences of becoming and being mothers are inextricably linked to 'race', social class, age and socio-cultural location and as a result are diverse and fragmented. In contrast, dominant forms of knowledge and associated practices shape the context in which mothering occurs. These are largely based on notions of mothering as biologically determined, instinctive and therefore universally experienced. In this chapter the complex and changing contexts in which transition to motherhood is experienced in contemporary Western society will be explored. This will be undertaken through a focus on the interwoven processes of medicalisation and late modernity, together with consideration of the ways in which ideologies and normative practices have shaped expectations and experiences in the Western world. How are the themes of late modernity played out? What are the implications of these – uncertainty, risk and responsibility – for women as they construct biographical narratives of transition to motherhood? The contested terrain of reproduction and motherhood has provided feminists with a rich arena in which to explore constructions of motherhood and theorise women's gendered and embodied experiences. This body of work, which importantly draws our attention to the ways in which notions of individuality and control are grounded in particularly Western and culturally bound ways of thinking, will be referred to throughout.

In Western cultures, the period of transition to motherhood, from confirmation of pregnancy to feeling like a mother, is both a public event and a very personal experience. As was shown in the previous chapter, the ways in which motherhood is framed in these societies shapes expectations and experiences. Women are confronted with an array of expert, public and lay knowledges through which their expectations and experiences of motherhood will be filtered. The medicalisation of childbearing, in conjunction with the pervasive ideologies and practices that shape expectations of motherhood, can be seen to powerfully reinforce notions of appropriate ways of preparing for becoming a mother and how a good mother 'naturally' acts. However, for some women, the experience of becoming a mother does not resonate with expectations. The gap between ideologies and lived experience can appear bewilderingly large and difficult to reconcile and to voice. In most societies, motherhood and family life are closely related to being a moral person and 'moral identities' may be perceived as being at risk if difficulties are experienced and/or disclosed (Ribbens McCarthy et al., 2000). The links between perceptions of risk and responsibility, or indeed being regarded as irresponsible, are particularly salient in relation to childbearing and motherhood, and will be returned to later in this chapter.

As we have already seen, the term 'late modernity' is used in this book to mean a period that has superseded the modern era, and is characterised by rapid change and uncertainty. Features of late modernity centre on 'institutional and individual reflexivity combined with the reorganisation of time and space' (Lupton, 1999:73). Transformations in late modern societies, for example changes in family living arrangements are, it is argued, happening at an unprecedented speed (Giddens, 1990, 1991, 1999). Old traditions and habits no longer provide the same certainties they once did. This has led to increased perceptions of risk as long-term certainties are called into question (Giddens, 1990, 1991, 1999; Beck, 1992; Beck and Beck-Gernsheim, 1995; Lupton, 1999). As notions of risk become heightened, individuals are increasingly exposed to expert bodies of knowledge and knowledge claims. At the same time the need to explore personal and social change reflexively has become a more pronounced feature of Western living. And this may indeed involve placing trust in expert bodies of knowledge and 'experts'. As Lupton has observed, 'individuals have greater recourse to expert knowledges in constructing the project of the self' (1999:76). As noted in chapter 1, in societies where traditions and practices have shifted, leading to greater personal uncertainty, making sense of our experiences has become, for many, a reflexive component of everyday life. This is achieved through the process of constructing and continuously revising our own individual biographies as part of the reflexive project of the self. This is an engaged and active project which moves beyond reflexivity as an intrinsic part of all human action. As noted earlier in chapter 1, it seems that we increasingly need to make sense of who we are, of our personal experiences, in order that 'ontological security' is maintained (Giddens, 1991; 1999). In relation to changes in gender, family and occupational roles, it has been argued that individuals must now seek out and negotiate relations that would previously have been part of gender fates (Beck and Beck-Gernsheim, 1995). Claims made about late modernity and the process of 'individualisation' are highly contested and alternative ways of seeing the social world have been put forward (Jenkins, 1996). Lawler, for example, recognises that changes in the way we live and the choices that we make could be seen to 'suggest that authoritative, expert knowledges are losing their ground' and that 'the proliferation of expertise and various forms of contestation between experts means that "expertise" is itself breaking down'. However, she concludes that 'these crises may be more apparent than real' (Lawler, 2000:19). Certainly in relation to reproduction, childbearing and mothering, the uncertain and yet morally underpinned context in which women come to motherhood continue to lead many to seek out and prioritise what they see as expert knowledge. But it is of course important to note that different groups will be touched by, and experience dimensions of, late modernity in different ways (see chapter 7).

So, how do the features of late modernity map on to the terrain of reproduction, childbirth and motherhood in Western societies? Clearly, changes in the ways we live mean that for many women becoming a mother is no longer regarded as a gender fate. Even so, motherhood continues to be central to the ways in which women are defined, whether or not they actually become mothers. For those who do become mothers, their expectations will be shaped by and through expert systems of authoritative knowledge as they negotiate the 'risky' and morally underpinned path to 'responsible' motherhood. The experiences of past generations have become less relevant as technological developments change the contours of pregnancy and childbirth in the Western world. These 'developments' ironically appear to have led women to perceive greater uncertainty and risk in their journeys into motherhood. This is at a time when biomedical, expert knowledge has apparently provided greater scientific certainty and predictability. Perceptions of risk in pregnancy and childbirth are not new. For example, wealthy women in the UK and USA employed doctors during the nineteenth and twentieth centuries specifically to protect them from the risks of childbirth. However, perceptions of risk have not diminished in late modernity but rather become inextricably bound up with safety and responsibility: a potent mix in the morally underpinned climate in which contemporary pregnancy and motherhood are lived out. Further, as Lupton has noted, 'risk-avoiding behaviour therefore becomes viewed as a moral enterprise relating to issues of self-control, self-knowledge and self-improvement' (1999:91). During pregnancy, childbirth and motherhood, avoiding risk, and so being seen to be responsible, continues to involve placing trust in experts.

To resist such engagement, to avoid screening tests, clinic visits and expert advice would be regarded as irresponsible behaviour. Such actions would be seen to jeopardise the woman's own health 'and more importantly, that of the foetus she is carrying and expected to protect and nourish in a proper maternal manner' (Lupton, 1999:90). For women in Western societies transition to motherhood is usually experienced against a backdrop of professional, expert management and self-monitoring. Women are compelled to take expert advice and avoid risk through appropriate behaviours and self-management. In turn, transition to motherhood challenges our sense of who we are as identities, and experiences shift and coherent biographical narratives become more difficult to construct: becoming a mother changes everything.

The medicalisation of childbearing

The area of medicine and related practices, then, provides a rich arena in which to see the characteristics of late modernity played out. In relation to reproduction and childbearing, perceptions of risk are increasingly 'filtered through contact with expert knowledge' (Lupton, 1999:77), and the reorganisation of time and space plays out in particular ways in relation to women's embodied experiences of becoming mothers. For example, regimes during antenatal preparation, during labour and birth and following birth are all measured in terms of 'the calendar and the clock' (Adams, 1995:48). Endogenous, body time is only alluded to, for example, in establishing the intensity of contractions during labour, but regularity of contractions are measured against 'clock time'. And so during birth, 'the woman is forced to oscillate between the all-encompassing body time of her labour and the rational framework of her clock-time environment' (Adams, 1995:49). The placing of childbirth within a medical, expert context and hospital setting, increasingly shaped by deference to 'authoritative knowledge' and particular constructions of time, is well documented (Oakley, 1979; Leavitt, 1986; Tew, 1990; Davis-Floyd, 1992; Jordan, 1993; Adams, 1995; Chase, 2001). A move away from home-based, midwife care to hospital-based, male-dominated care, has occurred in many industrialised societies. These changes have reinforced the illness view of pregnancy and childbearing and the need for expert knowledge, technology and management. By the 1970s, virtually all babies in the United Kingdom and America were born in hospital, the normality of pregnancy and childbirth only being acknowledged once delivery had taken place (Garcia, Kilpatrick and Richards, 1990; Davis-Floyd, 1992; Davis-Floyd and Sargent, 1997). It is now well documented that pregnancy and childbirth in the West have become medicalised and redefined as pathological, rather than natural states. As such they have become bound up with medical regulation and supervision and professional, expert management (Tew 1990; Nettleton, 1995; Foster, 1995). Along with the shift in place of birth, the development of routinised antenatal care has also occurred. Normative practices around preparation have developed, involving regular visits to health practitioners and hospital clinics. Women have generally come to accept these practices as an integral and necessary part of the childbearing process in which there is a 'cultural dependence on professional health care' (Oakley, 1979:15). Indeed, research in the UK and North America has demonstrated the ways in which women endorse the medicalisation of birth, leading to the conclusion that 'most women willingly submit themselves to the authority of the medical view' (Sargent and Bascope, 1997:185; Fox and Worts, 1999; Miller, 2000).

The shift in place of birth from home to hospital reflects both changes in wider society and the changes and continuities in women's lives in the Western world that have occurred over the last century. The placing of childbirth into the hospital setting has been explained in terms of patriarchy, male dominance and control over women's bodies (Oakley, 1979; Martin, 1990; Treichler, 1990; Foster, 1995). But it is also the case that in the UK women campaigned for the right to anaesthesia and hospital births during the earlier part of the last century (Lewis, 1990:15). Demand came from both middle-class and working-class women who, for very different reasons, wanted access to hospital beds and facilities for childbirth. In conjunction with this, a concern with high infant mortality and maternal mortality rates during this period, led policy-makers and doctors to conclude that 'the answer was to hospitalise childbirth' (Lewis, 1990:21). Similarly, in the USA of the 1940s, Davis-Floyd and Sargent document growing pressure from both wealthy women and doctors 'to convince the general public that the progressive "modern" way of giving birth was to divorce oneself from outdated servitude to biology by giving birth in the hospital under total anaesthesia' (1997:9). By 1946 54 per cent of all births in the UK occurred in hospital, and by 2003 the figure had risen to 98 per cent (*Social Trends*, 2003). This trend was echoed across other industrialised countries: 99 per cent of women in the USA currently give birth in hospital (*National Vital Statistics Reports*, 2000).

The lowering of both perinatal and maternal mortality rates and issues of safety and perceptions of risk have become inextricably bound in defending the shift to hospital-based deliveries and the expert management of pregnancy and childbirth. It has been noted that 'state interests in maternity care often use the language of safety and paternity' (Treichler, 1990:128). The extent to which safety, measured in terms of lowered perinatal mortality rates, can be attributed to better maternity care has been challenged (Tew, 1990; Campbell and MacFarlane, 1990; Foster, 1995). However, notions of risk and safety continue to be used to justify practices around childbirth across Europe and North America (Szurek, 1997). The practice of medicine in attributing better safety in childbirth to improved medical care has also been challenged in the light of other factors such as women having fewer children and the population as a whole being healthier (Oakley, 1993). Similarly, the relationship between outcomes and increased use of technology has also been explored. In the USA, the use of electronic foetal monitoring equipment was found to have resulted 'only in higher caesarean rate(s), not in better outcomes' (Davis-Floyd and Davis, 1997:316). Yet perceptions of risk, safety and responsibility remain persuasive factors in the antenatal period and the shaping of women's 'choices' in relation to place of birth. The concept of choice is of course particularly problematic in a pronatalist society. Davis-Floyd and Sargent have also noted the ways in which 'race, religion and socio-economic class still circumscribe most choices in overwhelming ways' (1997:11). They point to the dominance of technobirth in America, in spite of 'the apparently vast range of options for childbirth in America in the 1990s' (*ibid.*:11). The same observation holds for women becoming mothers in the UK. For a woman expecting a child in late-modern societies, then, interaction with the medical model, that is, services and health professionals during the antenatal period, can be seductive, as compliance is equated with safety and behaving responsibly.

As noted in the previous chapter, in both the UK and USA, biomedicine is increasingly regarded as providing 'authoritative knowledge' in relation to antenatal preparation for childbirth (Jordan, 1993; 1997; Browner and Press, 1997). Women who do not use antenatal services in 'appropriate' ways, or do not conform to particular societal expectations, may be regarded as 'feckless' or irresponsible (Miller, 1995:17). By attending clinic appointments, submitting to routine blood and urine tests and other technological interventions, a woman is perceived as preparing in an appropriate way for motherhood. In return, responsibility for the pregnancy is in some way transposed, a 'safe birth' becoming part of an equation in which a woman's control and power may be eroded (Lupton, 1994; Foster, 1995). Yet, as Tew has pointed out, 'scientific research in recent years has shown that most of the medical elements of antenatal care are ineffective ... antenatal clinics are, however, very effective in inculcating the rightness of and necessity for, obstetric intranatal care and so maintaining control of the maternity service by obstetricians' (1998:379). We can see, then, that a dependence on bodies of expert knowledge has evolved, reinforced by antenatal practices, which has led to the reconceptualisation of childbirth in terms of risk and 'clinical safety'. At the same time, the forms of authoritative knowledge that shape reproduction and childbirth have correspondingly shifted (Davis-Floyd, 1992; Tew, 1998).

The development of new technologies around reproduction and child-bearing has further reinforced claims of expertise. These developments have provided practitioners with the tools to detect 'abnormalities' and monitor pregnancy and childbirth. For example, screening has become a normative practice, a routine part of medical, antenatal care. It has enabled the detection of women and their unborn babies who may be 'at risk' of particular disorders and has contributed to 'the production of "authorita-tive knowledge" about pregnancy' (Davis-Floyd and Sargent, 1997:18; Reid, 1990; Georges, 1997; Rapp, 1999). Yet whilst screening has become an integral part of pregnancy, the social and moral issues it raises in societies where powerful pronatalist ideologies exist, are complex (Rapp, 1999). As Reid has pointed out, 'one of the critical issues inherent in any discussion of screening concerns abortion' (1990:313). And whilst women may eagerly anticipate their first ultrasound scan – taking along partners and other family members and purchasing the resulting photograph – far from being routine, the ultrasound may reveal serious deformities and place the pregnancy in jeopardy (Reid, 1990; Rapp, 1999). Screening then represents a further aspect of the medicalisation of pregnancy and childbearing and again encompasses the themes of power, risk, responsi-bility and expert knowledge. And whilst many women willingly engage with routine screening antenatally, and derive comfort from results con-firming the 'normality' of their unborn child, the continuing shifts in how pregnancy is expertly managed are in danger of further distancing women from knowing their own bodies (Boston Women's Health Book Collective, 1978; Treichler, 1990; Lupton, 1994). Clearly this has implications for the period following the birth of a baby when women may feel that they do not instinctively know what to do, that they have lost a sense of control in their lives (Lupton, 1994; see chapters 5 and 6, this volume).

The medicalisation of childbearing has been a gradual process. It has involved claims of safety and perceptions of risk being used to justify the relocation and the reprioritising, from midwife to obstetrician, of who has responsibility and who cares for, childbearing women, and impor-tantly, where (Robinson, 1990; Oakley, 1993; Annandale, 1998). More recently, in the UK attempts have been made to reverse this trend and for midwives to re-establish their previously held positions in relation to childbearing women (Page and Sandall, 2000). This movement has also been active in Northern European countries (De Vries *et al.*, 2001). However, the vast majority of women in Western societies continue to give birth in hospital and debates around medicalisation have continued. One graphic measure of the 'medicalisation of birth . . . is the caesarean section rate', which has increased rapidly across North America and Europe (Sargent and Bascope, 1997:192). In the UK 21 per cent of births were by caesarean section in 2001 whilst the rate was slightly higher in the USA at 24 per cent (Parliamentary Office of Science and Technology, October 2002, no.184). Rates for caesarean section have risen dramatically since the 1950s, when only 3 per cent of births in the UK were by caesarean section. This trend clearly raises questions about professional perceptions of risk and growing concerns over litigation. It also prompts us to think about the ways in which women have come to regard their bodies. Of course, debates on risk, responsibility and expert bodies of knowledge are played out in the context of gendered knowledge claims, against a backdrop of patriarchy. Feminists have differed on the positions they have taken to explain the shifts which have occurred around childbearing and the place of childbearing itself in women's lives. This, 'like the competing claims of patriarchy and capitalism as controlling structures, has been a theme of debate for feminists' (Oakley, 1993:11). However, shared by most feminisms is the 'understanding that patriarchy privileges men by taking the male body as the "standard" . . . and, through a comparison, viewing the female body as deficient, associated with illness, with lack of control and intuitive rather than reasoned' (Annandale and Clark, 1997:19; Martin, 1990; Davis-Floyd, 1992; Helman, 2001). It is on this basis that feminists and others have argued that male control over reproduction and childbearing has been achieved and maintained.

But whilst feminisms may share a common understanding regarding patriarchy, 'motherhood holds different meanings for different feminists' (Chase, 2001:9). An extreme and well-publicised position was expounded by Firestone, who argued that women would only be liberated from oppression 'when technology released them from pregnancy and childbirth altogether' (Chase, 2001:9; Firestone, 1971). This position has given rise to the misperception that feminists don't like men or babies, a myth that Chase and Rogers (2001) set out to challenge, demonstrating in the course of their book that 'the preponderance of feminist approaches to motherhood have been positive' (2001:4). Addressing the wider context of medicine, Lupton has usefully encapsulated the tensions that have existed in feminist writing over 'the uniqueness of women's embodied experience and the desire to deny that any such uniqueness exists' (1994: 131). Whilst radical feminists have argued that 'patriarchy seeks to control reproduction' (Annandale, 1998:72) and some talk of the oppressive nature of entering motherhood, others have celebrated the unique power of women's bodies to produce children. Here, reproduction is seen not as oppressive, but as offering women the possibility of experiencing a 'pure and original femininity' beyond patriarchal and social control (Daly, 1973; Chodorow, 1978; Gilligan, 1982; Annandale and Clark, 1997). The dilemma for feminists, however, has been 'how to retain the empowering or pleasurable aspects of motherhood without reinforcing the straitjacket of traditional gender arrangements' (Blum, 1993:292). The 'profound ambivalence' experienced as a mother – and a feminist – has been described by Gieve, who writes of 'the unexpected passion and joy and physical attachment on one side, and on the other side the relentless obligation and the necessity to respond which has deprived me of my own direction and brought the fear that I myself would be extinguished' (1987:39). Journeys into motherhood, then, have implications for our sense of who we are. Old recognisable selves can become subsumed within different identities associated with being a mother and motherhood. This pathway continues to be a tricky one to negotiate, both for women becoming mothers, and for those of us who, from different disciplinary positions, set out to document the journeys.

Ideologies of motherhood

The implications of the medicalisation of childbearing for women have been to shift 'the focus of birth from the social and emotional to the physiological and medical' (Garcia, Kilpatrick and Richards, 1990:3). Yet the ideologies which can be clearly discerned before and long after a child is born also remain a powerful force in shaping expectations. The biological fact of giving birth within Western cultures simultaneously leads to a redefinition of an individual's identity, an identity which is inextricably linked to family and motherhood – implying that a woman's fate is tied to her biological role in reproduction (Oakley, 1979; Richardson, 1993; Romito, 1997). This transition occurs 'against a background of personal and cultural assumptions that all women are, or want to be mothers' (Letherby, 1994:525). And whilst these assumptions have increasingly been challenged, and attempts made to separate motherhood from female identity, the tendency to conflate these identities has continued (Phoenix and Woollett, 1991; Ireland, 1993; Letherby, 1994). In the context of societies underpinned by pronatalist ideologies, it has been argued that whether women become mothers or not, 'motherhood is central to the ways in which they are defined by others and to their perceptions of themselves' (Phoenix and Woollett, 1991:13). The category mother is clearly problematic and dynamic, for as Lawler notes, 'the advent of new reproductive technologies potentially destabilizes the category "mother" (2000, 19). Yet, whatever the potential for different constructions of mother/motherhood, dominant ideologies remain: powerfully rooted in assumptions of biological determinism and the inevitability of women's destiny to become mothers. Fundamental to such ideologies is the notion that mothering is instinctive and therefore universally experienced and constant. Yet historical, social and cultural variations have been clearly demonstrated, which 'confirms that mothering, like other relationships and institutions, is socially constructed, not biologically inscribed' (Glenn, 1994:3).

Ideologies, then, also shift over time, and ideas about what a 'good' mother should do – stay at home and devote herself to childrearing and housework – shift according to public and political changes and economic demands. Good parenting, and specifically good mothering, is premised on ideas of being with children, fulfilling the demands of intensive nurturing, whilst at the same time it involves taking up paid work and providing financially for a child. Current policies in the UK and the USA, for example the New Deal in the UK, appear to encourage (certain groups of) women to combine mothering with paid employment (which may indeed be paid 'mothering' of other women's children). Once again, this serves to redefine the roles and expectations of what constitutes a 'good' mother (Phoenix and Woollett, 1991; Segura, 1994; Miller, 1998; Duncan and Edwards, 1999). This link between shifting policy and ideological commitments and particular constructions of maternal bodies and motherhood is echoed across post-industrial societies (Stacey, 1996; Chase, 2001). But class, race and culture have also always underpinned individual expectations and experiences of mothering. The notion of the 'good' mother, who stays at home or experiences guilt or ambivalence as a result of combining mothering with paid work outside the home, has been premised on particular groups of white, privileged women. Such constructions lack relevance for 'less privileged women (for instance, immigrant women, women of color) who have historically been important economic actors both inside and outside the home' (Segura, 1994:212). The material and cultural circumstances in which women live their lives is, then, a crucial feature in any analysis of motherhood. As Collins has argued, 'for women of color, the subjective experience of mothering/ motherhood is inextricably linked to the sociocultural concern of racial ethnic communities – one does not exist without the other' (1994:47). Equally, as noted in earlier chapters, for women becoming mothers, or mothering, in the developing world, day-to-day survival may well be a primary concern overriding any (Western) notion of individualised control in a life. So, contexts differ, but within the Western world dominant ideologies surrounding motherhood can be seen to represent the ideas and beliefs of more powerful groups and do not recognise or accommodate the diversity of women's lived experiences. And they are pervasive, and powerfully shape the cultural scripts and public and 'meta narratives' (Somers, 1994) which both inform normative practices and women's own expectations, of what mothering will be like.

Since the 1960s, feminists have challenged essentialist constructions of maternal bodies and motherhood. Attempts to theorise motherhood without recourse to 'natural or biological explanations' have been attempted (Glenn, 1994). Using psychoanalytic object relations theory, Chodorow (1978) has sought to demonstrate how being mothered transmits and reinforces a pattern of female mothering. This is not biologically determined but a product of the dynamics of the mother–daughter relationship, which differs from the mother–son relationship. In order to change expectations around mothering, Chodorow has argued that men must participate more equally in childrearing to redress the gender balance of nurturing/caring. Ruddick (1980) too has argued that mothers' concerns for nurturing and protecting their children can be explained through 'maternal practice'. The physical, emotional and intellectual dimensions of mothering are not, then, biologically determined but arise through constant practice. The positions taken by both Chodorow and Ruddick have been criticised for, amongst other things, universalising experiences of motherhood and not challenging the status quo, and the debate continues (Phoenix and Woollett, 1991; Delphy, 1992; Glenn, 1994; Chase and Rogers, 2001). In particular, Chodorow has been criticised for conflating motherhood with femininity, so that 'female desire is thus analytically erased' (Elliott, 2001:110). In stark contrast to these positions, pro-family ideologies, which have been dominant in America and bound up with the political Right in Britain and more recently New Labour, are rooted in perceptions of motherhood as biologically determined. The belief associated with cultural feminism, that women's capacity for motherhood provides 'an essential, unifying principle', reinforces such ideas (Chase, 2001:14). Similarly, conservative and pro-family feminism has focused on the 'life giving values associated with mothering' (Delphy, 1992:18). These positions have served to emphasise 'mothering as women's primary and exclusive identity' and in so doing locate women firmly in the home, the private sphere (Richardson, 1993; Glenn, 1994).

It is these essentialist constructions of mothering as biologically determined and shared and shaped in relation to patriarchy, that other feminists have long argued turn mothering into such an alienating and oppressive experience (Rich, 1977; Oakley, 1979). And yet such challenges have not radically changed the dominant ideologies that powerfully and pervasively surround and shape motherhood. Even though household and living arrangements have changed dramatically in recent decades, ideologies around 'good' mothering persist and override current living arrangements (Garcia Coll *et al.*, 1998). Change, then, has been slow and 'while divorce rates and women's paid employment have increased, women still do not have adequate day care, enough support from male partners, and workplaces attentive to employees' family responsibilities' (Chase, 2001:18). Clearly, the challenges persist, for the problem according to Romito 'is that despite twenty-five years of the new feminism, motherhood still retains its sacred aura. Mothers still do not dare to admit how burdensome the constraints and difficulties of their condition can be' (1997:172). Reflecting on her own experiences of being a mother, Gieve has also noted that the 'fear of the knot of motherhood has made us turn away from confronting it' (1987:39). And therein lies the paradox for women. The unique positioning of childbearing – at the interface between the biological and the social – both shapes expectations and renders experiences which do not conform to some idealised notion of motherhood difficult to make sense of, to confront and to voice. The compelling and confusing contexts in which transition to motherhood is lived and experienced in late modernity provide a particularly challenging backdrop against which to do this. The focus on individualisation apparent in late modern societies encourages reflexivity, through actively working on the self to make sense of new experiences in the absence of 'traditional norms and certainties'. Yet, it is the absence of these 'traditional norms and certainties', together with unrealistic expectations, which can make experiences of first-time motherhood particularly 'baffling' (Frank, 1995; Lupton, 1999).

Ideologies that surround and shape notions of motherhood are, then, pervasive, dynamic and linked to power. Yet this is to ignore that women are able to exercise some agency in their lives, albeit dependent on their structural location and material circumstances (Barclay *et al.*, 1997; Rajan, 1996; Fox and Worts, 1999; Duncan and Edwards, 1999). However, such powerful ideologies override individual experience, and continue to reinforce idealised notions of motherhood, that in turn fail to accommodate the diversity that exists in experiences of mothering. Commenting on the importance of theorising women's differences, Phoenix and Woollett caution that failure to do so 'helps to maintain the status quo as "normal mothers" being white, middle class, married women and other mothers being deviant/aberrant' (1991:226). As noted in chapter 1, the women whose experiences provide the first-hand accounts in this book apparently conform to stereotypes of 'good' and 'normal' mothers. They are white, educated and partnered, but their early experiences of motherhood were diverse and different from their own expectations and at times difficult to make sense of (Chase, 2001).

Yet, however invidious the ideologies, women continue to become mothers and 'to hold images of what motherhood and childhood should be like' (Ribbens, 1998:28). Having been socialised into roles that continue to anticipate mothering, a majority of women at some time in their lives become mothers (Abbott and Wallace, 1990). Indeed, in most societies to choose to remain childless is perceived as somehow 'unnatural', so deeply inscribed and culturally scripted are essentialist ideas of womanhood. The current decline in fertility rates across many European countries and the USA might eventually lead to different, less essentialist constructions of womanhood, or conversely, may further reinforce notions of 'unnaturalness'. However, for those women who anticipate having at least one child during their lives, studies have shown that expectations of motherhood often do not resonate with experiences. Despite many years of academic study and calls for change, it is noteworthy that women continue to come to motherhood with 'quite unrealistic expectations' (Boulton, 1983; Oakley, 1993; Richardson, 1993; Barclay et al., 1997; Chase and Rogers, 2001; Mauthner, 2002).

Normative practices

As was noted in chapter 2, in Western societies women becoming pregnant are 'exposed to a variety of ideas about pregnancy, childbirth and childcare' which will be filtered according to cultural location, social class, age etc. (Phoenix and Woollett, 1991:66–7). Preparation for most mothers is located within highly developed systems of preventive antenatal care, which is clearly located within a biomedical context: the clinic and the hospital (Miller, 1995; Graham and Oakley, 1986; Oakley, 1993; Browner and Press, 1997). It is interesting to note that attempts to redefine women as 'consumers' of maternity care within the UK, with a 'right' to choice, control and continuity of care have failed (The Winterton Report, 1992; Page and Sandall, 2000). This may in part be due to the nationalised system of health care that exists in the UK, in contrast to the largely privatised system of health care in the US, where more women would identify with the term 'consumer', whilst others are wholly reliant on Medicaid. However, given the diversity of women's lives, both within and across different societies in the West, services around childbirth continue to be provided in particularly uniform ways. For example, the hospital is regarded by most women as the 'natural' place to give birth (Treichler, 1990; Szurek, 1997). In many ways this confirms, were confirmation needed, the power and dominance of 'authoritative knowledge' as discussed in the previous chapter. By focusing on the normative practices in the West that have resulted from particular forms of authoritative knowledge, we can see when, where and how constructions of the expert are played out. The acceptance by a majority of women of the hospital as the natural place to give birth, reflects both the dynamic qualities and power of authoritative knowledge in which 'all participants come to see the current social order as a natural order, that is, the way things (obviously) are' (Jordan, 1997:56).

As already noted, even before the birth of a child, women begin to be defined in accordance with notions of 'good' mothering. They are expected to prepare appropriately – attend antenatal classes, wear appropriate clothing, change socialising patterns and behaviours to conform to some 'ideal type'. Clearly, antenatal practices and 'the rituals of obstetrics' help to transmit and reinforce gendered values held in Western societies (Davis-Floyd, 1992). Beyond regular antenatal visits, women (and their partners) are invited to attend parent-craft classes in order to prepare appropriately for parenthood. Yet, as was demonstrated in the preceding chapter, the perception of need for such classes is filtered through cultural ways of knowing, and preparing for childbirth: the Bangladeshi women did not think they were necessary (Miller, 1995). Following the birth, care in the postnatal period is much less highly developed in the UK. It is operationalised within the clinic setting *and* the private sphere of the home, and in relation to essentialist ideas of mothering (Glazener, MacArthur and Garcia, 1993; Garcia and Marchant, 1996). Although medical regulation and supervision characterise normative practices during the antenatal period, the medical gaze switches swiftly from the mother to the baby in the postnatal period. When Lawler writes of the 'apparent' rather than 'real' demise in the position of expert knowledges in late modernity, she concludes that 'there seems little evidence that there has been a loosening of surveillance of mothers and their children' (2000:20). Clearly, a whole host of different experts – midwives, doctors, health visitors – are involved in monitoring the antenatal and postnatal periods but, according to Lawler, this monitoring has become increasingly 'bound up with processes of self-surveillance' (2000:20). In the postnatal period this is expected to come to the fore. Certainly, from conception and sometimes pre-conception, expert advice is offered on what is best for the child, and mothers are expected to act responsibly in providing care and meeting their child's needs (Jessop, 2001). Being a mother involves responsibility, an intrinsic feature of which is self-surveillance. This involves evaluating one's self against others, in a confusing context where 'normal' mothering is not defined but powerfully reinforces expectations.

In the postnatal period, the form of monitoring shifts and the focus of early postnatal check-ups 'is almost entirely on the baby, or the mother in relation to the baby; her independent status as a woman is discounted'

(Urwin, 1985:177). The development and introduction of the Edinburgh Postnatal Depression Scale in the UK is one attempt to focus on women's mental health in the early weeks following childbirth. A health visitor administers the questionnaire when she visits the mother in her home. Boxes are ticked according to how the woman says she has felt over the preceding seven days. Responses are then coded and a 'diagnosis' made. Whilst this initiative could be welcomed as an attempt to collate women's experiences of early mothering, it is a blunt instrument with which to gather sensitive material and questions have been raised about its usefulness (Barker, 1998). Indeed, it could be seen as yet another practice that medicalises and, in turn, problematises *normal* early mothering experiences. Many women would agree that they felt tearful and at times unhappy in the days and weeks and sometimes months following the birth of their child. Patterns of care following the birth of a child are, then, largely normatively preoccupied and task-based, with an emphasis on routine measures being taken to indicate a 'return to normal'.

The close supervision and sense of shared responsibility engendered by professional antenatal practices and experienced from confirmation of pregnancy, ceases in most Western societies shortly after the birth. Any feelings which had been placed as secondary to authoritative, medical knowledge in the antenatal period are now expected to come to the fore: women are expected to instinctively know how to be mothers. Whilst women may be socialised from birth into gendered, 'female' roles, the experience of becoming a mother may not resonate with earlier expect-ations. Births are often different from what had been expected, and the tasks of early mothering can seem daunting and the responsibility for a small baby overwhelming. The dominance of particular ways of knowing in the antenatal period, which reinforce particular notions of good mothering, can be seen to be potentially disempowering and 'may make it difficult to take back control after the birth, when (a mother) may have no real knowledge of her own feelings, or her baby' (Lupton, 1994: 148–9). Indeed, the technologies and practices involved in the medicali-sation of reproduction increasingly separate women from knowing their own bodies. Thus 'the history of Western obstetrics is the history of technologies of separation (and) it is very, very hard to conceptually put back together that which medicine has rendered asunder' (Rothman cited in Davis-Floyd and Davis, 1997:315)

Narratives: making sense of personal transition

As noted in chapter 1, the need for individuals to make connections between the personal and the social, and thus make sense of their experiences, is increasingly regarded as a feature of changing Western societies in which choices have become more complex. In the face of these greater uncertainties and complex choices, there is an increased need to create and maintain ontological security and 'new certainties for oneself' (Beck, 1994:14; Lupton, 1999). This is achieved by the production of biographical or ontological narratives. Through these a recognisable sense of self is shaped and maintained, through a process of continual reflection and reworking. Individuals, then, make sense of experiences and project particular self-identities through narratives that are shaped by the material, cultural and political circumstances in which they live. As we have seen, during pregnancy the themes of late modernity are clearly played out as trust is largely placed in experts, and expert knowledge is ranked above that emanating from the experiences of family and friends. Ontological security is maintained throughout this period of transition based on a relationship of trust in experts and the knowledge that appropriate and responsible preparation, which implicitly diminishes risk, is being undertaken. But at this stage it is important to note that women anticipating the birth of their first child do not have the reflexive grasp that comes from experience. They are *anticipating* motherhood but are not yet mothers and so can only appeal to idealised notions of motherhood, or accounts from family and friends. Ideas about the type of mother women want to be are formed at this time from an array of sources, but it is the birth of a first child that is a crucial turning point. The experience of giving birth and being a mother usually leads women to reflect that their lived experiences are different from their expectations and to question their 'expert' preparation. They do not necessarily feel like the type of mother they had envisaged being, and shifting identities involving a temporary loss of an old, recognisable self, can add to this period of confusion (see chapters 5 and 6).

At some point during the early weeks and months of becoming a mother, early experiences of mothering that do not resonate with expectations have to be made sense of and reconciled. For a woman reflecting from this newly held position, the trust placed in experts during the antenatal period can gradually come to feel misplaced. Becoming a mother usually turns out to be different from what had been anticipated, as expectations are replaced by experiences. Plans that had seemed plausible before the birth have to be rethought as a sense of a pre-baby self (the old you) becomes subsumed within the new identities associated with being a mother. The conflicting and sometimes overwhelming feelings of love, guilt, exhaustion, joy and fear are not uncommon experiences in the early weeks and months of becoming a mother. But they need to be understood, and made sense of, recognised and accepted as *normal* responses to early mothering experiences and motherhood. For the many women who find that their experiences are different from what they had expected, the need to produce culturally recognisable accounts of early mothering, demonstrating that they are 'good' mothers who are coping, can appear paramount. Women may feel that they must conceal difficult or contrary experiences because of the morally underpinned context in which we mother. This also has implications for social action and women may confine themselves to the home, where new mothering is easier to manage. The birth of a child instantly leads others to identify women as mothers, and yet for the individual the process may be much more gradual. It is clear, then, that the powerful knowledges and practices that shape the context in which women become mothers, provide a challenging backdrop against which to make sense of and narrate early experiences. Cultural scripts and expectations do not necessarily fit individual experiences and yet women are expected to naturally know how to mother. It is only after the passage of time, leading to a shift in perception of who is the expert around reproduction and childbearing and the regaining of sense of a pre-baby self, that difficult and challenging accounts of transition eventually can be voiced (see chapter 6). Over time, women come to know their babies and feel able to differentiate between competing expert and lay knowledge claims. Eventually, they become the experts in relation to their own children, and they know that they are doing 'good enough' mothering.

Becoming a mother in late modern society

Becoming a mother in late modern society is, then, a highly complex experience. We must be cautious about any claims made in relation to universal experiences, and at the same time acknowledge the embodied act of birth and its cultural inscription and social location. In exploring the pathways through the landscape of childbearing and motherhood, feminists are continually faced with challenges. The key challenge is summed up succinctly by Linda Rennie Forcey, who observes the need to 'seek balance between the essentialism lurking in simplified notions of "mothers" as a homogeneous group and the equally important need for political unity and an ethic of care' (Forcey, 1999:304). Yet the context keeps changing, and we have to pay close attention to the ways in which changes infiltrate and shape expectations and ways of doing and being. So, whilst debates continue to surround the place of reproduction and childbearing in women's lives, the context in which childbearing takes place reflects other shifts that have occurred across many Western societies. Patterns within women's lives have shifted, with many women having children either much earlier or later in life, alone or partnered, combining work and mothering, or choosing to remain childless (child-free). These general trends are echoed across other Western societies (Eurostats, 2000; *National Vital Statistics*, 2000). Fathers have also been identified as a new consumer group (Barbour, 1990) and their role throughout the childbearing process and after has become a focus of research and debate (Laqueur, 1992; Ruddick, 1992; Mitchell and Goody, 1997; Helman, 2001). In the USA and across many European countries, 'the family' is increasingly repositioned as the cornerstone of society and policies to support particular types of family are promoted, whilst at the same time, families of choice and other ways of living are also being championed. In the UK, the rights of the child have also been increasingly recognised and detailed in legislation (for example, Children Act 1989) and meeting children's needs has become an ambiguous government concern. Parenting has been redefined in terms of skills to be learned and practised and parenting classes are increasingly offered or prescribed (Webster-Stratton, 1997; Home Office, 1998). Across many European countries maternity and paternity leave has been increased or introduced although not necessarily financially supported. But for all these changes, in almost all societies the rearing of children continues to be predominately undertaken by women, a significant number of whom parent alone and in poverty.

The context, then, in which women negotiate their journeys into motherhood and in which mothering is experienced, continues to shift. Writing in another context, Plummer has drawn our attention to the possibilities of challenges to 'old stories' and the 'obdurate grip' of others (1995:131). It is the 'obdurate grip' of the myths around motherhood which provides a recurrent theme across the chapters of this book. Feminists have, over several generations, debated and called for changes in the conditions in which mothering is experienced. Yet it appears that the difficulties of 'telling the hard things about motherhood' (Ross, 1995:398) remains, and essentialist notions of 'normal' and 'natural' transition make confronting and voicing difficult experiences particularly problematic (Nicolson, 1998; Mauthner, 2002). Wider social changes have translated into mothering occurring at different times in women's lives. The significance of mothering to women's lives within the context of changed educational opportunities for (some) women and the resulting shifts in patterns of employment, also has implications for constructions of motherhood. There is an increase in the number of single mothers and others who follow 'non-traditional' ways of living and parenting (McRae, 1999). In all late modern societies, contemporary mothering arrangements are more diverse, yet often remain unrecognised in areas of family policy and practice (Stacey, 1996; Duncan and Edwards, 1999). This is apparent in relation to mothers whose mothering challenges stereotypes. The experiences of mothers who have found themselves to be marginalised: teen mothers, immigrant mothers, lesbian mothers, homeless mothers, welfare mothers and incarcerated mothers, have been studied in recent years (Garcia Coll *et al.*, 1998). These 'types' of mothers all represent groups who challenge the ' "good" mother narrative [which] attempts to assert uniformity where there is diversity; consensus where there are differing perspectives' (Garcia Coll *et al.*, 1998:12). But the difficulties of making women's different and differing voices either heard or count have remained. Feminist and other research has continued to explore the differences and commonalities of contemporary mothering experiences. Yet the practices around motherhood in the West remain grounded in assumptions of mothering as biologically determined, instinctive and natural.

Conclusion

Transformations in Western societies have led to different ways of living and organising personal lives and intimate relationships. These changes differentially impact on individuals' lives, according to the ways in which lives are embedded in particular power relations. For some, and particularly those in the West, there is a pattern of greater self-reflexivity, which emerges as a mechanism for making sense of a life in the increasing absence of traditional, taken-for-granted, gendered fates. Individuals, then, increasingly seek understanding of their experiences and lives through the construction and reworking of biographical narratives. Becoming a mother changes lives in all sorts of ways, both anticipated and unexpected. But the contemporary context can make constructing and voicing biographical narratives difficult. This is because motherhood is 'mainly lived out in a private, domestic sphere', but it is measured according to societal norms and professional normative practices, which ignore the diversity of women's experiences (Phoenix and Woollett, 1991). Because motherhood and family are closely associated with an individual's moral being, moral identities may be challenged and compromised during transition to motherhood. Disclosure of experiences which do not resonate with expectations, both personally held and socially constructed, may, then, be perceived as too risky. The complex and contradictory dimensions of motherhood – the embodied physical act of birth, essentialist notions of mothering, the social and cultural contexts in which mothers and their children live their lives – make understanding and voicing normal difficulties problematic. Yet, paradoxically, the very act of not voicing difficult experiences maintains and perpetuates the myths that continue to surround motherhood. Women becoming mothers for the first time come to terms with their individual experiences within these shifting and contradictory contexts and from different positions within the social world. In the following three chapters the experiences of a group of women can be glimpsed, as their journeys into first-time motherhood unfold.

4   Anticipating motherhood: the antenatal period

> They've always done all the checks all the time so I'm quite confident that everything's been monitored.   (Clare, antenatal interview)

Transition to motherhood involves women embarking on uncertain personal journeys: anticipating the birth of a baby, becoming and being a mother, motherhood. The previous three chapters have helped to set the scene conceptually, theoretically and methodologically. The following three chapters shift the focus to women's own lived, embodied, 'fleshy' accounts of their experiences of becoming mothers for the first time. The arguments set up in the previous chapters are now revisited in the light of the experiences of the women in this group. How far are features of late modernity – uncertainty and risk, trust in expert bodies of knowledge, and reflexivity – discernible in the accounts produced? In what ways do these features shape the ways women talk about their experiences? For example, how do cultural constructions of risk translate into responsibilities and actions? What can a detailed focus on this period of transition tell us about the ways in which selves are experienced, maintained and narrated? How is reflexivity experienced and played out? As noted in the previous chapter, notions of normal and good and bad mothering permeate the contemporary context in which transition to motherhood is experienced and understood within the Western world. This extends to the antenatal/ prenatal period, in which appropriate ways of preparing to become a mother are culturally and socially shaped and experienced. Such a context leads to contradictory accounts, for example, expectations that are grounded in ideas about the natural capacity of women's bodies ('you want to do it yourself naturally'), desires to do the appropriate thing ('I just assume that I'll go to the hospital and let them do it') and acceptance that expert practices may dominate the birth ('You're going to be stuck with the medical way of doing things, but then I'm happy to go along with that').

The empirical data are prioritised in this and the following two chapters. Whilst the theoretical implications are raised across these chapters, these will be more fully drawn out and explored, in chapter 7. In these chapters women's accounts of their experiences move centre stage. We follow them on their journeys into motherhood. This focus enables us to note the ways in which they anticipate and prepare for motherhood and position themselves in particular ways in relation to dominant bodies of expert knowledge: how they construct and narrate their experiences. Although these chapters are organised according to the arguments outlined above, it is also interesting for the reader to trace individual women's accounts within and across the three chapters. In this way, individual stories of anticipation, tentative hopes, fears and experiences of becoming a mother, can be captured. In presenting the data in this way, I am also imposing a neat order through a focus on narrative trajectories whilst acknowledging that lives are lived in messier, less coherent, ways. The narratives are organised around linear time, chronologically. This mirrors the stages in transition to motherhood, which rely on medically defined language, i.e. antenatal (or prenatal) and early and late postnatal periods. It is also important to note that the longitudinal dimensions of this study both enabled, and indeed invited, reflexivity and to once again urge caution in relation to the assumptions and claims we make in relation to reflexivity (see chapter 7). This is because it assumes a capacity for active and engaged reflexivity, beyond the reflexivity that is an intrinsic dimension of all human action. Theories of reflexivity may not take sufficient account of oppressive structural and material conditions which shape lives and possibilities (see chapters 1 and 7). That we should not presume the reflexive social actor was brought home to me early on in my research. In one interview, I asked Faye how she would describe being pregnant and she replied 'I'm not very good on words and things like that.' I was aware that Faye had been surprised that I had not arrived with a questionnaire but a short interview schedule, and she seemed bemused that I should be interested in her experiences, even though we had talked through the format when arranging to meet. In subsequent interviews Faye seemed much more at ease with the interview format and talking about her experiences. However, in the end-of-study questionnaire Faye made the following comment 'sometimes I would have preferred a little time to think about the questions. I realise that initial response is important but I found myself thinking about some of my answers later and wishing I had added other things'. This shows the ways in which the interview encounter can prompt reflection both during and after the interview. Yet, whilst all this is to caution against assuming the actively reflexive, experienced storyteller, it should not deter us from noting how changes in late modernity in Western societies increasingly lead individuals to be reflexive, *at some level*. In gathering these women's accounts of transition to motherhood I was known by the participants to be both a researcher and a mother. This information will have shaped both the interview encounter and the ways in which expectations and experiences were narrated: what was said and what was left unsaid (see chapter 7).

Antenatal care (as it is referred to in the UK, although prenatal care is the term used in the USA) is available to all women in the UK, irrespective of the ability to pay, under the National Health Service (NHS). The differences that characterise access to, and quality of, prenatal care in the USA do not exist in the same way in the UK. Even so, there is a wealth of literature available to show that inequalities continue to be a feature of the access to, and services provided by, the NHS, that the 'inverse care law' continues to exist (Tudor Hart, 1971; Lazarus, 1997; Shaw et al., 1999). Deference to medical knowledge and engagement with those perceived to be experts, are features of late modernity. These will be explored in relation to debates on risk, trust in experts and individual control, and these themes will also be returned to in subsequent chapters. The layers within narratives have also provided markers to the ways in which women negotiate between the lived experience of mothering and the institution of motherhood (Rich, 1977). Finally then, the aim has not been to uncover 'truths' about transition to motherhood, but rather to listen to and explore the ways in which women gradually make sense of and narrate their experiences of this period of personal transition, the authenticity of accounts being 'created in the process of storytelling' (Frank, 2002:1). This approach involves engaging with the substantive data within the framework of exploring how and why narratives are constructed and presented in particular ways, how women make sense of this period of transition. The complexities of narrating experiences of periods of personal transition will also be explored. This will be achieved through a focus on different layers of narrative as both engagement and resistance are discerned in accounts. Substantive areas which have emerged from the data will be used to illustrate how narratives anticipating motherhood are constructed in relation to individuals' perceptions of 'expert knowledge' and changing perceptions of self. The two following chapters will show how these perceptions can be seen to shift over time, leading eventually to the reconstruction of previous accounts or the production and voicing of counter-narratives, linked to a shifting sense of self. The participants' attempts to make sense of this period of transition are most clearly demonstrated in the following areas: preparation and engagement with 'experts' (preparing appropriately and anticipating the birth), the shifting sense of 'selves' and anticipating motherhood. These areas will provide the focus of this chapter. Whilst they will be largely explored separately, they are also interlinked and interwoven, and underpinned by differential experiences of wishing to retain control.

Preparing appropriately

The moral context in which mothering occurs is hard to escape, its influences being felt for some even before conception. It clearly shapes the antenatal period, that is the medically defined stages, which pregnant women pass through. In the UK and the US there is a cultural expectation that all women expecting a child will take up and use antenatal services 'appropriately' and this involves regular interactions with health care professionals (Miller, 1995; Browner and Press, 1997). Most of the women in this study purchased home test kits from the pharmacy to establish whether they were pregnant. However, all presented themselves to their general practitioners (GPs) to confirm their pregnancy. Also, many spoke of the now routine ultrasound scan providing absolute certainty of their pregnancy and reassurance:

That was really reassuring because up till then I hadn't really sort of believed in it you know. (Peggy)

I suppose I didn't actually feel that pregnant until you actually see that baby on the scan, then yes, it becomes more real. (Linda)

Engagement with health professionals and associated practices were openly undertaken at an early stage by all the women. This was regarded as the appropriate thing to do when expecting a child. As noted in earlier chapters, how 'choices' are perceived and made is bound up with dominant ideologies about appropriate behaviours. These in turn are reinforced and perpetuated through interactions and mediated by social class. Thus 'all participants come to see the current social order as a natural order, that is, the way things (obviously) are' (Davis-Floyd and Sargent, 1997:56). This extends to place of birth, with the hospital regarded as the appropriate, 'natural' setting for birth. In the following extract, Felicity talks about her reasons for not contemplating a home birth and recognises the contradictions in her account:

The one thing about birth that really worries me is the mess. The mess and the smell ... and yes, OK, I slag off the medical profession but I'm going to be damned glad that they'll be there if anything goes wrong.

Kathryn too emphasises her perception of the hospital as being the safest place to give birth, and her responsibility for her unborn child:

I would just never forgive myself if something went wrong and I could have saved the baby.

These extracts resonate with others in the study and indeed other research findings in the UK and US, which show engagement with, rather than resistance to, a (potentially) medicalised birth (Lazarus, 1997). The uncertainty of what giving birth will involve, especially when expecting a first child, leads the women to engage with those they perceive as expert, and to demonstrate through their accounts and actions that they are preparing responsibly. Birth should occur where both expert professionals and expert equipment are located: the hospital. Greater interaction with the medical profession was also regarded as evidence of better care, and experienced as reassuring. The expert and reassuring nature of the relationship was summed up by Sarah:

> ... goes to the hospital and the woman there was brilliant, she was really nice. And there was a midwife there and a ... some guy who deals with genes, and a trainee doctor who just nodded a lot, and somebody else, some other kind of expert ... as well as the ultrasound person and ... and they were brilliant. The fact is that all of those women and men, they know exactly what they're doing, it's their job ...

Stories of engagement with the experts, through contact with G.P.s and/or midwives, or health visitors at parent-craft classes, provided a central part of the plot in the women's anticipatory narratives. Whilst the women all spoke of getting information from other sources, for example, relatives, friends and books, these were regarded as less reliable, less expert, than that provided by health professionals, as the following extract shows:

> I don't like getting information from other people because it's always so subjective and they always want to harp on about their little story, and so I have actually avoided other people ... I've steered away from those, those are the most unhelpful, personal experiences that I've steered away from. But I think the books, and the midwives and my doctor, my doctor's been good. (Rebecca)

Information from friends was seen as either 'unhelpful' or as in the extract below, potentially 'wrong'. Ironically, the cautious silence on the part of friends who were already mothers helped to perpetuate particular myths of motherhood:

> Well, a lot of the friends that have had babies say that they don't like to say too much because they could say the wrong thing. (Faye)

Information from experts, those in whom cultural authority is vested, is ordered as being a better source of knowledge. Information giving could also act as a catalyst leading to greater reflexivity. Gillian describes her experiences of attending parent-craft classes:

> they've been useful in that they've prompted me ... it's just made you think or it's made you think in order ...

But this opportunity to 'think' was of course bounded by the medical context in which particular ideological messages are conveyed. The interplay between acting responsibly and being seen to do the right thing is emphasised in the ways in which the women spoke about their feeding intentions. This involved seeking guidance and reassurance from the experts that their intended actions were appropriate. In the following extract Angela talks of her intentions, but within the context of having to seek *confirmation* from the expert, the midwife:

There's things like ... 'cos I can't make up my mind whether I'm breastfeeding or bottle feeding. So, I'd like to have a go at breastfeeding but you've got to know all the bits and bobs that go with it, like I didn't find out until the other day that, I want to go half and half so that my husband will be involved, and what I was going to do was do half formula and half breast, but I found out that if you've got eczema or asthma in the family, they don't like you doing a mixture, well, I only found that out Monday ... so looks like I'm going to do totally breast but I can't confirm that with the midwife until I see her.

Similarly, Wendy talks of not getting the permission she had sought in regard to the feeding practice she had planned. But she is apparently happy to be told what to do:

I'm going for the breast first to see how I get on. I did actually say to the midwife that I wanted to do both, I wanted the bottle and ... but she said you can't actually do that ... (but) it's been good. They just tell you everything.

Perceptions of the dimensions of expert knowledge are implicit within the extract: '*they* don't like you doing a mixture'. Wanting experts to give guidance was expressed by many of the participants who, at times, resisted being drawn into decision-making interactions, wanting to be told what to do and emphasising their non-expert status, as Peggy remarked:

Don't keep giving me decisions to make, I don't know, I've not done this before.

As I have previously noted, professional care in the postnatal period in the UK is organised under the National Health Service. It involves a number of home visits made by the midwife and then health visitor in the period following discharge from the hospital. This is a practice which may be less culturally acceptable in the US. In the following extract, Gillian talks in terms of establishing a relationship with the health professionals who will be 'responsible' for her following the birth of her baby:

It also gives you a chance to get to know the health visitor ... I mean I know which one will be mine afterwards ... just to sound out a few of their ideas and things and how you ... they're going to handle you afterwards, that type of thing.

Establishing a relationship with members of the health care team was seen as an important part of antenatal preparation. Anticipating and preparing to become a mother in culturally appropriate ways was not a solitary endeavour. Rather, it was expected that it would involve regular, formal interactions with different experts, who would monitor progress. The women produced accounts which showed their particular constructions of the relationship, although their expectations were not always met, as Rebecca comments:

The midwife came round the very first time when I'd just found out I was pregnant and I was very, as I said, confused and very unsettled and she was not that interested. They're very good now, they're very interested and they keep a tab on everything, but at the very beginning, I suppose because people miscarry in the first three months so they don't spend a lot of time with you then in case it's all for no reason. But I did feel very left on my own. They saw me once and then they didn't see me for a month and I didn't know when I was supposed to book up for classes, the antenatal parent classes, and I didn't know when I was meant to see them and how often and what I was supposed to be doing, and that kind of thing, and I just felt at the beginning I could have done with more support because I really needed it then. Not so much physically, but emotionally.

Here we see different frames of reference being operationalised in terms of lay expectations and professional, expert practices. Having anticipated interaction with the midwife once her pregnancy had been confirmed, Rebecca describes her confusion when this is not forthcoming in the ways she had anticipated, and said that without them she didn't know 'what [she] was supposed to be doing'. The uncertainties which surround the process of becoming a mother for the women in this study were discernible to varying degrees in all the accounts collected. The women had all experienced dimensions of agency within the context of being working women with some control over their lives. Yet uncertainties, together with ideas about preparing appropriately, led to dependence on authoritative expert knowledge and related practices. Through engagement with the medical profession and the regular monitoring of their pregnancies the women could be seen to be preparing to become mothers, in appropriate ways, reducing risk and acting responsibly. And whilst the participants said they did not have expectations of what pregnancy would be like, once again reinforcing the consequences of broader social changes, the narratives they produced were clearly shaped in relation to cultural messages, for example:

I didn't have any expectations whatsoever ... It wasn't really in my scope of thinking ... *I'm just doing what you're meant to do.* (Sarah, emphasis added)

I wanted to just carry on as much as I could as normally as possible. ... I didn't want it to sort of take over or anything. (Diana)

Although implicit references to expectations of pregnancy were apparent amongst the women, their non-expert stance in relation to other experts was acknowledged in all the accounts. In the following extract

Philippa comments on her early interactions with the health services and professionals:

I did feel very confused to start with because I think they assumed ... There was also, there was kind of confusion over just very silly things like, I remember where you had to sort of take your notes with you and they kind of assumed things like you knew you had to take a urine sample with you and stuff and there was a bit of kind of ... and I didn't on the first occasion and they said, oh I can tell it's your first baby, and I thought, no one ever told me. I don't know, there were just little things like that that I just found irritating, this kind of assumption that it was ... you were kind of stepping in to something and you'd automatically know where to go and who to see, and what sort of ... And I got a note from [hospital] saying come for your booking in, and I thought, what's a booking in? And I had no idea. So there was, I think that was, there was a lack of kind of explanation of the process that I'd be going through in terms of the health care I'd be receiving, but once I kind of got my head round it and asked questions, that was fine. And actually the health care itself was not the problem, it was more kind of procedural.

This extract captures the ambiguities and contradictions in the relationship between those in whom authoritative knowledge is vested and women beginning their journeys into motherhood. It also illuminates the assumptions made about what women should instinctively know. Once again, different professional and lay frames of reference are operationalised. Interestingly, whilst Philippa challenges the assumptions that are made about her level of knowledge as a pregnant woman, and what is perceived as expert terminology for example 'booking in', she concludes that it was not the health care itself, but the procedures that were ambiguous. Philippa, however, is also tentative in her criticisms: 'so there was, *I think* that was, there was a lack of *kind of* explanation of the process'. The differing perspectives on what pregnant women know, or are expected to know, are interwoven with essentialist assumptions around women's abilities to naturally mother. Although this is more apparent during the early postnatal period (see chapter 5) such assumptions clearly underpin aspects of antenatal care, which paradoxically occur within an increasingly medicalised context. This contradictory position has also been recognised in other work. For example, Lazarus notes from her extensive research on childbirth in the US that women 'regardless of social class or ethnicity ... spoke about childbirth as a natural process, but at least to some degree, they accepted the medical view of birth: that any number of things could go wrong and that ultimately they had to rely on authoritative knowledge and concomitant technological expertise of their physician to ensure that they had done everything possible to have a healthy baby' (1997:133).

The women's narratives throughout the antenatal period can be seen as tentatively constructed. They draw on both essentialist assumptions of women's abilities to naturally become mothers and the need for expert medical guidance and to be seen to act responsibly. As noted in the previous chapter, the experiences of previous generations have become less relevant. This is because technological developments have changed the contours of pregnancy and so other experts are increasingly looked to for guidance. Rather than a demise in reliance or trust being placed in expert bodies of knowledge in late modernity, as some theorists have suggested (Beck, 1992), within the arena of reproduction and childbirth there is continued and even increased engagement with expert bodies of knowledge and practices. The women in the study considered the procedures involved in their antenatal care to be ultimately reassuring, helping to allay fears around perceived risks. Even so, they found the ways in which information was given and the availability of tests (to confirm absence of possible risks) to be at times inadequate. They wanted their pregnancies to be monitored by the experts. They wanted more information not less, and whilst aspects of monitoring could involve some anxiety, ultimately engagement was perceived as reassuring, as illustrated by Clare:

I think it's been quite adequate. I mean, I had quite an easy pregnancy and there's never been any ... well there was one ... I had to have another scan because they thought the baby might be a bit small, which ... worried for a week until I had the scan and it was perfectly normal ... because it's been so normal I think I've never had to really ask many questions. They've always done all the checks all the time so I'm quite confident that everything's been monitored.

A focus on how women make sense of this period of embodied, physical change reveals that some narratives are more complex than others, challenging – whilst engaging with – the medical profession. Felicity (bravely) challenges the expectations she perceives to surround her pregnancy and begins to stray into the largely uncharted area of what can and cannot be said in relation to our (even unborn) children:

It's almost as if you have to play along with this game, you have to be really pleased in order to be a proper mum.

Later she talks about the midwife giving her a book on pregnancy, which contained pictures of the birth:

which just made me burst into tears, I don't want to do it.

Felicity feels that those with authoritative knowledge could provide more helpful parameters to help her think about the birth:

I'd be much happier if they actually said, you know, well I expect it's going to hurt like hell, how long it's going to take, sort of maximum and minimum, what they're going to do, but they haven't.

Yet, although she constructs an account with elements of resistance, Felicity does not challenge the medicalisation of childbearing, but rather finds that *she* must be responsible for privately purchasing further tests for Downs Syndrome, which she thinks are necessary:

The National Health Service has been awful in terms of ... we actually went to see a genetic counsellor to allay any fears [of Downs Syndrome] and she, the counsellor, was very patronising, 'don't worry, dear, go away and enjoy your pregnancy'.

Diana also talks of her needs not being met in the way she thinks they should have been:

You really need to make informed choices and not many people in the medical profession I've found tell you very much about it ... in fact I found my GP to be less than forward with any information, they just don't want to tell you anything.

The complexities of the relationship between health professionals and women are drawn out in the previous extract, and show competing frames of reference being used. Health professionals can be seen to assume some level of instinctive knowledge on the part of the women, whilst at the same time giving only that information which they deem necessary for the women to have. It could be that the profoundly embodied experience of pregnancy leads the experts to assume some level of instinctive, bodily knowledge. But this needs to be set against the ways in which women's knowledge of their own bodies has been shaped over generations. Barbara Katz Rothman has spoken of 'the history of Western obstetrics (as) the history of technologies of separation' (cited in Davis-Floyd and Davies, 1997:315) and here is another context in which the effect of separation is played out. The women are unclear about their needs, both wanting and resisting information that they are given or believe is being withheld.

Anticipating the birth

The seduction of formal, medicalised preparation is discernible in the narratives constructed by all the women as they contemplate the birth. This seduction is rooted in notions of risk, safety and being seen to act responsibly. The women produce narratives based on their perceptions of what 'good' mothers do, which is to achieve a safe birth without pain relief, and what their own experiences might entail. The contrasting threads of resistance and engagement are apparent in many accounts. These are interwoven with the contradictory implications of it being a 'natural' process and therefore one that a body can bear, or has the capacity to bear. The words 'natural', 'naturally' and 'instincts' are repeatedly used within the context of anticipating (hoping for) a 'good' (easy) birth, and acceptance of what the medical profession and technology may be able to offer. Hopes then were carefully and tentatively voiced in these anticipatory narratives. Yet as will become clear in the following two chapters, in contrast to what is voiced here, many of the women had thought they would be able to cope with the birth. All the women were well versed and informed about the different forms of pain relief that were available to them. Most had ranked them according to their perception of their acceptability. In the following extract, Gillian anticipates the birth of her child. The complexities of constructing an acceptable, culturally recognisable narrative around an experience which is unknown, uncertain and also inevitable, is clear:

And also you don't want to be induced either. I'm sure that's a strong feeling that one, you want to do it yourself naturally and second, you have a higher incidence of forceps . . . and pethidine. Talking with a very open mind on the matter, yes, my instincts say that your body will look after itself . . . it might need a little help and that's all. Ehm . . . but at the same time if things go wrong I'm quite happy . . . I'm going to hospital [name], if things go wrong then . . . have an epidural, do this, do that . . . then I will. I don't think, 'no, I don't want an epidural' . . . in my mind I think 'no, I shall manage'. I might try this TENS thing, and I'm quite happy to have some gas and air, so I feel in control. I don't like the feeling of being out of control, ehm and I'm not happy about having pethidine, I think I'd rather have TENS, or gas and air or if things go badly wrong then I'll have an epidural . . . pethidine, I think that with a lot of people it makes them out of control and I don't like that feeling . . . I think it's the lack of control for me, I think I might be physically and mentally so well under that I wouldn't be on the planet, whereas with gas and air you can just stop it if you feel you're getting out of control and with epidural although physically you lose a lot of control, mentally you still keep it, in fact probably better because you are not distracted by the pain . . . But I don't want to be so pushed over having a natural birth that I shall be terribly disappointed if something goes wrong and I need help. I want to try and keep it very open.

In this extract, Gillian rehearses various scenarios, balancing the need to keep an 'open mind' within the belief that 'your body will look after itself'. Interwoven within the account is the acknowledgement that she might 'need help' and doesn't want to feel 'terribly disappointed' if she does. The complex interweaving of contrasting hopes and anticipated outcomes were discernible in all the accounts, for example:

I thought right at the beginning when I thought I was having one (twin pregnancy since confirmed) I didn't . . . I wanted to try for natural labour . . . well, I would like (a) go, see if I can do it. But then obviously I'm . . . I'm not . . . I'm not a fool. I know that if I did get in pain then I'd rather have anything that will help me. I'm not sort of this person who wants to be perfect and do it all properly. (Sheila)

Yes, it scares me, it does, it does scare me. I'm not too worried about the pain ... I think I can handle the pain, but as I said it's, you know, the thought of the body coming out of that little hole. I wasn't quite sure what to go for as they've got so many different things you can take ... I was going to have peth-idine, 'cos I thought I don't really want a lot of pain if I can help it, but then at the last antenatal class they said the [hospital name] don't sort of push that, so now I am going for gas and air ... so, but it all depends how it goes, really, it might be a piece of cake. (Angela)

I mean my whole instinct is to crawl away and to have it on my own ... I mean obviously ... I would absolutely love to be one of these people that just floats through and gets by with a few puffs of gas and air ... And I'd ... I'd like that but I'm not going to say that's what I'm going to do because then I'd be really dis-appointed if I need something else ... I don't like the idea of an epidural at all but then I don't know ... I might think it's the best thing ever when I come to it. (Peggy)

If you are tense and nervous and not particularly positive you can create, you know, problems of anxiety ... I don't condemn anybody [but] I think that our bodies were geared, and made in a certain way that we can give birth naturally. (Helen – interesting because Helen eventually had to have a caesarean birth)

... and I don't really want any of their drugs. I don't want to have an epidural or any of that ... I don't mind anything else, but I don't want that, and I mean, hey, nature you know. (Sarah)

The women construct narratives by drawing on their own hopes and fears, grounded in essentialist constructions of maternal bodies, that women can naturally give birth without medical intervention. At the same time there is acknowledgment that some 'help' may be necessary. This is couched in terms of trying to retain some 'control', and trying to 'enjoy' the experience. Yet these hopes are tentatively voiced. Implicit within the extracts is an awareness that even how women achieve birth has implications for perceptions of the type of mother they will be: a 'good', 'perfect' mother, who gives birth 'properly', or a 'guilty' mother who 'fails' and needs medical intervention. It is interesting that whilst a 'natural' birth (without drugs) is seen as the best type of birth, engaging with some form of pain relief is, at the same time, seen as offering a means of retaining control over the birth.

The hospital, as a place in which births are managed, is perceived to offer both the possibility of a natural birth and at the same time the possibility of a medically assisted birth enabling women to retain 'con-trol': indeed, ideas around these are conflated. Loss of control for these women, who have experienced dimensions of agency in relation to the world of work, was a particular concern and one that is class-related (Lazarus, 1997). Pain relief, then, becomes potentially liberating, offering a means of retaining control. And whilst the extracts above suggest that women anticipated that control and some autonomy could be retained within the context of 'keeping an open mind', the medical profession were still perceived to be the experts, experts with 'rules' which might have to be followed, as Lillian says:

Yes, when I've found out that . . . if they're happy about people changing positions and things like that, because somebody was saying to me that sometimes they get you into a position that they want you to be in rather than you want to be in and you know, like, so I want to find out [the] rules.

Similarly, Gillian comments:

You're going to be stuck with the medical way of doing things, but then I'm happy to go along with that. I don't know what to do if I have problems, I want them to tell me what to do, and it's only if everything goes smoothly and you don't have any problems that you should be perhaps allowed to do what you want to do.

These constructions reinforce notions of expert, authoritative knowledge and associated power. Yet the women did not resist such notions but colluded and engaged with them. Indeed, the ways in which the participants operated with a hierarchy of forms of pain relief and saw potential take-up as a means of giving them control, showed the women to be sophisticated consumers rather than passive victims. These findings are also echoed in research from the USA and Canada and increasingly may be less a phenomenon of class position, but rather a demonstration of the 'success' of medicalisation and technological birth (Fox and Worts, 1999; Davis-Floyd, 1992).

In many societies, powerful moral and legal sanctions exist for those who are regarded as not preparing appropriately to become a mother, or more importantly, to be acting irresponsibly, and putting the life of their unborn child 'at risk'. The exercise of agency and choices made by the women in this study must, then, be considered within the context of a powerful medical/health profession and associated authoritative knowledge and practices. These are then reinforced through culturally and socially circumscribed beliefs in appropriate ways of becoming and being a mother. The anticipatory narratives constructed during the antenatal (prenatal) period were both complex and, apparently, unproblematic. Women presented accounts in which they spoke of their appropriate actions around preparation. They attended antenatal clinics, went to parent-craft classes, had ultrasound scans and changed their diets and socialising habits. Interestingly, having claimed not to have expectations of what being pregnant would be like, the women produced narratives which were built upon shared assumptions and stereotypes of what pregnancy entailed. When the women described less enjoyable aspects of their pregnancy, they quickly reverted to language they perceived to be more acceptable. In the following extract Linda, apparently sensing that the account she has narrated has been rather negative, containing lengthy descriptions of how she did not like the physical changes to her body and her sense of her body being 'fat', concluded in the following way:

But I know that there's going to be a bundle of joy at the end of the day and that's what I'm looking for . . .

To talk negatively about the pregnancy was construed as not preparing appropriately, not being a 'good' mother-to-be, risking being seen as irresponsible. In the following extract, Rebecca talks about not passing her 'apprehensive' feelings about the pregnancy on to her unborn baby:

But I've never ever throughout the whole pregnancy, and I hope I don't, thought, oh this is a mistake and I don't like the baby, or anything like that. I've always kept positive and talking to him or her and that kind of thing, because even in the womb, well I think they can tell if you go off them and feel vindictive towards them in any way, well not vindictive – it's too strong a word, but . . . and I don't want to ever do that . . .

Rebecca's own 'policing' of her account is interesting here. But showing the complexities and contradictions within narratives, Rebecca had earlier commented:

So I was just in the middle of changing my mind when I fell pregnant, so I did have mixed emotions actually. To start with it was quite difficult, and also the hormones bit I think made a difference, it does, doesn't it? And so I think I was probably quite grumpy and tearful and a bit moody, as well as all these other very real worries and that kind of thing. So I was excited but had reservations as well . . . in fact that was the good thing because when I first started telling people everybody was so pleased, so pleased, that it made me pleased. That was actually the turning point for me because up until then I'd been not exactly negative but very, very apprehensive, I mean really apprehensive. And it was when I started telling people that I actually felt better about it, because everybody thought, I don't know, I suppose they thought I would be a good mother or something, because I do take it very seriously, and I was quite pleased that they obviously have confidence in me.

Positive reactions to Rebecca's disclosure of her pregnancy to family and friends help her to envisage her self as a mother. She is reassured by their perception of her capacity to be a 'good mother'. The interactional dimensions of selves are apparent here and will be returned to in subsequent chapters.

Shifting selves

Interwoven in the accounts of engagement with those with authoritative knowledge were both implicit and explicit references to the women's shifting sense of their selves. These story lines were discernible within all the narratives collected. Transition to motherhood was experienced not only as physical change, but also as involving changing perceptions. These were experienced interactionally, in terms of how the women saw their selves, and how others saw and responded to them. Factors such as whether a pregnancy was planned, whether a woman feels supported by a partner and/or family members and friends, whether a woman feels positive about her changing physical shape, all contribute to the overall experience and what is voiced and what is left unsaid. Experiences which are perceived as negative may only be tentatively voiced. For even in the antenatal period the risk of appearing too negative may be construed as not preparing to become a 'good' mother. Transition to motherhood, then, is regulated and monitored, within the public sphere but experienced as a very private and personal transition, which also requires self-surveillance and personal policing of a self (Lawler, 2000). In the following extract Felicity describes the struggle that this has presented for her:

It's very difficult to sort them out into one coherent sentence ... it's an experience that I'm glad I've had, but it's an experience that I don't want to repeat ... yes, it's been very ... very bizarre. It's been a complete learning curve as my husband says. All sorts of things that I didn't expect to happen are happening. To me, I don't feel any different. OK, yes I've got this ... but I'm still me. You know, OK, I will hopefully some time in August have a healthy child, but I'll still be me ... so it's like this internal/external battle, and either having to constantly reinforce your internal feelings to the outside world or just giving up. And sometimes yes, sometimes I just sort of smile and go 'yes', yes I've been guilty of that.

The perceived need to retain and still be 'me' for Felicity is clear from the extract, but so too is the difficulty at times of achieving this. The struggle to retain a sense of self, an identity that is not conflated with being a mother or motherhood, is voiced by many of the women. What they acknowledge in their narratives is that others now see them *just* as pregnant women, that this becomes an overriding identity, but it is not how they experience their selves. The implications of not being seen as independent, working women, with some control over their lives, indicate the ways in which motherhood is constructed, anticipated and experienced in many Western societies. In the following extracts, the participants reflexively explore their shifting sense of self:

I've stopped being me, people just see me as a pregnant woman and I don't like that, and I know it's going to get worse, people will soon just see me as a mother ... I want my life back ... I just feel I am not me anymore, I'm just a pregnant woman now, I don't exist anymore in some people's eyes. I just carry a baby. I don't like that ... I don't like not being me ... I am not me at the moment. And you focus so heavily on 'week 40' your whole bloody life disappears ... (Abigail)

I know I'm not going to be me anymore ... I'm not going to be an individual anymore ... my life's totally changed the minute I found out I was having twins. (Sheila)

I think it's all bound up with the fact that you ... there's something else going on that you haven't got any control over, that you are not the person that you were anymore, and you know from now on you're going to be a mother. (Felicity)

I think you have to fight more to keep your individuality ... You know you have to fight to be the person that you ... rather than everybody's preconception of what a mother ought to be, or what a pregnant woman ought to be, or what you ought to be doing. (Peggy)

At one point, I don't know if this is because I was feeling emotional, I feel as though like me and myself is sort of like taking a backstage at the minute. I find that really sort of ... I find that hard, you know sort of like, you know, mmmm, and that's quite ... that's not very nice ... you know you lose a little bit of your identity. (Lillian)

Oh God, it's the end of my life as I know it, and I still feel that on bad days. (Philippa)

It was noted in chapter 1 that 'the physical facts of menstruation, conception, pregnancy, childbirth and menopause generate a series of moral problems related to identity and self concept for women', and in these extracts we can see aspects of this being played out (Almond, 1988). The women construct their narratives in different ways and in relation to their particular experiences of agency, dimensions of which will be both different and similar for other women coming to motherhood for the first time. Indeed, the need to actively 'fight' to retain a sense of individuality reinforces the struggle that is involved in maintaining a sense of their selves as they move ever closer to becoming mothers. The image of the 'me and myself' having taken 'a backstage' in Lillian's narrative is very powerful and resonates with many of the other women's experiences of transition to motherhood. Yet Lillian's narrative also encapsulates the contradictions experienced in the transition to motherhood, especially in relation to the perceptions of others:

I mean, I don't know if it's me that's imagining it, but like my father looks at me differently. He can't look at me as if it's a little girl any more, I'm a mother, I'm going to be a mother. And he's ... so that's quite a nice ... that's a positive aspect of him looking at me as an adult. And then some people look at you saying, you're a mother now, you haven't got like your own sort of intelligence I suppose really.

A few of the women presented their transition to motherhood at times as unproblematic and in positive terms:

I don't know, because I have been well and everything, it's not really changed me and obviously my size, but it's not been too much of a problem .... (feel) happy with myself sort of thing. (Faye)

Seeing me as a potential mother rather than a professional – my image has changed. To start with I rebelled against that but now I'm kind of quite looking forward to it and happy with it. (Rebecca)

Talking about her experiences of pregnancy, and the pregnancy diary in which she has noted down her changing feelings during pregnancy, Helen comments that it's

Better than I'd imagined it to be ... I mean I love the look of pregnant women, I think they look absolutely gorgeous ... I have stayed very trim, I desperately wanted to get big and fat. (Helen)

The potential struggles involved in making sense of a changing sense of self, through experiences of transition to motherhood, are also discernible in relation to control and changes in the body. Control, or loss of control, emerged in relation to the women's struggles to maintain a sense of their selves. Struggles around attempts to maintain a sense of self ('me') and the recognition of the difficulties in achieving this were centred on embodied change, involving presentation of a changing self in a maternal body. In the following extracts some of the participants talk of their experiences of these changes:

I don't like losing my body, not the shape of it, but just feeling ... the having something inside it, and not having control over it is odd to say the least. (Abigail)

I feel that from being the person in charge work-wise, to the person that is being taken over by something else, or someone else is quite a lot to take in. It's as if your whole identity changes from here on. (Linda)

Yes, I didn't like the idea of getting fatter. It's fine now because it's obvious that I'm pregnant, but at the beginning I had real traumas because people didn't know I was pregnant. I take pride in my appearance and that was hard ... I mean, my perception of my body image and the clothes I wear which make a statement, because I think the clothes you wear do make a statement, don't you? So, having to wear these peculiar floaty dresses which isn't really me . . . (Rebecca)

These extracts reflect shared concerns with changing shape and the implications of this for the women's sense of self. The complexities and contradictions in narrating personal experiences of change are also apparent in extracts from Helen's account. Helen talks about her changing shape at an early stage of the interview:

I've had a very sort of positive reaction to, you know, my body and how I've been growing and everything . . .

Helen later comments:

I have to say it's been one of the most uncomfortable physical states that I've ever been in and it's so difficult to describe to anyone . . . I feel like my body has been taken over by something else . . . it's a bit like being an alien . . . people touch you, touch your stomach, stare at you . . . you just feel that you're sort of not human.

And towards the end of the interview she concludes:

as far as I am concerned it's such an amazing thing of, you know, nature taking control and, you know, producing this little . . . being.

These extracts once again demonstrate the inconsistencies in producing accounts of personal change, and the ways in which we dip in and out of culturally recognisable ways of describing pregnancy. They also raise questions about how narratives are constructed for particular audiences. For example, in the first extract, Helen appears to conform to what she perceives to be appropriate ways of talking about pregnancy. As the interview progresses and she becomes more comfortable with me as the researcher, she voices her experiences in ways that could be perceived as less acceptable – 'being an alien' and 'not human'. Finally she reverts, as the interview draws to a close, to more culturally recognisable ways of talking positively about pregnancy, 'producing this little . . . being'.

Constructions of motherhood will be dependent on multiple factors. As noted earlier in chapter 3, constructions of motherhood and what 'good' mothers do change over time, in relation to social and economic demands (Duncan and Edwards, 1999). Amongst this group, many women anticipated combining mothering work with previously held jobs outside the home. This was seen as offering 'a return to normal', a return to something familiar, in contrast with the uncertainty of pregnancy, childbearing and motherhood. At work, where the women were positioned as experts, they felt in control. A return to work, then, was seen as a way of retaining/regaining a sense of a recognisable, practised and familiar self. In the following extracts, constructions of motherhood are variously played out in terms of responsibilities and right ways of doing things. These are premised on gendered assumptions around caring. This group of women are in a privileged position of having jobs, job satisfaction and security, including the ability to choose. Of course, for many women such choices do not exist. Notions of what life with a baby might be like are rehearsed in these extracts. For those anticipating a return to work, motherhood is constructed as not providing sufficient stimulation, and being at home, full-time, as potentially boring. A return to the public world of work is seen as offering the possibility of women regaining their 'identity', a sense of their pre-baby self and so being 'me again'. Other constructions attempt to reconcile ideas of what 'good' mothers should do, 'stay at home', with the woman's own needs, 'you might go insane'. Others construct motherhood in terms of a job to be done 'properly':

You can see these people who are so focused on [the] child ... there's nothing wrong with that but it's not me. I've struggled losing my identity as it is and I can't go ... I can't go forever just being someone else, I've got to be me again. (Abigail)

I am one of these people that their self, identity, is locked into what they do ... in terms of my own self, I would like to do something. (Felicity)

I mean in an ideal world I wouldn't go back to work, I mean I've always ... before I got married I always said that I felt that a mother should stay at home but I think as you ... I mean this is another sort of an ideal ... an ideal that's changed over the years. I mean, I love my job and I really enjoy the stimulation and I think ideally I would go back to work part-time if that were possible – and they've said it is but ... I've said that I'll go back full-time and do my best and if that doesn't work then ... (Kathryn)

I've sort of started thinking about childcare as well when I go back to work ... [Partner] thinks I'll be bored, not bored [with baby], but bored with being stuck at home. (Clare)

I will do definitely [return to work], but only part-time, because I think you should put in ... I mean, what's the point in having the baby unless you're going to look after it ... [but] yes, definitely, otherwise you might go insane. (Sarah)

I didn't particularly want my children to go to a childminder's or a crèche or something ... doing it this way [temping on a part-time basis] hopefully we'll be able to do it between ourselves and I'll still have my identity as well. (Sheila)

Others are undecided whether they will return to work, or they see full-time mothering as their new job:

Because we decided we would either have children or I would apply for promotion and that would have been a big change because I would have been in a very, much more important job and being looked up to as a more important person, and I decided not to go for that. I decided to go for motherhood which also I think if you do it properly you're respected and looked up to and trusted more, I think, in a way. Because you're not the young, frivolous person that I was before anyway, but because you're a mother, you have to be a responsible person, or should be. (Rebecca)

It really depends how bored I get. I've kept my job open so I can go back ... I keep saying if it's awful I'm going to get a full-time nanny and go straight back to work. (Peggy)

I may actually adore it and think I'd love to be a full-time mother and I'll find that completely satisfying, but at the moment I can't really imagine myself feeling like that. (Philippa)

The nuances and subtleties of cultural messages imbue these women's narratives, as clearly gendered notions of responsibility, caring and child-rearing shape the accounts. Ideologies of intensive mothering are both drawn upon and resisted but their dominance and power remains resolute, shaping both engagement *and* resistance.

Anticipating being a mother/motherhood

All the narratives discussed in this chapter are constructed in the context of women anticipating having a baby and becoming a mother. In the following section women look ahead and envisage themselves as mothers, doing mothering. Once again, as in discussions around the birth, the ability to 'cope' is linked to the process being 'natural', which for the women means that they should be able to cope. Yet their accounts remain tentative; words such as 'worried' and 'frightened' are interwoven into the narratives:

... and she [a friend] was ever so worried about not being able to cope. But I think once it comes it all goes ... it is natural ... uhm, I was ... frightened ... - will I be able to cope? (Angela)

It all seemed so easy nine months ago ... as if it was something that would just come naturally and now that I'm very aware it might not and I'm a bit worried that I won't cope. (Diana)

But I think maybe when the baby comes I'll ... it will be very natural to me ... I would say that my personal views on motherhood are, you know, very positive and yes, uplifting. (Helen)

... and I think how on earth am I going to get everything done. Yes, I mean that does worry me, because as I said before, because I like things so well ordered. You can't control a baby, you can't say, stop crying now. (Kathryn)

Terrified ... the responsibility, doing things right, just looking after a whole human being ... but then again it's ... well, everybody else can do it and I'd rather just do it by instinct. (Sheila)

Lots of changes ... I think we both worry about ... well, not worry but it's going to be very different having a baby there ... you know we've been together for nearly ten years, just us, and then there's going to be a little person as well. (Faye)

There's this idea that as a mother you will love your child, and as a child you will love your mother and that's not necessarily the case ... It would just be nice if we get on and we both survived, I think. (Felicity)

These extracts are clearly grounded in powerful cultural messages about 'right' and 'good' ways to mother. They are also shaped by the moral context in which mothering occurs, and reinforced by 'texts, images, interpersonal interactions, codes and laws' (Garcia Coll *et al.*, 1998:1). Individual concerns about the ability to 'cope' are voiced tentatively within the context of the assumption that mothering is dependent on 'instincts' and being 'natural'. Anticipating mothering involves uncertainty and at the same time anticipatory narratives are constructed within the context of essentialist ideas that mothering is 'natural'. The women's concerns, then, about not being able to cope, suggest that failure to get it right will have implications for both their sense of self and the ways in which they are perceived by others. It was noted in an earlier chapter that whether women have children or remain childless they are defined in relation to motherhood as the identity of woman and mother are so often conflated (Romito, 1997). Part of what we see in these extracts are the women struggling on the brink of becoming mothers to retain a sense of self, whilst negotiating the cultural contours of womanhood.

Conclusion

Contemporary constructions of motherhood, discernible in the women's anticipatory narratives, are clearly shaped with reference to dominant ideas about doing the right thing. Such notions are morally, socially and culturally underpinned. They are played out in terms of being seen to act responsibly, and to narrate experiences and expectations in culturally recognisable and acceptable ways. Acting responsibly and thereby diminishing risk involves engagement with those in whom cultural authority is vested: the experts, and expert bodies of knowledge. It also involves elements of self-surveillance, which extend to the ways in which anticipating being a mother is narrated, and what can, and cannot, be voiced. Clearly, reflexivity becomes particularly salient in relation to events which are perceived to be risky, for example first-time pregnancy and childbirth.

As Lupton had observed, reflexivity 'involves the weighing up and critical assessment of institutions and claim makers, including those who speak with expert voices about risk' (1999:15). In this chapter we have seen the ways in which women carefully and tentatively weigh up various and sometimes competing claims and construct anticipatory narratives around their experiences of transition to motherhood.

Clearly, the location of childbearing and motherhood at the interface of the social, cultural, moral and the biological, has critical implications for the ways in which women anticipate and narrate their experiences of transition. Narratives are both coherent and contradictory, constructed in relation to largely medical, authoritative knowledge and at the same time appealing to instinct and essentialist ideas about birth and women's 'natural' capacity to give birth and to mother. Women, then, tentatively make their journeys into motherhood through a gamut of public expectations and assumptions and private experiences, and these may not always coincide. The resulting narratives reflect both the wish to be seen to be preparing appropriately to become a mother and the uncertainty that a period of personal transition can bring. And, rather than there being a diminished reliance or seeking out of expert knowledge or a breaking down of 'expertise', this period of transition is characterised by active engagement with experts, actions which are equated with acting responsibly and avoiding unnecessary risks. In the context of childbearing this is achieved through the regular, expert monitoring of a pregnancy. Responsibility also involves some level of self-governance. Over twenty years ago Reissman argued that women have not simply been passive victims of medical technology (but) rather they have actively collaborated 'in the medicalisation process because of their own needs and motives' and this continues (1983:3). Medicalisation might very well have contributed to heightened perceptions of risk in relation to childbearing. But whatever the order of events, women continue to seek out and accept medical expertise and technology (Lupton, 1994). Similarly, with the hospital regarded as the appropriate and 'natural' place to give birth, the 'cultural dependence on professional health care' appears complete (Oakley, 1979; Davis-Floyd, 1992).

Uncertainty and perceptions of risk help shape women's expectations and experiences around childbearing, and translate into practices involving engagement with experts and expert bodies of knowledge. The ways in which preparation for motherhood is engaged with have implications for perceptions of women as future mothers. Similarly, becoming a mother can lead to greater reflexivity, over and above that which is intrinsic, as changes in a life are anticipated and heightened by embodied change and interactions with others. The narratives explored in this chapter begin to reveal the tenuous and shifting dimensions of self and offer insights into the ways in which selves are experienced, maintained and narrated. But this is just the beginning of the journey into motherhood. (Compare for example these antenatal accounts with those in chapter 6, the late postnatal accounts.) In these antenatal narratives the personal is only very occasionally voiced; telling your story during this period is all about presenting an acceptable and culturally recognisable narrative of preparing appropriately and responsibly for motherhood. Yet, as we shall see in the next chapter, birth changes everything.

5   Making sense of early mothering experiences

> I think I kind of expected to be more in control of the situation and I wasn't really at all. In fact I just didn't know what to do, it was all completely new to me and I felt very kind of overwhelmed by the whole experience.   (Philippa, interviewed seven weeks after the birth of her first child)

The subjective experience of being a mother, in contrast to anticipating motherhood, can throw lives into temporary confusion. As noted earlier, transformations in patterns of living and changes in the timing and frequency of childbearing have implications for constructions of motherhood in late modernity. In the Western world, changes in family size and ways of living mean that many women come to motherhood with little or no first-hand experience of its dimensions. At the same time, geographical mobility and more women working outside the home translates into traditional patterns of family support not necessarily being readily available. In this chapter, the ways in which new mothers make sense of their early mothering experiences are explored through the narratives they construct. These continue to draw on recognisable cultural notions of right ways of doing and being. Presenting a self as a responsible mother involves self-governance around what can and cannot be voiced. As noted in the previous chapter, the narratives produced in the antenatal period were tentative, drawing on essentialist ideas of women's natural capacity to give birth and instinctively cope, whilst at the same time acting responsibly, through interactions with experts and expert practices. However, experiences which do not fit with expectations can be difficult to cope with and lead women to question their own abilities as women. For if childbearing and mothering practices are natural and instinctive, as the antenatal narratives suggest, then how do women make sense of subjective experiences which are found to be counter to these essentialist ideas? As will become clear as we continue to follow the women through their journeys into motherhood, the need to produce recognisable accounts of early mothering and to be seen to 'do the right thing' can become paramount at this stage in the journey. The women at times struggle to produce narratives that resonate with what they take to be 'normal' responses to becoming a mother, demonstrating to those around them that they are coping and in control. Now the responsibility for a dependent child becomes a reality. It is something that must be performed and managed and ultimately evaluated, within both the private sphere of the home and the potentially more risky public sphere outside the home.

In this chapter the women's accounts are once again prioritised as we engage with fleshy, embodied experiences of birth and the early weeks of 'mothering' at home. The theoretical focus remains implicit as the chapter continues to map the ways in which selves are constituted, maintained and presented through narratives of compliance and resistance. This occurs against a backdrop of competing lay and professional time-frames. The birth of a child can be seen to provide a narrative 'turning point'. Crucially, anticipation becomes experience, but the context in which narratives are constructed must be continually acknowledged (Frank, 1995). It has been suggested that motherhood provides 'an opportunity for renewed narrative movement par excellence' (Bailey, 1999:351) and whilst at one level this is indeed the case, such claims fail to take account of the difficulty of voicing what are perceived to be different or abnormal experiences. The narratives constructed during this period are more complex than those constructed in the antenatal period. Expectations can be narrated by drawing on culturally recognisable and socially acceptable ways of preparing to become a mother. But experiences may be more difficult to place, and indeed to voice, in relation to the available repertoire of birth and mothering stories. Many of the women produced their stories within the context of asserting that they were '*now* feeling better', '*now* able to cope'. Lived experience, in contrast to anticipation, which of course also involves physical, embodied changes, provides a significant ontological shift in the ways in which becoming a mother and motherhood can be narrated.

The birth

The early postnatal narratives centred on the overriding sense that the birth had not been as the women had thought it would be. They felt, on reflection, that the experts had not prepared them adequately or in appropriate ways. Yet it was not just the experts who had concealed what giving birth might actually be like. The conspiracy of silence which some now felt had surrounded their preparation involved both health professionals and friends and family members. In the following extract, Faye relates a conversation with her sister-in-law, who is expecting her second child:

I said to her when Emily ... the day Emily was born, I said, what the hell are you going through that again for? And she hadn't told me.

I too was seen to have been complicit in this silence, as one participant said to me, 'to be honest, even *you* didn't tell me what it would be like' (Felicity). The following lengthy extracts are included to both challenge the conspiracy of silence and profoundly illustrate the contrast between expectations and experiences:

So everything I'd planned went completely wrong ... The pushing bit was abso- lutely the worst thing that I have ever experienced in my entire life because it was three or four different sensations to me all at once ... I had an epidural which I didn't want beforehand but at that stage I would have done anything because I was convinced I was going to die, literally. (Felicity)

Eventually Felicity has a forceps delivery:

... awful, it was the most ... it's the worst thing that I've ever had to go through. I just felt completely violated ... I just can't believe that for somebody who's usually so healthy and doesn't have any tablets, or anything, that I've had all this medication and medical intervention over what's supposed to be a natural event ... I thought I'd give birth naturally, quite easily because everybody said you've got childbearing hips ... so it's turned out completely wrong for me.

Similar accounts of expectations and plans being abandoned and control handed over to/taken over by the experts were narrated by other women:

So then, you see, they threatened me with forceps, but once I was threatened with forceps I suppose I pushed harder, and out she popped ... but I thought my birth was going to be easy. I don't know why, I just thought that ... I expected a sort of four-hour labour, I didn't really expect stitches or anything like that. I thought ... I just thought my body would be very good at that, and it wasn't ... I think I did lose control. On the gas and air, I had quite a lot of gas and air because I was just on it for so long. (Gillian)

... and after about two hours I was just in agony and I couldn't stand it anymore ... I thought about it [requesting pain relief] at one stage, that was when it was nearly all over, so I thought well, I've gone this far, I don't really need to bother ... but it was pretty horrendous, mind you ... You can't really explain the pain of it ... I mean it's horrendous, but ... (Faye)

... and I said, oh, you know, I've got this twinge ... if this is what it is, then this is fine because this doesn't hurt at all! I can cope with this! But then they started getting stronger and stronger ... So I just tried to carry on and have a bath and walk about a bit and that kind of thing, but by about 2 o'clock in the morning, they were really getting quite painful, more so than I thought they would be, because having done yoga and everybody saying how fit and healthy I was, I thought oh well, this is going to be a cinch, it will probably be all right, I'll just keep the breathing up, but it really, really hurt, I thought, so I was getting slightly panicky, thinking oh goodness me, I'm not really doing very well ... Because people had said if you keep the breathing it's bearable – well, it was bearable because I bore it, but . . . So I was there thinking, this is so painful, I'm surely going to have to have a caesarian or forceps or something like this, surely it can't be this painful . . . I think if I'd have just known that I was having a normal delivery but it was painful, I think that's what I would have liked to have known. (Rebecca)

I wanted to have a water birth originally and because I was induced I couldn't, that's why I was stuck on this bed. And I had like . . . I had everything in the end, I had an epidural . . . I knew that . . . you know . . . originally they examined me and they said you're only three centimetres, you can't have an epidural yet, and I was absolutely desperate . . . and they made me hang on for another two hours, and I was like . . . I just thought I was going to die. (Clare)

I was admitted and I wanted to . . . I didn't want to have the baby in the water bath but I wanted to spend as much time in the water bath as possible. But by midnight I was getting really tired with the gas and air and I just said 'I'm sorry, I need an epidural' because by that time I'd been going almost twenty-four hours . . . And then the anaesthetist or the doctor who was going to do the epidural took . . . he was doing something else and he took an hour and a half, and that was the worst bit, waiting for him . . . It was a long time and I remember being in absolute agony . . . he was absolutely stuck fast, and after pushing for an hour and ten minutes they called in the doctor and they got . . . they turned him with a venteuse and then gave me an episiotomy and forceps delivery. So he was born at 9.03 on the Saturday . . . I sort of felt in a way that I'd failed by having to go for an epidural but I just knew that I couldn't go on any more . . . I'd been to all these sort of aquanatal classes and everybody said that going sort of swimming helped . . . helped the pregnancy. And I just . . . I just thought, you know, I'm really fit. (Kathryn)

I mean I think secretly I sort of thought I'm quite strong, I'm quite resilient, I'm quite fit, I should be able to get through this really. I mean I didn't really . . . I don't think I ever really said that to anybody but I think that was kind of how I felt about myself, I sort of thought I'd never . . . I thought I dealt with pain – could deal with pain – quite well. But it was just beyond anything that I kind of could deal with, really. It was certainly much more agonising than I expected, and even now I can't remember how agonising it was, which is the funny thing, you sort of forget it, and I'm kind of tempted if people say, how was your labour, I just say oh all right, and I think it wasn't actually at all, and you know I have to say . . . if anyone says to me . . . you know if you catch me saying it's not that bad, remind me that it is. (Philippa)

I just want an epidural, I thought this is it, I can't cope with this, this is ridiculous, in fact give me a caesarian, just knock me out . . . I didn't scream in hospital because I was more sort of . . . I felt I had to like try and control myself. (Diana)

At a later stage in the interview, Diana comments:

. . . and knowing afterwards I thought, well, you know, I wish I'd realised, I would have maybe felt a bit more in control, because as it was I felt completely out of control.

Clearly, the women had thought their bodies would be able to cope because they were 'healthy', had 'done yoga' and 'aqua-natal classes'. In contrast to their antenatal narratives of preparation in which some had voiced the possibility of medical assistance, we now see that they had not actually seen themselves as women who would need medical help: 'I just thought my body would be very good at that', 'somebody who's usually so healthy and doesn't have any tablets'. Relinquishing to medical intervention involved mixed feelings for the women, but the most palpable were of gratitude and defeat: 'I'm sorry, I need an epidural'. As Felicity says, 'it's an odd mixture of being between relief and resentment of the medical profession'. The tentative voicing, antenatally, of choice around different forms of pain relief enabling control to be retained, is not realised during the birth. Most of the women spoke of handing over or succumbing at some point during their labour to the experts:

Yes, well, because they were worried about her, although she showed no signs of distress at any point, but meconium in the waters means you've got to have what they say which is ... the drip ... well, I don't know if ... much choice. But by that time I was thinking, I want her out and whatever you think is best and get on with it. (Gillian)

And I was desperately trying to breathe in and that, and I just couldn't, lost it totally. And I had the epidural, told the anaesthetist he was God ... Because I tried gas and air, revolting, disgusting, let's throw up, it was obscenely revolting. And the TENS machine was well, a total waste of time, I think, but it felt as if you were in control, and so I had no pain relief at all basically, other than the epidural when I eventually succumbed. (Abigail)

When he [the consultant] said to me I think we should do such and such, and I just said yes, whatever, you know best. I just took ... gave it totally over to him ... I knew that I would just want somebody to take control and take over from me. (Sheila)

Yet even requesting or accepting some form of medical intervention did not have to mean that all aspects of control were lost or handed over. As the earlier extract from Diana shows, she requested a range of forms of pain relief, yet didn't allow herself to scream in hospital because 'I felt I had to like try and control myself'. Yet both the complexities of narratives and cultural dimensions of birthing behaviours are clear here and later when she talks of feeling 'completely out of control'. Aspects of control, then, are either seen to have been 'lost', 'taken over' or given over and/or retained during parts of the birth, in contrast to what had been anticipated (see chapter 4). The women reflect on their antenatal preparation and the failure of experts and others to prepare them for what birth might really be like. But as the following extracts show, they are able to acknowledge the difficulty of doing this:

Yes, I suppose looking back on the ante-natal care, it was as good as I suppose it could be, given the fact that the midwife who was leading it had no idea basically of what we were all going to go through. She knew the kind of experiences that can be gone through. (Rebecca)

I just think they could do with being a bit more realistic without frightening you, you know, because I know that they don't want to tell you what it's really like because it can sound quite terrifying if you try to say, you know, the pain is like indescribable and it is, but you forget, you do forget, I know that it was horrible but I can't really remember how horrible. (Diana)

Everybody was saying that they don't tell you enough about the birth and what it's like. (Faye)

Engagement with experts and expert bodies of knowledge characterised the antenatal period and the procedures involved in labour and birth. Yet resistance rather than engagement characterises the accounts of two women who exceed their 'due dates' and come under pressure to have the birth induced. However, although they initially adopt strategies that question and resist expert practices, eventually they succumb as choices apparently run out. Antenatally, Helen had spoken of her belief that 'our bodies were geared and made in a certain way that we can give birth naturally' and so when her pregnancy reaches forty-two weeks it is not a surprise that she actively resists medical induction:

And it went on and on and on and basically she was . . . she was at forty-two weeks and they had booked me in at this time to actually come in and be induced, but I was . . . had quite a strong opinion on the fact that I really wanted it to be spontaneous. I felt as though that we'd waited nine months and she was going to come, you know, when she's ready as long as I wasn't putting her at any sort of risk at all, so I'd spoken to the consultant sort of like at forty-two weeks and he said, well, you've got enough fluid around the baby and the placenta's still healthy, come in on a daily basis . . . so anyway we went to three weeks over . . .

Although she had been 'booked in' to be induced, she challenges this and proceeds to await a spontaneous start of labour. Helen's resistance is bound up with her strong beliefs and earlier assertions of birth being a natural process, for to resist expert knowledge within the medical arena could be seen as involving risk. Helen speaks to the consultant and negotiates her way around induction by agreeing to visit the hospital on a daily basis to be monitored. Philippa can also be seen to resist and indeed challenge the basis of expert knowledge. At almost forty-three weeks pregnant she finally gives birth but only after a verbal struggle with the experts, whose knowledge is increasingly questioned. They are unable to provide a satisfactory reason as to why Philippa should have a caesarian. At forty-two weeks pregnant Philippa is booked in to have her labour induced, but the attempts to get her labour started do not work:

So they said, come . . . well, no actually, what happened, the registrar said, well we could go to the consultant or whatever and they said have a caesarian this evening, which I was just, like why? Tell me why I have to have a caesarian, you know . . . I mean we sort of tried to work out why. We were just . . . the only thing I could think of is that they kind of . . . they have . . . they booked . . . you're booked in to have a baby on that date and if you don't have it . . . one means or another! And the registrar seemed to disagree. I mean, I said is this normal policy or whatever or is this what you normally do and he said, well, I've never really come across this before and I've never used this method of induction before, I'm just doing what your consultant says and all this sort of thing, so it was a bit . . . I just felt a bit kind of removed from the person making the decision and yes, it was all . . . and no one could tell me why I had to have it, they said well, you're fine and the baby's fine and why couldn't we just leave it and that'll be it. And they said, well . . . well, basically they said stay in overnight and see how you feel in the morning, but we would recommend you have a caesarian tomorrow morning. And I was just really unhappy about it. I mean had the baby been in any danger or had I been ill or anything I think I would . . . it would have been fine to have a caesarian. I didn't really mind in a way, but I just thought why do I have to have what is fairly major surgery, you know, and I knew it would take me longer to recover from it as well. I also wanted, you know, wanted the opportunity to do it myself naturally.

Both women are driven by their belief that birth is a natural process that they and their bodies should be able to achieve at the appropriate time, without medical intervention. These beliefs are, however, tempered with acknowledging that elements of risk must also be considered. The apparently arbitrary basis on which expert knowledge was being used to make decisions was challenged by Philippa: 'no one could tell me why'; the registrar said, 'I'm just doing what your consultant says'. The hierarchical nature of expert knowledge is also illustrated in Philippa's account, where the registrar admits that he is deferring to the consultant, and some of the midwives applaud her resistant stance:

I mean, a few of the midwives sort of said, good for . . . you know, good for you.

Both women eventually give birth; Philippa avoids a caesarian birth, unlike Helen. Helen's beliefs in her own ability to give birth 'normally' and 'naturally' are retrospectively made sense of in relation to her mother's and sister's experiences:

You know, I suppose that you always look at your sister and your . . . your family and your mother and . . . you know, never had any problem whatsoever, always had normal ... you know normal labour and normal childbirth, to the point where you know, ignorantly I had never ... you know all the books and everything, I think that I was quite well read through the pregnancy, but whenever I got to the part about the caesarian I flicked over it because I thought, well, it wasn't going to happen to me.

Having resisted medical intervention, Helen talks about finally having a 'medically run labour':

So at this point I knew that it was going to be a medically run labour, because they'd said, you know, the only thing that we can really do is ... is start you off on the drip, give you an epidural and take it from there, all the things that I said that I didn't want I ended up having. There was me ready with my aromatherapy oils and TENS machine and ... because I knew that everything was pointing towards a caesarian ... they had taken control ... But in fact I don't feel disappointed about it in any way, I suppose because it was taken out of my hands. I wasn't allowed to be in control. The time that I was in control I did everything that I possibly could and ... so I wasn't allowed to be in control. I suppose once they started me on a medically induced labour, it was ... it was over to them at that point ... I mean they had really taken control sort of from the time that they gave me or administered the first epidural and I knew that it really wasn't down to me at that time, and ... But it was quite an emotional time ... because things weren't going to plan.

Helen weaves a complex plot, voicing her hopes and expectations for 'a natural birth', and her experiences, which involved an 'emotional time', but which at the same time she says she doesn't 'feel disappointed about ... in any way'. The taking over of control is acknowledged, but in the light of Helen having done all she possibly could and then not being 'allowed' to be in control. Yet interestingly, Helen, having reflected and produced a narrative of becoming a mother which contains elements of resistance, reverts to a more culturally recognisable way of talking when she comments on the birth weight of her baby:

They weighed her and found out she was 8.11 [lbs] which is quite nice ... Well, she was forty-three weeks so ... I know, be grateful for small mercies, I think. Yes, and to be perfectly honest with you it really has been plain sailing since then. That day was very up and down, very emotional, it was like a ... you know, a whole story, you know, from start to finish, but since then it's all been ... it's been fabulous.

The notion of a 'whole story', implying that this episode is now finished, is interesting; so too is the implication that she got something right by giving birth to a large baby: 'be grateful for small mercies'. Helen can reveal her unanticipated birth story in the context of the assertion that 'it really has been plain sailing since then' and 'since then it's all been ... it's been fabulous'. The tensions and layers beneath the 'fabulous' time she is claiming to currently be enjoying are only revealed in her final interview and the end-of-study questionnaire (see chapter 6). It is only when her baby is nine months old, when she is again interviewed, that the struggles and difficulties she is encountering during this interview – to produce a 'coherent' and acceptable account of new mothering – can be voiced.

Hospital to home

The women spent varying lengths of time in the hospital following the birth, from a matter of hours to a week. The interests of the medical profession shift swiftly following the birth: the baby or other expectant mothers on the wards were now the focus of the medical gaze. As Felicity notes:

[They] don't give a damn ... so I think in a way I feel as if they were completely obsessed by me and my body beforehand. Now they don't care. It's almost as if ... you know ... now I'm not an incubator, then I've just got to get on with it, really.

The women were now mothers. They were expected to naturally know how to mother and elements of the antenatal narratives suggested that the women shared this expectation. Professional practices involved more limited engagement following a successful birth, childrearing being a largely private activity and responsibility in the West. Yet the following lengthy extracts illustrate both the scale of the changes which women can experience around the time of the birth and the competing perceptions amongst those involved. Wendy is in hospital to have an elective caesarian. She is expecting twins following successful IVF treatment:

I had baby blues in hospital ... I stayed in there for a week ... .Well, they told me that I could go home on the Friday. I had them on the Monday and they said I could go home on the Friday. But I said, no I'm staying, and they let me stay and said I could stay for a bit longer if I wanted to. They were saying about this mother and baby place I could go to, in Taybury or Norbury? Because they said we should have been counselled, because they were IVF babies, but we never had anything. Because you just go in and you think, oh my God, I'm having these two babies tomorrow and they're just there and you think, God, what do I do? You just have to know it all. I don't think they've got much time for you up there because I was trying to breastfeed Alex and I used to ring them to help me to fix him on and that, and it used to take them ten minutes to come along. Fifteen minutes and you think, I can't cope with this and I just used to give him a bottle. I had to beg them one night to take them off me for one night and the next night I thought, well, I'm not going to ask them again because you just think, do they really want them? It's really bad. They kept saying it was part of postnatal depression, but it wasn't. They sent a psychiatric woman in to see me and she said, do you feel suicidal? and I said no. I was on the seventh floor. I said if I did I'd be jumping out that window by now. We went in on the Sunday and that's all they kept talking about, because

I was quite tearful anyway when we went in and she kept saying I've got to tell you about postnatal depression, and I said I haven't got it. I'm just teary because I'm in here and I'm going to give birth in the next twenty-four hours . . . I wasn't the only one up there crying. There was quite a few of us. It was weird though, having these two babies just lying there and thinking, God, what do I do.

Wendy's sense of not having been properly prepared, 'because they said we should have been counselled, because they were IVF babies, but we never had anything', and being unsupported once the babies were born, 'well, I'm not going to ask them again because you just think, do they really want them?' is profoundly felt and voiced. But she was not alone in feeling 'teary', 'I wasn't the only one up there crying. There was quite a few of us.' Wendy rejects the diagnosis of postnatal depression and the need for a 'psychiatric woman', rather she makes sense of her own feelings, like those of many women, within the context of the scale of what she is going through and the associated responsibilities, 'and they're just there and you think, God, what do I do?'. Felicity also talks of her experiences in hospital following the birth of her baby. Her (lack of) interactions with the staff only serve to reinforce her sense of personal failure and isolation following a birth that required medical intervention:

In the hospital – I mean this is another thing about the isolating experiences – they stuck me in a ward with four beds in it and I was the only one there. So I'd had this horrible experience and then I was stuck in this room on my own and I just felt as if I was the only person in the entire world and nobody wanted to know me. It was awful. And they kept doing things like forgetting to bring my meals because I was the only one that . . . 'oh we didn't know anyone was in there'. So of course there was just floods of tears: 'I'm not even worthy of them bringing me a cup of tea'.

The shift from hospital to home marks both the beginning of a return to 'normal' and the gradual disengagement of medical and health professionals. Felicity describes trying to convince the hospital staff that she could cope in her bid to be allowed home, 'you know, I have to show them that I'm fit to go home with this child'. In the West the different localities of hospital and home represent different public and private spheres: the hospital, in which experts are seen to largely have control and manage childbirth, and the home, where mothering naturally occurs and the private responsibility for childcare is undertaken. Yet for the women in the study being at home with a new baby was not experienced as natural and the sense of not knowing what to do was profound. Describing the early days at home with her new baby Philippa says:

I just wanted to go back to hospital actually the whole time . . . after being home for a couple of days, I thought I just wanted to go back, I want someone else to be in control.

During the early postnatal period in the UK, midwives continue to be responsible for mothers until ten days after the birth, at which point the health visitor takes over and makes home visits, which are targeted according to professional judgements of coping. In many ways antenatal interactions prepare women (sometimes inadequately) for the birth of a baby, but not for coping with being a mother. For many women, mothering does not come naturally and the early days at home are a confusing and challenging time, as the following extracts reveal:

I'm thinking, 'oh my God, it's a baby, oh God, oh my God ... mum's changed its nappy' and I'm just looking at it thinking 'oh God'. (Sarah)

I think I have a right to feel upset and tearful because of, you know, the experience ... the enormity of it, I think that's what made me cry in the first place. (Felicity)

Yet although most of the participants found the early days at home a challenging time, Peggy did not. In the extract below she places her own experiences in context:

It's just like when you get a new dog or a cat or something and you know, settling it in ... It doesn't sound very good, does it? It doesn't sound very maternal, but ...

What is interesting here is not the apparent ease with which Peggy has settled her new baby in, but her recognition that comparing the settling in of her new baby to previous experiences with her dog and cat, does not 'sound very good' or 'very maternal'. Here Peggy acknowledges that there are publicly acceptable ways of narrating experiences of becoming a mother, and this description may not be perceived as 'very good'. Of interest too, and showing the complexities and contradictions in accounts, is Peggy's earlier comment:

[Antenatal classes] didn't really prepare you for actually what you'd got to do when you'd got the baby. Which wasn't really much use because you just wanted to be told, you know.

The relationship between the experts and the mothers shifted as they moved from the hospital to home, with different frames of reference being used. For example, the women still felt they needed expert guidance and someone to share the responsibility with and, at times, take control, whilst professional practices involved limited home visits. The women felt confused by this new twist in the relationship, as the following extracts show:

I must admit that one thing I didn't like was that because my emotions were all over the place and I'm a very organised person, I found that it was very difficult for me to get my head round who was supposed to be in charge of me, who I was supposed to ring up and all the rest of it ... and I was under the impression that she [the midwife] was going to keep coming for ten days, and after the second day she said, you're fine, I won't come anymore. And I have felt a bit abandoned really, and she knew that I was feeling quite emotionally tender, so I think perhaps that could have been dealt with a bit better ... and I did feel a bit abandoned ... the midwife just dropped me after two days, saying that I was fine, the baby was fine and everything was all right. But I didn't feel emotionally all right. (Rebecca)

And I've found the whole way through that they're fairly reactive but then that's OK, once you get used to it. I think I went ... I kind of had the attitude ... or felt that everything should be a bit more black and white than it actually is and that people would actually tell me what to do, and I've found ... I mean even in hospital no one told me how to sort of bath the baby, for example. I had to, you know, say how do you do ... how do I do this? And they said gosh, hasn't she been bathed for two days, you know, or whatever? Well no one's shown me, no-one's given me a bath or whatever, I don't know. And I think emotionally as well, I mean they were quite supportive. The occasion when I'd seen the midwife one day and everything was fine and then she said right, I won't come tomorrow if that's all right ... have a day off, and I called her and said come round, because we'd had like this sort of twelve, I think twelve hours feeding almost continuously right through the night, and I just didn't ... I mean I didn't know what I was doing wrong, whether it was just she wasn't getting enough or whether she just wanted the comfort or whatever. And she was great because she sort of came round and she actually put me to bed and latched the baby on and made me a sand-wich ... and I felt quite depressed about, you know, 'oh my God, what have I done', because she [the baby] was obviously taking up all my time and all [my husband's] time as well and we were both like 'what have we done to our lives?' We quite liked our life before and we were just never going to know ... we just couldn't imagine ever being beyond this kind of twenty-four-hour baby care. (Philippa)

The sense of wanting to know 'who was supposed to be in charge of me', illustrates the dependent relationship which has developed through a protracted period of antenatal preparation and support. Ironically, it is these early postnatal days that the women identify as being when they most need emotional and practical support. During these early days they are struggling to make sense of the scale of the changes that have occurred, in a context that has changed much since their own mothers or grandmothers gave birth. Finding that experiences of early mothering do not resonate with expectations has implications for the ways in which narratives are produced. Timing is also important, and self-governance leads women to voice difficult experiences within the context of '*now* feeling able to cope', or 'things *now* being better'. Voicing experiences of not coping is perceived as too risky. Because mothering is largely taken to be a natural ability, to admit to 'failure', to not coping, is to risk incurring moral sanction and a questioning of one's capacity as a woman. The content of the womens' narratives produced at this time serves to confirm that, if they have experienced some earlier difficulties, they are *now* coping. Clearly, the temporal ordering of events is important in how we present accounts of ourselves to others.

In the following extract, we can see the ways in which Helen uses various devices, temporal and linguistic, to produce what she feels is an acceptable and coherent narrative of her early mothering experiences. Helen begins by reflecting on the antenatal preparation,

The only thing that I . . . I could possibly sort of criticise on now . . . I wouldn't say it as a criticism, but I was not prepared for at all [was] the emotional changes of when you come home and suddenly you're living this story life when you have the baby and suddenly when you come home and after all the visitors have started to dwindle off and it's just you that's left, as to how your life is possibly, you know, going to change, that there is going to be no normality whatsoever . . . I suppose I've been, you know, quite a controlled . . . well, I was in control of my own life, I knew what I was doing and every day I was quite organised and things, and that's completely gone out of the window. And I would say that I hadn't really been prepared for those feelings of actually being out of control, which I would say probably only the last week that I've actually got on top of it and I'm actually starting to feel a little bit more in control.

Helen tentatively voices some concern, 'I wouldn't say it as a criticism' of her antenatal preparation. But crucially her voicing of earlier difficulties is within the context of 'only the last week . . . actually starting to feel a little bit more in control'. To admit to, or to actually experience feeling out of control, may mean that it is impossible to construct a coherent, or publicly recognisable, narrative. To admit to others, particularly professionals – or even researchers who are known to be mothers – that you are experiencing difficulties, has all sorts of implications for how women are perceived. Whilst some women talked of their difficulties of asking for help, others spoke of the competing perceptions of 'normality' in the early weeks following the birth of a baby:

They're really worried about postnatal depression, she's [the health visitor] really hot on it. And she did keep trying to tell me that I was postnatally depressed, when I don't think I was . . . I was in floods of tears continuously . . . and I think it was just normal. (Sarah)

Midwives came for ten days, well, the ten-day period, this is another thing. Because I felt so dreadful I would have liked them to call every day to check sort of my tail end every day, but they assumed that because I was again . . . I suppose they think this is a fairly nice house, you know you've got everything sorted out, [my husband] was home, they kept saying 'I'll not call tomorrow, eh, I'll leave it for a day or two', and I kept . . . it was almost as if I couldn't say, no actually, I want you to come back and talk to me tomorrow. So I had to go, OK yes, that's fine. (Felicity)

But I still felt as though it wasn't normal somehow to feel like that ... you know my whole life's falling apart and I can't do anything and they're [other mothers] coping so well. (Diana)

In a later extract Diana talks of her fears of being perceived as not coping and being labelled by the experts as:

... postnatally depressed, we're going to take the baby off you, and that's something I did worry about.

The irony here is that a friend of Diana's who was another participant in the study (Helen) was also experiencing difficulties. Yet neither felt able to voice concerns or difficulties to each other: these were concealed. The myths, then, of how women should feel, and act, on becoming mothers are perpetuated *because* women feel vulnerable, and unable to challenge dominant ideologies of early motherhood. As Helen recounts in the extract below:

I suppose I've been, you know, quite a controlled ... well, I was in control of my own life ... and that's completely gone out the window. And I would say that I hadn't really been prepared for those feelings of actually being out of control.

Helen then (unknowingly) shares some sense of her life being out of control, 'falling apart', with her friend Diana, yet when she relates that the midwife had found her to be "bordering on post-depressive", according to the Edinburgh postnatal questionnaire,[1] she asserts that: 'I actually do feel a lot better now, I'm starting to feel in control.' A sense of being in control, then, of having regained control implies that life can begin to return to 'normal', perhaps that aspects of a previous life start to become visible again. Yet as the following chapter will reveal, many of these women were producing accounts of their early mothering experiences which in fact bore little resemblance to what they were actually experiencing during this time.

A shifting sense of self: being a 'mother'

A narrative turning point occurs when experience replaces anticipation, leading at times to a reordering of past events. The biological act of giving birth means that in a very short space of time women shift from being pregnant and anticipating motherhood to being mothers, with all the responsibilities associated with a dependent child. Yet this biological

---

[1] The Edinburgh Postnatal Depression Scale has been designed in questionnaire format 'as a screening tool for the detection of postnatal depression'. It is administered in many parts of the UK to mothers by health visitors at between six to eight weeks postnatally.

shift is not always mirrored by such a swift ontological shift. Beginning to feel like a 'mother' is often a much slower process. Women can find it difficult to reconcile the differing biological and social time-frames which exist around mothering, and which may differ from professionally based time-frames. The potent mix of cultural, social and moral knowledges and practices which surround perceptions of motherhood, together with the biological act of giving birth, do not in themselves lead women to feel like mothers on the birth of a child. Indeed each woman needs time to come to terms with and develop a social self as a mother; to jettison previous expectations of an essential, instinctive self as mother. Yet to those around her, family, friends and experts, as soon as her child is born, a woman becomes a mother, this powerful new identity overriding all others.

Fear of a loss of control in relation to experiences of transition to motherhood provides a recurrent theme running across and between the narratives constructed by these women. As noted earlier, they had all been working women and spoke of having control in their lives and sometimes control over others at work. The unexpected experiences of birth and the new responsibilities of the early weeks at home all contributed to a sense of loss of control in their lives. This included a loss of a recognisable self. At the time of the early postnatal interviews most of the women were trying to come to terms with, to make sense of, the changes in their lives. The following extracts reveal their struggles:

My role in life has changed ... I mean I was saying this to [a friend] yesterday, I don't really know who I am yet ... There isn't anything in my life that I could say is any sort of constant stability to ... in reflection to what it was before. (Helen)

The change to my life I think is complete and absolute, there's nothing left of my life that resembles ... I have [the baby] all the time and it doesn't matter how much you love your baby, if you've had a life it's very difficult to give up all of it, and I think I started to get really resentful because I was struggling to cope, just generally day to day I just felt like she demanded all of my attention all the time. I couldn't do anything for myself. (Diana)

You realise what a totally different ... you know, you're in a different world at the moment, you know ... (Lillian)

I felt as if I didn't have control over what was going to happen to me anymore. (Felicity)

Although she's ... I mean she's never been a problem, but I'm certainly, as I say, the last couple of weeks been thinking that there's more to life sort of thing ... the last couple of weeks I've sort of felt that I can do more. (Faye)

This period of transition: 'a different world at the moment', which lacks any 'constant sort of stability', is differently experienced by the women as they each try to come to terms with becoming a mother. Lillian talks of being 'in a different world at the moment', and Helen of not knowing who she really is yet. It is interesting that Faye pre-empts her acknowledgement that over the last couple of weeks she has felt that 'there's more to life' with the qualifying sentence 'although she's . . . I mean she's never been a problem'. Feeling able to cope, of regaining some control, provides a turning point in terms of the narrating experiences of the early weeks. However, actually having a sense of being a 'mother' is something that for some is only much later experienced and acknowledged (see chapter 6). This is experienced as a 'mothering career' (Ribbens, 1998) advances and a social self as a mother is gradually developed through practice. In the following extracts the women draw on different images of motherhood, but they are not categories they can yet identify with:

I don't really see myself as kind of an earth mother type . . . I still don't really think of me as a mother a lot of the time, you know I think of me as looking after [the baby] . . . but in terms of my mothering skills, I'm not sure . . . I'm quite keen to keep some sense of my pre-baby self. (Philippa)

I'm beginning to feel like a mother, but that's only recent [baby eight weeks] . . . but there are some bits of my life that I miss . . . it didn't come naturally. (Diana)

I've tried to maintain that sense of self, but I know there is this . . . that I will always be perceived as a mother . . . but when I go out I try not to look mumsy and I think that's partly to do with how I feel about myself. (Felicity)

I've only just started saying 'my child, my baby'. But I don't know if I feel like a mother. I don't know what you're meant to feel like. (Sarah)

I mean it's like how do you define a mother? Yes, I'm doing all the practical things of a mother. But it hasn't actually sunk in . . . It's like I'm living this part in a play and in fact I'm going through all of the motions, but is it actually reality and is this what motherhood is all about? You know, my mum's a mother, but am I? . . Although you probably ask anybody that knows me and they'd say oh gosh, she's like a duck to water and she's very natural and relaxed with her and it just seems like I can't . . . you know I can't have life without her. And that's . . . is how I do feel, but I wouldn't say, no I wouldn't say that I really feel like I'm a mother . . . I was very ready to become a mother . . . but in fact I have lost control of my life. (Helen)

In these extracts the doing of mothering work, doing 'practical things' and 'looking after' are drawn upon, but are seen as distinct from being or feeling like a mother. Some women at this time were struggling to hold on to a sense of their pre-baby selves and their lives prior to the birth. Yet whilst they struggled to make sense of this period of intense transition, others around them saw them as mothers. In the extract above, Helen talks of others' perceptions of how she is coping as a new mother, 'like a duck to water' and that 'she's very natural'. The difficulty, then, for Helen, and other women whose experiences do not resonate with their own earlier expectations is feeling able to reveal that they are struggling. Helen uses the analogy of living a part in a play; the implication then is of pretence, of 'going through all of the motions' but not actually feeling, as she thinks she should feel, like a mother. The complex interplay between essentialist and ideological assumptions and social and cultural constructions of mother-hood are evident in these extracts. Narratives are produced within the context of mothering being perceived as 'natural' and mothers being guided by 'instincts'. When these are not experienced, reflexive difficulties may be experienced, for as Somers has noted, 'struggles over narrations are (thus) struggles over identity' (Somers, 1994:631).

As noted in earlier chapters, selves exist and are interactionally con-structed in relation to others. For example, in Sheila's extract below we see her referring to herself as 'Mummy' when talking to her twin sons, but also the implication that this new dimension of self would take time to get used to. Other women experienced their new self as mother differently:

I walked in I said, 'All right, Mummy's here.' And I thought 'oooh', it sounded so weird to be saying that. But yes, I do thoroughly enjoy being a mum. (Sheila)

[on being asked if she feels like a mother] I suppose so, I don't really feel any different, you know ... well I suppose ... I don't know really what a mother feels like. I mean, I suppose so, but you know ... I don't really have time to sit there thinking what I feel like. Yes, I suppose so. .... You get on with your life and you get on with the baby and you just do it. (Peggy)

[on being asked if she feels like a mother] Yes, it's come really naturally to me, which I wasn't sure whether it would or not ... but then I think that because we planned it all and we knew what ... that this was the right time. It wasn't too early and we were ready for it. (Faye)

Faye's comment is interesting because she had earlier asserted that only in the 'last couple of weeks (she'd) been thinking that there's more to life, sort of thing'. The implication had been that she was now feeling more able to cope and to get out, yet in the extract above she talks of mothering coming 'really naturally', implying she had not experienced difficulties. Diana recounts the range of emotions she has experienced since having her baby:

A lot of people probably feel the same, but I couldn't believe how invisible I became after I had her [and later] I can't believe how happy having a baby has made me feel, even though it has made me extremely unhappy at times.

Clearly there are complexities and contradictions in the narratives we produce, such is the condition of human life. Different accounts may be produced for different audiences, and reworked and changed over time, and in accordance with a shifting sense of self. Similarly, some individuals may be more reflexively engaged beyond the intrinsic reflexivity that is a component of all human life than others, for example, as Peggy says above 'I don't really have time to sit there thinking what I feel.' Arguments about reflexivity and its masculinist and gendered dimensions are explored further in chapter 7.

Performing motherhood outside the home

A sense of being a mother was only gradually experienced by many of the women as they came to terms with the practical tasks and responsibilities that shape mothering in many Western cultures. Doing the practical things around a new baby could, after time, be managed in the home. But the outside world presented different challenges. Potential scrutiny and judgement by others was regarded as risky amongst those who did not yet feel confident or skilled in their mothering abilities. Managing a performance of being a mother in the public sphere, especially when facets of self were experienced as uncertain and tenuous as a consequence of transition, led many women to stay at home. Being perceived as a competent social actor, a 'real' mother, in public places was regarded as too daunting by many of the women, and led to limited social action in the public sphere. Interestingly, withdrawal from social networks has been identified as a factor in the development of 'postnatal depression' (Mauthner, 1995, 2002; Nicolson, 1998). In the following extracts some of the women relate how, because their experiences of early motherhood did not resonate with their expectations, they did not actually feel in control or like 'a mother' and they regulated their interactions in public spaces. It was considered risky to be visible in a public place, while not feeling able to confidently present as a 'good' or 'proper' mother, as Philippa describes in the following extract:

So I didn't go out very much, which really made it hard ... I don't think I went out, literally set foot outside the door, for three or four weeks or something which is quite ... it was a long time, and that was too long actually, because I didn't ... but I just felt ... I didn't feel very confident taking her out because I just thought she was going to cry the whole time and I felt a bit sort of self-conscious about it, I suppose, and I thought at least at home I can always feed her and I didn't feel confident about feeding her out of the house and things ... I mean even now I sort of feel if I take her out shopping and she started crying ... this woman in a shopping queue said to me, 'they hate shopping', and they're so sort of accusing and I felt like saying 'well, I have to eat' ... I mean I am sure she didn't mean it like that, but I took it as, you know, you're inflicting this awful thing on your child. But I mean I sort of feel I get disapproving glances. I'm sure you don't at all, but I can't ... that's how I interpret it.

Being perceived as a 'real' mother, and being able to give a convincing performance in the public sphere, was a concern for many of the women. Felicity relates an early outing to the doctor's with her young baby:

We had to go to the doctor's and both of us went, Robert and I went with the baby and then I got a prescription. Robert went to get the prescription. I said, I'll come home because the estimators were coming for the removals. And I'd done ... you know I'd got one of the changing bags like you're supposed to, taken a bottle of milk with us in case he got horrible, and he had in the doctor's, and Robert had started to feed him and then we'd left and he was quite happy. But I was coming home and he started to get hungry again and Robert had the bottle in his pocket and had gone off to the shop to get the prescription, so I had this screaming child in the middle of [town] on, I think it was a Thursday afternoon, and it was hot and the tourists were there, and I felt like shit and I couldn't walk very fast, and I had to virtually run from the middle of town to here, over the bridge, and you could tell everyone was, 'poor child', 'what's that woman doing with that child'. And I thought, I was convinced somebody was going to like stop me and say you've pinched that child, that's not your child, you aren't a mother, you don't look like you can cope with him, this baby, you should be doing something to stop it crying.

Other women spoke of gradually gaining the confidence to leave the safety of their homes and do mothering in the public sphere:

... but it's taken eight weeks to be confident to walk along with a pram with a screaming child. (Abigail)

... but it's absolutely exhausting, yes, I was quite sort of lonely to start with when he wasn't doing much and I didn't really feel confident enough to go out. (Clare)

I know I'm a mother but I don't quite feel like a mother yet ... I went to [the shop] once and she screamed the whole way round, then I did feel like a mother because all these old ladies were there and they were going ... 'that baby shouldn't be out', 'it's too hot for that baby to be out'. I could hear them rabbitting on behind me. So then I did feel very much like a mother ... a dreadful mother. (Gillian)

I know, sort of, how long she can go without food so if I want to go down town or something I can sort of time it ... so I don't have to feed her when I'm out. (Faye)

You know, you just feel so tied to this one little thing, and tied to the house, just ... and also I think because I'm ... I'm so organised and such a ... like, sort of, things well planned, I found it impossible to be able to make appointments ... I was never quite sure when he was going to feed and when he was going to sleep, and I think because I couldn't control him I was worried about making any appointments, whereas now I think, well, I'd take him with me and if he cried so what ... whereas at the beginning I think I thought if he cried it was my fault and I was very aware of people thinking, you know, he's crying, why doesn't she pick him up ... and that made me feel guilty. There's this awful guilt, sort of ... oh, it's dreadful. (Kathryn)

Clearly then, striving to make sense of the intensely private experience of becoming a mother within the context of public expectations is both challenging and potentially baffling. Difficult experiences may remain unvoiced and social action be regulated. Concerns about being perceived as a 'real' mother were also implicit in other accounts, where women felt that their 'pretence' of being a mother would be found out. In the extract above, Felicity talks of her fear that others will think that she has 'pinched' her child, and other women voiced similar concerns:

... but I still feel I've borrowed him, that I'm not his mother, that he's not mine. (Kathryn)

We kept looking at them and thinking no, somebody's going to take them away because they are not ours really. (Sheila, mother of twins)

Coming home with him was odd in that we both felt that we'd kidnapped him and even though I'd been pregnant, it didn't really feel right. But we were both very natural with him. So there was complete conflicting things, that we must have stolen him but he was ours and we coped with him really well. It was really odd ... really bizarre, freaky. (Abigail)

The complexities of becoming a mother, in circumstances where changing familial arrangements have reduced the likelihood of women having previous experiences around babies and childrearing practices, have become more intense. One consequence of such transformations has been a greater emphasis placed on individuals and the monitoring of their actions through reflexive practices. Yet as was noted in chapter 1, being a mother is always more than 'playing a part' and in these extracts we see the women trying to come to terms with conflicting experiences. Becoming a mother involves embodied, visceral experiences and responsibilities for meeting the needs of another dependent human being. However, the very things that patterned these women's pre-baby lives – planning, coping and having control – are the very constituents of a life that now, at times, elude them. Reflexively sustaining and maintaining a sense of self through this period, whilst necessary for ontological well-being, is complicated by the essentialist constructions of motherhood that continue to dominate Western societies, knowledges and practices.

The relationship between mothering and paid work outside the home was explored in an earlier chapter. The relationship has, historically, been subject to change according to societal needs, and has always differentially affected different groups of women (Hill Collins, 1994; Segura, 1994; Duncan and Edwards, 1999). The women's decisions in this study about whether to return to work or to mother full-time, drew upon a range of recognisable discourses. For some, returning to work was seen as offering the possibility of regaining dimensions of a pre-baby, recognisable self, in an environment where they would not be 'just a mother', their 'performance' at work being measured according to different parameters:

... that's why I want to go back [to work], is to be me. (Abigail)

I'm looking forward to it in a way 'cos it will give me a break, I think, 'cos it's surprising how much work it is, you're on the go all the time. I think I have about an hour [a day] to myself. (Angela)

... because I think work, well for me it was very much a part of my identity, it's part of who you are, and I think that I didn't really realise that until I didn't have it, and having the baby has made me realise I do need something back for myself, because I have lost my identity – to everyone else I'm Sonia's Mum and that's what I am, who I am, and I don't think I will regain any of that feeling of having my own identity until I get back to work, which is why it's important, I think, for me to go back to work. I'll never be the same because I can never be at work what I was before because I'm still Sonia's Mum, but I will always have something a bit different, something for myself, and when I get back to work I know that I will have something for myself like I'll go to the gym when I'm at work and I'll chat to people and I'll have a bit of a laugh and I'll talk about things other than babies, but then I'll come back and I'll still be Sonia's Mum and I'll still have to get up in the middle of the night or change dirty nappies and talk about baby things on the days when I don't go to work, but that's OK as long as I've got something for myself, I couldn't ... I couldn't survive without having that, I don't think. (Diana)

I'm not sure that I am cut out to be a full-time mother ... I don't know that I'd find it stimulating enough ... well, not stimulating enough, but ... I don't know really whether I would be good at it ... I need to do both anyway, I think. (Philippa)

For most of the women, work offered the possibility of regaining a sense of self, which is experienced as either 'lost' or submerged in full-time, intensive mothering. But one mother spoke of her satisfaction with being at home with her baby daughter:

... so the future at the moment just for me, I'm just concentrating on Emily at the moment, I'm afraid. I've just not really thought about what I'm going to do. (Faye)

Yet, interestingly, Faye finds it necessary to apologise, 'I'm afraid', when she voices apparent contentment in concentrating on her daughter: intensive mothering as an option also has to be justified.

Conclusion

Narratives produced during these early postnatal interviews are both complex and contradictory. Whilst antenatally, women tentatively construct and produce narratives of anticipation, the experience of giving birth and being responsible for a child precipitates both an ontological shift and a narrative turning point. The narratives produced in this early postnatal period are grounded in experiences of giving birth and early mothering. These experiences differ from or challenge previous expectations and dominant cultural and social ideas which permeate motherhood. The struggle, then, can be to reconcile individual experiences with earlier expectations and assumptions, whilst managing a competent performance as a coping mother, a performance which is highly gendered, embodied and contingent on dominant representations of mothers' responsibilities and meeting children's needs, and essentialist notions of women's capacities to mother. The act of giving birth did not necessarily, or often, lead the women to identify themselves as 'natural' mothers or childcare experts. Rather, most experienced confusion and struggled to produce recognisable narratives of mothering when they had not yet had time to develop a 'mothering voice' (Ribbens, 1998). A sense of who they now were and had been, and the connections between the two, had to be made sense of: a shifting and tenuous self eventually becoming integrated into an altered 'schema of self understanding' (Lawler, 2000:57–8). Almost overnight they were expected to become experts on their children. And whilst over the early weeks the women felt able to fulfil the practical aspects of mothering, many did not recognise themselves as mothers. Normal 'difficulties' associated with early mothering were compounded by confusion, as professional support was reduced: the experts and the new mothers worked with competing frames of reference around coping and a return to normal. One was task-based and normative and the other grounded in the everyday experiences of mothering and motherhood.

Narratives of early mothering, then, draw on, and are shaped by, dominant moral discourses of maternal responsibilities and intensive mothering, and representations of children's needs, which must be met. There is risk involved in not being seen to achieve these maternal demands. So, if normal difficulties are voiced it is always in the context of things now being better, 'fabulous' and under control. When narratives contain experiences that challenge or resist these dominant constructions of motherhood, more publicly recognisable ways of talking about being a mother are also interwoven. Narrating experiences of early mothering and motherhood involve reconciling unanticipated experiences and potent ideologies. As reflexive social actors the women employ techniques of resistance and self-governance, in order to conceal unhappy or difficult experiences, which ironically only serve to perpetuate the myths that surround transition to motherhood. As we shall see in the following chapter, it is only when the women have moved through and survived this early and intense period of mothering and motherhood that they feel able to retrospectively and safely voice contradictory accounts of their experiences.

> But yes, I feel much more like a mother now than I did . . . I suppose I do
> feel like a mother . . . You're a person with a baby, you become a mother
> and you feel like a mother.   (Gillian, final postnatal interview)

For women who have survived, and coped with, the early months of
first-time motherhood, new opportunities for narrating experiences arise.
In this chapter we trace the ways in which a stronger sense of a recognisable
self is gradually regained. This is achieved as most of the women both
re-enter the world of work and come to position themselves as the experts
on their babies. The passage of time enables the women to (re)construct and
present challenging narratives of mothering. Over time, they reflect on
and make sense of their experiences and now feel able to disclose unhappy
and difficult experiences, which had previously been withheld. In particular this chapter draws attention to the shifts that occur around perceptions of expert, authoritative knowledge as control in a life is felt to be
regained. Women become the experts, through practice, in recognising
and meeting their children's needs. Similarly, professional constructions
of normal transition to motherhood and child development are also
challenged. Perceptions of risk are re-evaluated from this more accom-
plished stage in the women's mothering careers (Ribbens, 1998). This is
in relation to their children, and how they manage their ownselves and are
judged by others as mothers. The ways in which a sense of a recognisable
self, reflexivity and voicing experiences are interwoven forms a backdrop
to the chapter. Once again the ways in which women collude in perpetu-
ating myths around motherhood, through practices of self-surveillance
and self-governance, will be returned to (Lawler, 2000). If early difficulties cannot be voiced as they are lived, or are not voiced, then the myth of
motherhood being intrinsically biological and essential, and therefore
natural, continues unchallenged.

In the previous two chapters the women engaged with ideas that were
rooted in essentialism as they prepared to become mothers. They later
produced accounts of 'doing the right thing' as many struggled to come
to terms with early mothering experiences which were not felt to be

instinctive. It is only now, after the passage of time that the extent of earlier (normal) difficulties can be disclosed. It becomes clear that distance from an event facilitates narration, that 'for a person to gain such a reflexive grasp of her own life, distance is a prerequisite' (Frank, 1995:98). The features of late modernity – uncertainty and risk, trust in expert bodies of knowledge and reflexivity – are played out differently in these later accounts of transition to motherhood. Risks, of course, have not gone away, but they are now differently perceived and interpreted by the women after they have successfully met their young children's needs over the first nine months of life. Cultural constructions of risk will continue to shape mothering and parenting experiences, but do not translate into dependence on experts or expert bodies of knowledge in the same intensive ways they had done during pregnancy and early motherhood. Disclosure of unhappy early mothering experiences can now be risked, although elements of self-governance will always shape the ways in which women feel able to talk about the everyday experiences of meeting children's needs in a morally charged climate. As Romito has noted, 'mothers still do not dare to admit how burdensome the constraints and difficulties of their condition can be' (1997:172). The largely private endeavour that constitutes childrearing in the West can be seen to perpetuate self-reliance. So, doing the practical things of mothering over time, and largely alone, leads the women to become the experts on their own children. Shifts in a sense of self are also discernible in relation to women gaining confidence in their mothering abilities, and for some returning to the world of work. Managing their own selves as mothers, women and workers leads to a greater sense of control in a life with glimpses, and sometimes more, of a pre-baby self and life. So, how are selves differently experienced, maintained and narrated during this later stage of the journey into first-time motherhood? How is reflexivity engaged with and played out in these final accounts?

Becoming the expert: practising mothering

It has been earlier argued that the dimensions of the contemporary context in which childbearing and mothering occur, promote a continued dependence on experts and expert bodies of knowledge. This is particularly the case during pregnancy and through the early confusing weeks of becoming a mother. But developing competence in doing the practical things of mothering and meeting a child's needs lead gradually to a reassessment of this relationship. Indeed, the disengagement in terms of professional support and interest which the women felt happened shortly after the birth, can now be interpreted as having fostered (forced) independence. Commenting on her contact with various health professionals, Diana observes, 'I find it quite amazing that they can be so in your face for like weeks and then just not there.' And whilst the underlying assumption which underpins professional practice, that is that women naturally know how to mother, differs from the experiences of the women themselves, gradually most women do become more confident in their own abilities to meet the needs of their children. The endeavour becomes less stressful, as Abigail and Helen comment below:

I don't feel that I need information as much now, because I don't know it all, obviously, because he is still only eight months old . . . but I do feel that for most stuff it's common sense. The stress goes out of it . . . you become less dependent on others because your own confidence builds . . . it's so easy with hindsight . . . somewhere along the lines it all clicks. (Abigail)

I think I feel a lot more sort of secure about myself and my decisions and what's the right thing to do and what isn't . . . so, yes, but I'm certainly more confident now. (Helen)

Growing confidence in meeting their children's needs leads the women to challenge those they had previously regarded as possessing authoritative knowledge. In the following extract, Sheila describes the gradual process of reaching a point at which professional expert knowledge and advice can be weighed up, challenged and discarded in the context of her own experiences. Competing constructions of normal development are also clear in these extracts:

That was, that's been my real . . . I don't know, it's just you don't know what you're doing . . . I always like to have, 'this is what you're doing' and I'm told and then I just do it. But with solids and everything, you just don't know what you're doing. You have to feel your way . . . on their eight-month check they are supposed to sit up, they're supposed to put their hands up to be picked up, and all these things they're supposed to do, and I just think, oh, I just don't care anymore. If they don't want to that's it, that's their little way of doing things. I know they're perfectly happy, healthy children. And that's what, you know, I've come to realise.

Sheila goes on to describe another occasion when she received advice from the health visitor:

She said, you know, 'oh you really should be giving them finger food because some children will get tactile' and I said, 'what do you mean' and she said 'oh well, they don't want to touch things'. So, I was like getting all uptight thinking oh, maybe I should be doing this thing . . . and then I just thought, oh, sod it, I'm just going to do what I feel and what's handy for me.

Here Sheila is able to weigh up the professional advice in the context of her life, and reject it: 'oh sod it, I'm just going to do what I feel and what's handy for me'. Peggy also talks of challenging expert advice in relation to weaning her baby on to solids:

I started him at fifteen weeks with the health visitor having kittens.[She] kept saying, you've got to wait until he's four months old and I said, well, look, I can't wait.

Unusually, after a relatively short period of mothering (fifteen weeks), Peggy also feels able to act in a way which is counter to the expert advice she has been given. But this action must be seen within the context of other information and support that Peggy has, as she explains:

Apparently my mother had the same problem with me of not putting on weight and getting nagged at all over the place, so she said 'don't worry about it'.

Supported by her mother, whose knowledge is grounded in experience, Peggy rejects the professional advice given. This is in contrast to the accounts constructed during the antenatal period. In these, the women prioritised professional, authoritative knowledge over that of other sources, including family and friends. But the women now speak of finding support from other mothers whose advice is crucially grounded in experience as mothers. They also speak of their own growing confidence in relation to meeting their children's needs, as the following extracts show:

I met a couple of girls through a postnatal group which I went to once because I felt I had to, and we've become quite good friends and I tend to see them, you know, every other week or so, and that's more helpful than the health professional, I find, but no, I haven't . . . I haven't seen anyone. You know, you never see hide nor hair of them, they just disappear, don't they? (Diana)

The health visitors are on the whole . . . certainly at the beginning were really good. I find now that he's older and therefore probably not prone to as many problems, I'm more experienced . . . And I think, you know, girlfriends, I tend to sort of ask them what they're doing far more than health visitors or professionals, think I'm much more confident now. I mean I . . . I think as a mother, you just have an instinct and you know what's right. (Kathryn)

I've got used to the idea now and it's coming more naturally . . . you become less dependent on others because your own confidence builds. (Clare)

When she was about four months, I sort of stopped seeing them as frequently. I kind of had her weighed a couple of times. She had a hearing test and things and I've seen one health visitor once since I've been back to work. And they've been fine, actually, you know there's no . . . I mean not . . . I think because you kind of go through the whole thing with your health visitor and your midwife to start with it's like . . . and they're much more involved, it's not the, you know, I just . . . just sort of go along so they say she looks well, she's gaining weight and that's it really . . . I mean, I just don't have any worries about her, really, and I think I know that I'm doing the right thing in terms of with feeding. I'm not worried about her developmentally. It seems fairly kind of common . . . a lot of common sense to me at the moment . . . Yes, I mean it's partly confidence and it's also . . . I think it's kind of easier. She seems like a more kind of robust being rather than this kind of fragile little thing . . . And also because she goes to nursery as well – this sounds really awful but I sort of think there are more people involved, it's not just me anymore. (Philippa)

It is interesting that whilst Philippa welcomes the shared responsibility of childcare now that she has returned to work and her daughter attends a full-time nursery, she believes that 'this sounds really awful'. Here the dominance and gendered dimensions of the discourse of intensive mothering is clearly discernible, shaping the ways in which Philippa, apologetically, describes her current childcare arrangements. Gradually then, women become practised in identifying and meeting their children's needs and develop their own informal support and information networks. The professional practices of monitoring and measurement which provide evidence of 'normal' development are increasingly questioned. The weighing up of risk becomes less fraught as responsibilities are coped with and met. Yet for all this advancement and success in their mothering – they and their babies have survived – the women continue to draw on dominant, gendered constructions of motherhood. They feel compelled to apologise for their actions, for example in relation to work, which they perceive as counter to constructions of good mothering.

Selves and the world of work

In chapter 1 the complexities of debates around the self were highlighted and the difficulty of treading a path between essentialism and engaging with 'fleshy, sensate bodies' acknowledged (Jackson and Scott, 2001:9). These theoretical debates will be revisited in chapter 7, but the empirical data presented here illustrate the ways in which tenuous selves are experienced and presented through a period of transition. According to Lawler, 'most Euroamericans incorporate various forms of understanding of the self into an overall schema of self understanding' (2000:57–8). The narratives produced by the women in this study show the complexities and fluidity of these schemas of self-understanding. Such understandings are grounded in a sense of a recognisable and practiced self, and it is these dimensions of a self that are fundamentally challenged for many women when they become mothers. This is because when childbirth and doing mothering are experienced as different from expectations and found not to be instinctive or natural, a social self – rather than an essentialist, instinctive self – as a mother has to be developed, worked on and practised. Different locations enabled women to reflect on and make sense of this confusing period. For example, a return to paid employment, involving movement in and out of different worlds, provided opportunities for the women to be their (old) selves again. By the time of the final interviews all but three of the women had returned to paid work outside the home. Interestingly, it was those who had not who drew a particular distinction between the different worlds of home and work. In the following extract Sheila talks of not having any 'out life':

My outlook on life is totally different. I still don't have any out life, any life of my own really . . . I miss the conversation, that's the major thing . . . I mean I love them dearly but I do miss . . . I mean not just normal conversation, I miss the office life.

Her decision not to seek work outside the home draws on ideas of doing mothering in a particular way:

I really want to be there for them, the old-fashioned style, isn't it?

Sheila then goes on to assert her happiness in her current situation:

I'm quite happy at home, I'm my own person now since I've got these [twins] . . . but I still want my . . . my independence.

Yet contradictions are woven throughout these extracts, as Sheila asserts that she's her 'own person', implying autonomy and independence, but talking also of wanting her 'independence'. Faye also rationalises her decision not to seek work outside the home, which results in her feeling a 'bit out of the world':

I wouldn't earn very much and I don't know whether . . . I know it would be for my sanity, but I don't really want to work to pay someone else to look after her . . . I sometimes feel a bit guilty about not going to work . . . you . . . sort of you feel a bit out of the world in a way because you're not getting up every day and going into work and the normal things you do.

Work outside the home offers the possibility of 'normal things', helping to maintain 'sanity'. Ironically, and in contrast to the women who have returned to work, Faye experiences guilt *because* she is not also working outside the home. The social negotiations in which women engage between motherhood and paid work have been explored in previous research (Duncan and Edwards, 1999; Brannen and Moss, 1988). Interestingly, in research which focused on lone mothers, Duncan and Edwards found that 'lone mothers' agency in deciding whether or not to take up paid work is essentially concerned with what is best and morally right for themselves as mothers and for their children' (1999:109).

Perhaps not surprisingly, these are the very same concerns that this group of partnered women weigh up in these late postnatal narratives. For those who have returned to work, contradictory feelings are also experienced. As Diana says:

The mixed feelings I had about going back to work – on the one hand I did want to go because I . . . I did miss the sort of wideness of the world, you know, the world becomes very small when you're at home with a baby because it's a baby, isn't it, and other mothers and it's not really . . . you don't have much to talk about. And . . . but on the other hand I felt that, you know, should I be leaving this baby who probably needs its mother more than anyone? Very mixed. But then I was lucky to be in a position to go back part-time, so you feel you can balance it a bit. You've got some work and some time with Sonia, but then the downside to that is that you . . . as I say, you just feel you're not doing anything . . . constantly feeling guilty, under achieving . . . under achieving mother, under achieving employee . . . I'm very organised and like to be in control and it's just never . . . you're never going to be in control again.

Returning to the world of work provides a temporary diversion from the otherwise all-consuming world of intensive mothering. It also offers the possibility to regain and be a different – old, enduring – self again. The ways in which different selves can be practised, performed and maintained in the different locations of home and work are apparent in the following extracts. In these the women draw on ideas of 'ideal types of mother and/or worker', what Duncan and Edwards have termed 'gendered moral rationalities', to narrate and locate their selves and their experiences (1999:109). Abigail explains her readiness to rejoin the other world:

I do like being a professional person and myself . . . I really felt by the end of my maternity leave that I was treading water and the whole world was getting on with their lives and mine was on hold . . . Even if I was achieving something with him, I didn't feel it was enough for me. That might sound selfish, I don't know? . . . I felt so trapped by the end of my maternity leave, I felt so isolated.

Abigail tentatively voices her experiences of motherhood, yet recognises that this might not be perceived as a culturally or morally acceptable way for a mother to narrate her mothering experiences, and adds, 'that might sound selfish'. Other mothers also spoke of mothering not being 'enough' for them, of needing something more:

I kind of thought I'll go back, never really kind of found myself like a real role as a mother, like a role just me and Georgia in the house together, we were fine, but I just . . . that wasn't enough for me, obviously. I mean I needed to see other people, I needed to make new friends, and I haven't really done that so I haven't really established myself as a kind of a social being outside the house, you know. And I was starting to think, you know, this is not enough for me really and I need more stimulation and adult company and things. (Philippa)

I still sort of want to get a part of my life back and not just talk nappies . . . it wasn't really me going to parent–toddler groups all the time . . . I mean when I'm at [work] I'm more my old self. (Clare)

I felt as though if I had a job I was doing something, whereas if I didn't, if I was just at home with baby, 'oh you're just a mother and a housewife'. And I know that's the wrong thing to think but you still can't help thinking it. (Rebecca)

The ways in which mothering work is (under) valued in Western societies and the pervasiveness of the contradictory messages which surround and shape women's lives, are clear in the ways these women narrate their experiences, reflecting on how mothering and work fits into their lives. For most, to be 'just a mother' and 'just at home with baby' is not perceived to be enough and Rebecca acknowledges that her feelings are linked to the 'status thing'. Others have not established themselves as 'social beings' outside the home as mothers, have not wanted to become subsumed within an identity of full-time mother. The (inaccurate) perceptions of what other mothers are like, and do, are not challenged by these women, but rather help to confirm their decisions to return to work where other dimensions of selves, beyond the maternal, can be experienced. The women spoke of meeting and interacting with other mothers, but they saw their selves differently, although at risk of becoming like them if they followed similar patterns of intensive mothering. For example, Wendy talks of meeting other mothers who do not work outside the home:

. . . and you talk to them . . . they are so boring, they've got nothing to talk about. I mean, God, I don't want to become one of them . . . I don't want to end up like that.

Clare and Abigail also talk of mothers' needs to meet together and talk, but distance themselves from such activities:

I mean being at home all the time you want to get out and meet people and you . . . So, I can understand why people do, but it wasn't me. (Clare)

I only ever palled up with one other [mother] and so once a fortnight, once a week, we'd have a coffee morning, but it was so focused on our children. How many teeth have you got? How many farts does he do, anything, oh for God's sake, what texture is . . . for God's sake, I don't want to know. So it's nice to have got away from that. (Abigail)

The narratives here draw on perceptions of work outside the home being more highly valued. A return to paid work, the 'out world', offers women the opportunity to re-enter a familiar world. This is a world where their competencies are measured according to criteria not usually as invidious as those operating around mothering. For these women who were fortunate enough to have a choice, a return to work offered an escape route from the responsibilities and more isolating and mundane aspects of mothering and an opportunity to be their (old) selves. Paid work was regarded by some as the easier option, as the extracts below show:

I mean, I admit this to you and it'll be on the tape, but at the end of the weekend I'm thinking, phew! thank goodness somebody else has got part of the day, which is an awful thing to say, maybe?. (Kathryn)

I do enjoy being a mother, I am enjoying it a lot, although I find it incredibly hard work. Having said that I do like being at work. (Diana)

I just sit there all day, like you've got a computer in front of you and it's . . . we're on a good section so . . . it's just good. Yes, I get away from the babies and I appreciate them more when I pick them up. Got my life back. (Wendy, mother of twins)

I think it . . . it is nice to go and do some work but the thing is at the moment, I'm not happy with where I am. I don't know if it's just temporarily, you know, that it's not a very nice atmosphere, but I still think it's good, you know, to do something. (Lillian)

I think . . . again, when I was at home with her for a long time I did feel that my identity was being a little bit kind of subsumed into this kind of fluffy thing that included her and me and . . . that I didn't really have a life of my own other than my role as a carer for Georgia . . . Actually a lot of the time I don't feel as much like a mum as I . . . as I used to as well, you know, because I do genuinely forget about . . . it's awful, but I forget about her when I'm at work. (Philippa)

The privatised and often isolating gendered practices that characterise childrearing in the West are implicit in these extracts. It is interesting too that Philippa censors herself with the words, 'it's awful' when she talks of forgetting about her daughter when she is at work. Over time, the women gradually develop aspects of social selves as mothers as expectations grounded in essentialist ideas of instinctive and natural abilities are re-evaluated. But for most, experiences of mothering do not resonate with dominant constructions of motherhood and the women differentiate themselves from other women they meet who are involved in full-time mothering. Most of the women actively resist becoming completely subsumed in full-time, intensive mothering.

Selves as mothers

The claim that motherhood provides 'an opportunity for renewed narrative movement par excellence' was countered in an earlier chapter (Bailey, 1999:351). This was because it did not sufficiently take account of the difficulty of voicing different or unhappy mothering experiences. Given both the moral minefield in which motherhood is lived out, and the 'gendered moral rationalities' that shape social negotiations around mothering and paid work, doing mothering is a complicated business (Duncan and Edwards, 1999). When asked about their feelings on becoming mothers in the earlier postnatal interviews (chapter 5), many women spoke of coping with the practical aspects of mothering. But they had ambivalent feelings about actually feeling like mothers in those early weeks. Many were still coming to terms with the, for most, unanticipated scale of what becoming mothers entailed. Yet during the earlier interviews women could be seen to juggle their contradictory feelings. They worked hard to make sense of the confusion they were experiencing and to confirm that by the time of the interview they were 'coping'. By the time of the final interviews an interlude of eight to nine months had elapsed since the birth of their children, and experiences remained varied. Interestingly, some women who had previously spoken of their immediate, 'natural' identification with being mothers, now produced contradictory narratives of their experiences. For example, in the following extracts Faye's words from the two interviews are juxtaposed:

Yes, it comes really naturally to me, which I wasn't sure whether it would or not. (early postnatal interview).

I don't know, how does . . . how does a mother feel? . . . No, I don't really consider myself as . . . I suppose when she starts calling me Mum or something like that. (final postnatal interview)

The precarious properties of narratives are demonstrated in these extracts. As individuals we reflect, reconstruct and produce narratives, at some level, to make sense of experiences within the context of other influences. The temporal ordering of events is interesting in any analysis of narrative construction. In the extract above we see how the lapse of time enables Faye to reflect and challenge assumptions around womens' natural abilities to mother. Having survived with her child to nine months, she is able to risk questioning how 'a mother' should feel. The following lengthy extracts are included to show the ways in which women experience their changing sense of selves as women and mothers, and the influence of cultural scripts on how women should feel and respond:

I worry about it the whole time. You know, I worry whether I'm a good mother, whether . . . whether I've got the right responses, whether I'm bonding enough with him . . . That's what . . . this is the bit . . . that comes back to the bonding thing. No, I . . . I don't know. No, I don't . . . my self-image hasn't changed. I don't feel . . . I don't know whether I do feel like a mother? No. And that's . . . that's what worries me is that . . . I still think . . . I still feel that I borrowed Rupert. It is... I still feel that he's not mine. That it's like baby-sitting, that I can... I'm going to be able to give him back, that he isn't mine, and this is the whole bonding thing, and it really worries me. (Kathryn)

I think I actually half expected that I was going to be an instant mother because I was so ready for it and so looking forward to having her. That really isn't the case at all... I suppose the basics are that I am [a mother], this is my new role. (Helen)

But I've really enjoyed the whole thing. I'm obviously a lot more maternal than I thought I was... I think I've recognised something in myself, you know, perhaps a sort of need to care for something... it's harder than... I don't know, its easier and harder. (Peggy)

Sometimes I do but I... I don't know. I mean I do because... in the sense that I know that Sonia is definitely my priority, but other times I keep thinking am I really a mother? and I've felt like that from the beginning, is it really... is it really me? You know, you just sort of don't really think you're grown up enough to be it, but as time goes on you realise you are because you have to cope with so much more every day, there's always something else, and you become more sort of mature, I suppose. So yes, I do feel like a mother, very mumsy. (Diana)

The reality of realising I was a mother came gradually. Being a mother, I think, instinctively happened. I didn't... it was a bit weird the first couple of weeks because you're like, well, what the hell am I doing, I just nearly died, I've got this screaming, demanding thing that doesn't show me any love, everyone says to you, 'oh you're going to love it straightaway' and you're like – that? And then you suddenly realise, oh I really, really, really love him and you wander round going, I love my baby, I love my baby. And I don't know, it just sort of happened. (Sarah)

I suppose it has been a gradual sort of thing and then really in a way, sort of, like things have sort of like changed, you know... suddenly, sort of, like, but then it really happened... it really dawned on me that... You sort of trudge along and then like all of a sudden I thought,... you know, this is really... (Lillian)

I feel like a mother. Not in the way I used to view mothers... I suppose I used to view mothers as very organised, well, like my own mother, sort of very organised, taking you to ballet, the person that took you to the ballet classes, took you to school, made sure that you had your wash or your bath or whatever... Whereas the way I feel like being a mother I suppose is just the cuddles... and the fun and just having a little person, a little friend. You know, she's like my little friend, but I am responsible for her as well, but there's less of a big gap and I think also that might be to do with the age difference because my mum was forty-two when she had me whereas there's less of an age gap between us. (Rebecca)

I do, but it's not... it's not always at the top of my mind that I am a mother. (Clare)

Yes, I suppose I do really, just because the babies have changed and they do things, like William will come and give me a cuddle... and you say 'give Mummy a kiss', they'll come and kiss you . . . so I think it's just because they are doing more. (Wendy)

But yes, I feel much more like a mother now than I did . . . I suppose I do feel like a mother . . . you're a person with a baby, you become a mother and you feel like a mother. And you call yourself Mummy, I suppose, don't you, as you're going about, you know you say, 'that's Mummy', and 'don't drop Mummy's bag again', then you call yourself Mummy so I suppose that makes you . . . But like now, I could almost forget that she's there and I do feel like me. But then when she's around I suppose I'm on duty again and you feel like a mother. No, I couldn't forget that I have her, but I could imagine life . . . I could imagine life without her, I could imagine going outside for a walk and forgetting her. Not that I would of course! Yes, but you know, that would be a possibility. (Gillian)

For most of the women, feeling like 'a mother' is a gradual process and one which, even at nine months, may not be perceived as having been achieved. As Kathryn explains 'I don't know whether I do feel like a mother . . . that's what worries me'. If mothering is assumed to be natural, then to not feel like a mother has implications for a sense of self as a woman. Kathryn voices her concerns that she is not a 'good mother' and that she might not have the 'right responses', or using professional language, have 'bonded'. Diana also doubts her own self as a mother: 'am I really a mother? and I've felt that from the beginning'. Helen also notes that, contrary to her expectations, she did not feel an 'instant mother'. In contrast, Peggy is surprised by her enjoyment of 'the whole thing' and her 'maternal' self. Interestingly, Peggy begins to describe her experiences of being a mother as 'harder than . . . ', but pulls back and admits confusion, 'I don't know, it's easier and harder'. The increasing responsiveness of their babies is noted by other mothers and is used to explain how, interactionally, their sense of feeling like a mother has developed.

Stanley and Wise have observed that 'reality is much more complex and multi-dimensional than we ordinarily suppose it to be, and it is contradictory' (1990:64). Not surprisingly then, the narratives produced as women make sense of their experiences of transition to motherhood are also fluid and contradictory. Whilst Diana talks of her doubts: 'is it really me?', she also confirms in the same extract that 'yes, I do feel like a mother, very mumsy'. Gillian talks of her different identities and the possibility that she could forget her baby but quickly asserts 'not that I would of course'; clearly for 'good' mothers such an act would be (almost) unthinkable. In Kathryn's extract, a thread of personal narrative is discernible when she voices her worries around 'bonding enough' and 'right responses', she asserts that her 'self-image hasn't changed'. Indeed, it may be that Kathryn has not (yet) incorporated a social self as a mother into her schema of understandings of her self. Similarly, to admit to feeling that you have 'borrowed' your baby is a difficult disclosure as it does not conform to culturally acceptable ways of describing experiences of mothering.

What can, and cannot, be voiced around experiences of mothering, then, is clearly shaped by wider influences, and inextricably linked to socio-cultural, 'racial', ethnic, gendered and structural positions. The experiences of the women in this study were narrated in relation to culturally dominant, moral constructions of 'good mothering'. The passage of time, and the temporal ordering of experiences, is clearly important in relation to what can be voiced about mothering experiences and our children. But self-surveillance may mean that some things are never voiced. An interesting interchange took place in a final postnatal interview with Abigail, which touches on the parameters of what can and cannot be said in relation to our children.

ABIGAIL: I guess we're just lucky, he's a nice child. But then have you met anybody who's not liked their child?

TINA: I know people that . . . there have certainly been a couple who've found it quite difficult to really fully feel even at nine months that the baby is properly theirs and . . .

ABIGAIL: But nobody surely criticises their child?

TINA: No, no, no one does, no, that is true.

ABIGAIL: Because I think he's lovely, but I'm bound to.

TINA: No, that is right, no one criticises. They might feel concern that they're not doing a good job necessarily or that things could be better or whatever, but no, the babies have all been . . .

ABIGAIL: Wonderful babies.

TINA: Well no, some have been little sods, I think, but . . .

ABIGAIL: *But do parents admit that?*

TINA: But no, and some have felt that . . . no, I mean, no, generally the babies have come out pretty well.

ABIGAIL: Yes, exactly. (emphasis added)

By the time of the final postnatal interviews some perspective could be brought to bear on the enormous shifts which had occurred during this intense period of transition. As Frank has noted, 'the chaos that can be told in story is already taking place at a distance and is being reflected on retrospectively' (1995:98). Whilst experiences had differed, and the time taken to feel 'back to normal' varied, giving birth to a child and coping with the responsibilities provided a new place from which the women could reflect upon their experiences. Nine months after the birth of their child many of the women felt they had regained some control in their lives.

This led to both the disclosure of less happy experiences and struggles around a sense of self, and also to a palpable sense of achievement. In the following extracts, more positive aspects of mothering are reflected upon:

All in all it's just been a life-changing experience . . . I don't . . . I think I've got a much more positive self-image than I did before because although I sort of feel all these emotions about not feeling I'm doing anything properly, really, ultimately, you only have to look at your baby to know that you are. And you know, I just feel sort of more confident, although I was never a wallflower, but I do feel a bit more confident about my ability. You feel like you've joined a club and that you suddenly know so much more than you did, and I don't know why. And I don't know, what else do I feel about myself? Well, I suppose I feel quite pleased with myself a lot of the time. (Diana)

There's times when I'd like to be able to turn round and tell them to stuff their job and there's more important things to life than you know, whatever the problem is . . . Yes, I feel more . . . more sure of myself. You know, it doesn't matter to me now if I don't go out . . . if I go out of the house without make-up on or you know I look a mess because there's some people who get their figure back by working out and they will always wear make-up and I think, yes, I want to look nice, but it's not the end of the world. People can take me for what I am . . . I've achieved something fantastic with him. He's, you know, the most incredible thing ever. I don't need anybody else to . . . to have a good . . . high or low opinion of me. It doesn't bother me. I know what I've done and if someone thinks I'm fat, well, you know, it's their problem. (Abigail)

But now I have more of a . . . I feel I have more balance, I mean it's affected me . . . I think it's changed my outlook. It certainly has changed my kind of confidence . . . I am probably more confident than I was before, actually, as a result of having . . . because I sort of feel I've . . . I've sort of done relatively well, you know, so I mean although it's really early days but, sort of thing, she's obviously thriving and . . . and I sort of feel a bit more . . . probably a bit more balanced rather than . . . but I certainly kind of have the same sense of my own identity . . . I mean probably . . . I don't know really . . . which is one of the reasons why I wanted to do something outside the home, definitely, I felt I needed that space and time, well not really space because it's . . . it's just filled with something else, but I need that time away . . . away from her, some of the time, and I just . . . so I think work has got a lot to do with it, but because I'm doing the two things now, it's probably kind of made me feel more . . . in a sense it hasn't actually made me . . . given me a split identity at all, actually, it's just kind of made the whole thing a bit more whole, a bit more . . . in a good way, I feel quite genuinely positive about it. (Philippa)

The women's growth in confidence in their abilities as mothers is linked to the development of their child, with comments such as 'she's obviously thriving' and 'you only have to look at your baby to know'. The enormous achievement of creating another human being overrides other concerns: 'people can take me for what I am . . . I've achieved something fantastic with him'. But not all the women feel as content with their lives and selves as mothers. Kathryn talks of feeling more positive about herself, but this is within the context of real concerns about her mothering responses (see previous extracts). Kathryn expresses unhappiness about the 'routine' of her life, although this is narrated within assurances of still 'coping', as the following extract shows:

Yes, I like myself better, and I think I feel that I . . . I remember saying this to you before, I feel I've got much more to offer. And I don't worry nearly so much about myself, my identity . . . I feel I'm coping. I feel I'm on top of it, but I don't enjoy my life particularly. It's . . . you know, it's back to this rehearsal. It's . . . I'm doing it because I've got to. I mean I remember bursting into tears last, whenever it was, Sunday with Christopher [husband] and I said look, it's the bloody routine, the whole . . . I get up, I feed Rupert, I get myself ready, I make my sandwiches, I walk to work, I do my job, I come back at lunchtime, I walk the dog – I have to fit in a walk and seeing Rupert at lunchtime – I come back to work, I come home, I bath the baby, I cook supper – and I'm knackered! . . . Oh, it is shattering. And every bloody day is the same. It's a routine. And if only it was different.

Whether women engage in full-time mothering, or combine mothering with paid work outside the home, doing mothering can be both exhausting and lonely. In the early postnatal interviews several of the women spoke of restricting their interactions in the public sphere because of a concern with not being seen as a 'real' or 'proper' mother. They were fearful that they may not be able to manage a performance as a mother because they did not yet feel practised in their mothering. In the following extracts, taken from their final interviews, Sarah and Clare talk of their confidence in having come to know their own children's needs and so coping in public settings:

And I don't know, it just sort of happened. But . . . like when we go to cafés or something it's like I need to . . . you have to explain to your friends, I need to sit in the non-smoking area with a high-chair, with a baby room, with baby food, and it's like you're sat on the bus and he starts screaming halfway through the bus ride, and I can sit there and let him scream because I know he's moaning because he's stuck on the bus, and it's not that he's in pain, and all my girlfriends go, what's wrong with your baby . . . I think it's just . . . and you can see that everybody else on the bus is freaking out and you think, chill out, everyone, it's just a baby, you know. (Sarah)

For ages I was conscious of, you know, when he was crying and things, but I mean now he cries, you just sort of laugh . . . laugh at him and . . . and everyone knows . . . and you think . . . you go round the shop and like where a few years ago if I heard a baby screaming I'd think, oh what's wrong, now you . . . just you know, dropped the toy, wants some food or something, you just think, oh well . . . (Clare)

Becoming more practised in 'good enough' mothering, and recognising their children's needs, leads to greater confidence in their own abilities; regardless of what others might think.

Reflection and narrative reconstruction

In these final accounts we glimpse a sense of how selves are differently experienced and made sense of and narrated. The narratives produced are both more revealing and more challenging of previously accepted bodies of authoritative knowledge. Elements of resistant, 'counter-narratives' – produced when experiences do not fit with more mainstream ideals – are discernible (Somers, 1994). Previous accounts of early mothering experiences are now withdrawn, reworked and re-narrated. By taking a close look in this section at how women construct and reshape versions of their experiences over time, we can see how narratives through transition are strategically used to present different selves. Initially, most women work hard to produce accounts which show they are coping and responsibly meeting their children's needs, being seen to be doing 'good mothering'. Later versions of their experiences often contradict or embellish these earlier versions. It is also important to note that an interview necessarily attempts to prompt reflection and may indeed serve to reproduce modernist subjects and these important considerations will be returned to in chapter 7 (Alldred and Gillies, 2002). Telling stories of transition to motherhood is not, as we have seen, unproblematic. In these final interviews a developing confidence in their own abilities, and the gradual transition to being the authority on meeting their own children's needs, empower the women in reflecting and challenging aspects of what had gone before. Distance from an event also provides a sense of safety: the risk of revelation is not perceived to be so great. Having experienced eight to nine months of mothering, difficult experiences can now be voiced, revelations made because they have been survived. In chapter 5 we saw the ways in which many of the women produced narratives within the context of *now* being able to cope, any difficulties having been resolved. Yet in these final interviews some women contest the stories they had previously constructed, and now present a different version of their early experiences of mothering.

In the following extracts Helen talks of her experiences of becoming a mother. The first extract is taken from her first postnatal interview in which she is asked about her antenatal preparation; she comments:

The only thing that I . . . I could possibly sort of criticise on now . . . I wouldn't say it as a criticism, but what I was not prepared for at all (was) the emotional changes of when you come home and suddenly you're living this story life when you have the baby, and suddenly when you come home and after all the visitors have started to dwindle off and it's just you that's left...and I would say that I hadn't really been prepared for those feelings of actually being out of control, *which I would say probably only the last week that I've actually got on top of it and I'm actually starting to feel a little bit more in control*... (emphasis added)

In her final interview, Helen feels able to disclose how she had been really feeling during the early weeks of becoming a mother:

The emotions were so intense, I think in every way, that my life just turned upside down...I don't think that there is anything that anybody can do to actually prepare you for the change it's going to have in your life. I talk to people about it now because I think that...*you know, it is difficult to talk when everybody is so wonderful that in fact you don't want to create any negative sort of impression* to, you know, people around you so you sort of go with the flow, but inside you're actually quite terrified, and yes, now I can talk to other people about it and they say 'gosh, but you, you would never have known – you know you had this real sort of positive, enthusiastic, unflappable way about you at that time', and maybe I did, but *I know now and I can express myself as to how I was sort of really feeling*...I know that a couple of questions you asked me, sort of, first I was bordering on bursting into tears, you know, *but I mean obviously I contained myself but you know I wouldn't let this other side, sort of*...Because I don't think I...you know I didn't express it to anybody. You know, not my health visitor, not...not Stephen [husband], you know, my sister and my mum, you know, have been great sources of support but they have been so capable. (emphasis added)

The difficulties of giving an account which does not resonate with the expectations of those around you, or your own expectations, are all too clear in this extract. The overriding need to contain personal experiences – to avoid giving any negative impressions – and to provide a coherent narrative of being a 'good' mother appears to be paramount, especially if those close to you have coped well and been seen to be 'so capable'. And this may not only be the case for new mothers. Helen goes on to describe the difficulties her husband had in voicing his experiences,

...it's a very trying, difficult time and I know that he had *emotions which he again didn't express then, but he does express now*, because he didn't want to make out to anyone that this...this lovely...rosy sort of glowing impression of *how it's supposed to be* in fact maybe wasn't quite as rosy, the reality of it when you get home... (emphasis added)

The importance of presenting an acceptable and culturally recognisable account of new parenting is apparent in this extract. The disclosure of other feelings – even to each other – is perceived as risky. Both partners then work to construct a different, and what they take to be, a more acceptable 'reality'. It is only retrospectively that such experiences can be voiced. Interestingly, Helen used the end-of-study questionnaire to again confirm the difficulties she had in voicing her early mothering experiences:

In the second interview it was one of the first times anyone had taken so much time in concentrating on my emotional state (even more than the health visitor) – but I now realise that I was not being 100 per cent honest with my answers and was too eager to attempt to create a feeling of control, relaxation and total happiness and contentment. In fact I was feeling quite disorientated and out of control. (end-of-study questionnaire)

Kathryn began her final interview in the following way:

And I think actually . . . I don't think . . . *I was pretending that I was coping better than I was. I must . . . I must admit that looking back on that interview I thought I hadn't done terribly well.* You know, I thought . . . sort of thought, oh I wished you hadn't interviewed me then because I don't know, perhaps I'd just had a bad day or I don't know, I just remember . . . Well, I always come across . . . more in control than I actually am. I'm a real sort of swan paddling below the surface . . . . I think we all . . . I think all new mothers feel that they've got to do terribly well. I mean, you know everyone says to me in a way I don't want it to change my life, I don't want people to think that I'm not coping or I don't want . . . you know, life's got to go on, that's . . . that's the general feeling. *And why should we all feel that?* (emphasis added)

Having begun the interview in this way Kathryn then goes on to voice her worries and concerns over her mothering abilities which continue to trouble her. Having challenged the need to contain difficulties, 'and why should we all feel that?', Kathryn proceeds to reveal personal layers of narrative which might have remained unvoiced. The narrative she presents is complex, as evidenced in the extracts which appear in other sections of this chapter. Her use of words such as 'which is an awful thing to say maybe?', 'do you think all mothers feel that?', show her seeking reassurance and (possibly) permission to voice what she feels are not 'normal' ways of talking about being a mother.

A comparison of Sarah's postnatal interviews also reveals interesting shifts in the ways in which experiences are narrated. In her earlier post-natal interview Sarah had continued to draw on essentialist ideas linking birth and mothering to nature and instinct. Her baby's birth had pro-ceeded rapidly in hospital without any need for pain relief, and Sarah again reiterated her belief that she had coped with the process of birth by adopting a positive 'state of mind':

And having him was fine, I didn't have any drugs . . . to be honest I think it's all a state of mind. I think some people if they're encouraged to know that they are . . . they're a human being and we've been doing it for thousands of years, then they can handle it and I've sort . . . people, I know, are like that, that's their mentality, but there again, if you're told oooh, oooh it's going to be really horrific, you better take everything available, then you will because you haven't been shown that there is another path to take, you know. And I mean I'm not knocking people that take epidurals and all that kind of stuff because I understand that it most probably... if you panic then, hey, God it must be horrendous. I panicked twice and I realised how much more horrendous the experience was when I panicked. *And then I thought to myself, wow! aren't I amazing.* You can control everything that's happening to you. You know, breathing, you can actually control the pain and I'd anticipated it being absolutely horrific, so it wasn't... it was worse than I thought but it wasn't as bad as I thought... I mean I think I was incredibly fortunate, you know. And I think it's maybe just because... maybe my upbringing has... has told me that, that you are in charge of yourself, and that you don't need drugs and this, that and the other, you can do it all yourself. So I mean that's... I was lucky, I knew I could do it, and there again I knew I could fall back on the drugs because it would be awful saying to people I'm having no drugs and then you get there and you think, God, I need it. (early postnatal interview, emphasis added)

Sarah's comments at the end of this interview were:

Yes, but I am very fortunate and I'm having a very good time. It wasn't good at first, *but now it's brilliant.* We're enjoying ourselves. (emphasis added)

In her final interview Sarah reflects on the previous months and talks of having experienced a period of what she now describes as prolonged 'shock' since the birth of her baby:

I actually feel that I was... maybe not postnatally depressed, maybe in shock, definitely. I feel I was in shock up to about a month ago because I've only just started tasting food again... And my mum said to me, 'oh that's a sign of shock'... is that you stop tasting things and smelling things. I've only started smelling things again since having him, it's really weird. But I don't think it was depression, I actually think it was shock, and change of the... you know. But no, I just think it's the shock of the whole... the whole sort of... I don't know... no, they don't sort of tell you these... not that they tell you, it's just... *the reality of it all smacks you in the face*, doesn't it, and you either... you either go one way in that you just hand responsibility over to other people and you then lose your child, because you can do that, or you take it all in your stride and *do it the right way*, which you should be doing, which you are capable of doing. But it's like I say, my cousin you know, she's having a really bad time, and the only way she can do... I mean, I believe that she is taking it to the extreme, that she is... she's got a chemical... a chemical imbalance in her brain definitely, she's ill, but she's got a good man. You know, like my cousin is a social worker and he's a really good man, and... She is in a position to say, take the baby, I can't handle it, which I would love to do, but I'm not in a position. I can't hand him to someone and say take him, and me run away, because... so I just feel it's the shock of giving birth. *Oh my God, it's the closest I've ever been to death, Jesus!* (emphasis added)

By juxtaposing these extracts, the contradictions between and within accounts are highlighted. The difficulty of voicing negative experiences is also apparent, and particular time-frames are used to place distance between the lived experience and narrating that experience. In one of the first extracts Sarah says that 'it wasn't good at *first*, but now it's brilliant'. In the final extract Sarah again places her experiences within a time-frame, the implication being that *now* everything is fine, 'I feel I was in shock *up to about a month ago.*' The intricacies of narratives are also apparent in this final extract. Sarah says that 'the reality of it all smacks you in the face, doesn't it?', apparently acknowledging that the lived experience, 'the reality' of being a mother, differs in some ways from expectations. Here she challenges the dominant ideologies which sur-round motherhood, but also colludes with them when she talks about there being a 'right way' to do mothering. Different ways of narrating the *same* event are also demonstrated in these extracts. Sarah's early postnatal description of giving birth and her later account do not appear to be descriptions of the same event. In the first Sarah says, 'I thought to myself, wow! aren't I amazing', and in her final interview she notes, 'so I just feel it's the shock of giving birth. Oh my God, it's the closest I've ever been to death, Jesus!'. The passage of time enables a reordering of experiences, and shifting perspectives can help to bring new meanings to past experi-ences, leading to previously withheld experiences being voiced.

The ways in which time is used to organise experiences into coherent narratives is also demonstrated in the women's accounts. As noted earlier, different time-frames – one professional and one lay and experiential – are used by the health professionals and by the women in their constructions of a 'return to normal'. Within narrative accounts, temporal ordering shows the ways in which events are woven into episodes, and experiences made sense of and given coherence. In the following extracts from Philippa's final interview we can see the way in which this reflexive practice is used:

Well, I remember . . . I sort of remember things in terms of like watersheds quite a lot and I think that three months was the first time . . . because *I remember feeling a bit more human again at that point.* So from sort of six weeks to three months I just probably, much rather saying, but getting a bit, kind of . . . a little bit easier and getting, you know, to grips. *I think also my expectations probably changed*, I thought I don't really mind sitting breastfeeding the whole time, you know, and things, but by the time she got to three months it kind of . . . *I found I was feeling a bit more like my old self again, I was getting parts of my life back*, I wasn't feeding twenty-four hours a day and sleep . . . getting more sleep and, you know, all those things. And then I mean after that I remember sort of six months being . . . well, between four and six months things just getting a lot more interesting and sort of *thinking this is more like what it's about*, if you know what I mean, and I just . . . she was much more responsive, I mean once she sort of started smiling and . . . God, all sorts of things, I can't remember! . . . I really can't remember exactly when anything happened. It seems very kind of murky. (late postnatal interview, emphasis added)

Philippa organises her narrative around what she calls 'watersheds'. These are times at which shifts were discernible, for example, 'I remember feeling a bit more human again at that point' and later, 'I found I was feeling a bit more like my old self again, I was getting parts of my life back' and 'thinking this is more like what it's about'. Her narrative documents a journey through early motherhood in which her expectations are challenged by different, unexpected experiences. An extract from her early postnatal interview provides a much more immediate account of Philippa trying to make sense of the early weeks of being a mother:

I mean in terms of my life changing . . . I feel both . . . I'm kind of enjoying what's happening now and I'm a bit kind of frustrated by the, you know, day after day on my . . . a bit on my own, I mean even though I do see people it's kind of for an hour or so or whatever, and I do . . . I sort of think, gosh you know, this is major decision, a major change, you know, I just can't . . . I can't turn the clock back or anything now. I mean . . . and I felt that very much over the first . . . that feeling's getting less and I'm sort of now . . . I'm getting more to the stage where I couldn't imagine life without her and I'm enjoying her a lot more, but *that's been kind of gradual. But there's a little bit of thinking, gosh, what . . . you know, what have I done?* Yes. So a bit of sort of . . . a few negative feelings and . . . *But you know, on the other hand I really . . . you know, I'm sort of enjoying her* and I sort of think, you know, in a way this is more what life's about than working or whatever, you know, which is what I had before. You know, some aspects of my life before seem quite sort of empty comparatively, you know . . . life without children, I think, and I think that's kind of . . . that's coming to the fore more and more, it's *just more of a gradual adjustment* rather than something that I felt immediately very strongly. And I sort of . . . I do go back to work and I sort of think I've no desire really to be here at all, you know, I don't . . . especially with nice hot days you know, yes. You know, I sort of think it's fairly . . . some of it's fairly petty and . . . you know, it's certainly not a hugely worthwhile job in a way, so it just seems . . . this sort of seems part of a bigger part of life, you know . . . (early postnatal interview, emphasis added)

The narrative Philippa produces at this point can be seen to veer between presenting as a competent and coping mother, and trying to voice her everyday experiences. Negative aspects are tentatively voiced 'but there's a little bit of thinking, gosh, what . . . you know, what have I done?', but always within the context of returning to more culturally acceptable ways of describing becoming a mother, 'but you know, on the other hand I really . . . you know, I'm sort of enjoying her'. The gradual and individual nature of transition is once again emphasised. In her final interview, Philippa reflects across her experiences of transition:

I surprised myself by how badly I coped in the first few weeks, actually, because I kind of . . . because I've always . . . I'm the kind of person that tends to cope reasonably well. I'm quite . . . I know that I'm quite balanced and I'm fairly laid back and I'm fairly competent and things, so I expected myself to have . . . *I had a kind of vision of myself* with children which was that it was all kind of . . . I mean not completely brilliant the whole time but I sort of thought . . . I thought it would be fine, I thought I'd be OK, so I'm not really surprised by that, but I was surprised by . . . because she just cried quite a lot in the first few weeks, that I was surprised by that, I just thought, oh my God, *I'm not sure that this was quite in my kind of vision of things*, which hadn't like a very kind of demanding, whingy, difficult baby, which is how she was. (emphasis added)

Her 'vision' of herself as a mother, her expectations, were not initially met and the difficulties she experienced were not part of her vision. Other mothers' accounts also revealed a reordering of experiences. Reflecting on their first eight to nine months of mothering enabled the women to make sense of their different, and for some unexpectedly difficult, experiences. This was the case for Linda, whose journey we now turn to.

Narrating chaos?

Arthur Frank, writing in the context of illness narratives, has argued that 'those who are truly *living* the chaos cannot tell in words. To turn the chaos into a verbal story is to have some reflexive grasp' (Frank, 1995:98). For Linda, the early postnatal period was an unexpectedly difficult time. Having been labelled as 'postnatally depressed', a label she rejected, she opted out of the early postnatal interview on the advice of her husband and health visitor. She resisted, or felt unable – or elements of both – to produce a narrative of her early mothering experiences. Linda had found out she was pregnant shortly after she had been made redundant from her office job and in the antenatal interview she had described her pregnancy as planned. In the following extract, taken from that interview, Linda describes her experiences of her pregnancy, drawing on different discourses to do so:

The first three months I didn't enjoy, I didn't enjoy at all. I mean I don't think the whole pregnancy throughout has been very enjoyable, but the first three months – I wasn't sick or anything like that, it was just like . . . I think it was because I was made redundant, and then I found out I was pregnant, that I think all those kind of things got on top of me, so I was not happy about the whole situation, even though I wanted to be pregnant, it was . . . it was just . . . I think it's the fact that something else has taken over your body, the fact that you have to give up things that are probably not so important, but you still have to, you know, change your whole way of life, really, to carry a child. I used to smoke and as soon as . . . I always vowed that as soon as I knew I was pregnant – I didn't smoke a lot, it was just an occasional thing – as soon as I knew I was pregnant, that was it. You give up smoking, you give up drinking, you give up the yoghurts, the . . . all the things that they tell you to give up . . . and I'm thinking this is not fair, you know. But now, because of you're feeling the baby and you get to sort of understand it a bit more – well, you can tell because ... so much bigger, that yes, I do ... *I'm looking forward to having the baby.* (emphasis added)

And later:

[It's] the thing about something else actually taking over your body ... out of control. Because I suppose I got pregnant quite late in my life ... I'm twenty-nine now. And most of my friends have actually sort of ... they've got children and they're three and five years old, you know, and they've got another one. Because I've had that independence, that way of life, that I could just please myself as and when, then you become pregnant, your whole body's taken over, you feel very sensitive to things that you could just sit down and cry sometimes, and the fact of becoming so large and ... not obscene but I never knew that ... *I suppose I shouldn't say this,* but I never knew that your backside could actually increase double the size just through being pregnant. That's happened to mine.... Yes, I'm really.... *I know that there's going to be a bundle of joy at the end of the day* ... and that's what I'm looking for, but I wouldn't go straight into being pregnant again. I think I'll have to be convinced that you know ... I feel that from being the person in charge, work-wise, to the person that is being taken over by something else or someone else, is quite a lot to take in. (emphasis added)

But Linda concludes by anticipating the support she will have from her husband:

... and I think Philip and I will actually work things out together and just get on with it ... Well, you make it together, so ...

Perhaps the seeds for a difficult time as a new mother are sown in this narrative of anticipation. Linda reveals her unhappiness in quite candid ways in comparison with some of the other women interviewed at this stage. But she also always returns to what she perceives to be more acceptable ways of talking about anticipating motherhood, for example, 'a bundle of joy at the end of the day'. As noted above, Linda opted out of the early postnatal interviews although we spoke at length, and on several occasions by telephone, during the early weeks following the birth of her child when her profound sense of being lonely and isolated was palpable. Eventually, Linda contacted me to rejoin the study and was interviewed when her baby was nine months old. Linda began this interview by saying, 'I have been to hell and back', 'I feel cheated of the months [the baby] has been growing up' and 'I never knew bringing a baby into the world could upset your life'. In this interview Linda makes no attempt to edit her experiences in the ways she had in the antenatal interview, where she had usually concluded with culturally acceptable ways of talking about antici-pating motherhood. Linda's difficult experiences have involved emo-tional estrangement from her husband, which she traces to the birth:

The birth, I felt, was horrendous, I really did. I think because of Philip ... I don't know ... we sort of ... on the birth of Nathan it was like we split. It was like the bond had gone between us and I could see on the expression of his face ... Literally at the birth ... ours has changed so much. And I wasn't prepared for that ... I think it is because everybody thinks that Mum and Dad are ... the Mummy and Daddy are just going to be a bonding family and everything's going to be perfect ... But it wasn't, it just wasn't ... we're still working at it .... Oh, I won't be having another one.

Linda, like some other women in the study, feels physically isolated from the world of work and her friends, but nine months after the birth is still coming to terms with the scale of the changes in her life:

I miss work, I miss ... not work, not my job, but I miss the brain ticking, the conversation ... Because you don't have that contact anymore and the contact that you do have ... I mean, I've got a really nice friend who lives in [town] and, you know, she's back at work or whatever and we don't talk about nappies, the price of baby food and boring things like that, because that does bore me, but you speak to other people and it's like, and how's your baby doing and my baby is doing this and blah blah blah, and yes, I don't mind listening to it but after a while you want another conversation ... Yes, I would like to go back to work, just part-time, and you know if I don't like it, then I've got nothing to lose. But, yes, I'd like to venture out again, dress up in a suit, make an effort and you know, speak to other people, yes ... I never thought I'd be carrying this [indicates baby on hip] all the time. My briefcase wasn't heavy at all in comparison to a baby but that was heavy enough. And you can put the briefcase down, that's the thing, can't you? Just leave it.

For Linda, and as found in other women's accounts, work outside the home appears to offer so much of what mothering does not: it is valued, something to 'make an effort' for, a different, less boring arena in which to interact and be yourself. The all-consuming dimensions of motherhood and responsibilities of mothering are also implicit in the analogy with a briefcase: 'you can put the briefcase down, that's the thing, can't you? Just leave it.' But Linda and her baby, with the help of her parents, have survived to nine months and she feels she is coping: 'I can cope, I mean I'm coping with it.' Having disclosed her own difficult experiences Linda feels able to challenge what other people might be concealing and she ponders:

And when you see other people, you see them for face value, but when they go home is it a different story and do they actually tell you? And no, I don't think they do and that annoys me because I think to myself, I know what I've been through, or we as a family have been through, and I'd love other people not to know that it's us but to know that it's not all hunky dory and *you've not failed if something has gone wrong* ... (emphasis added)

In the end-of-study questionnaire, Linda uses a question which asked the women to describe their experiences of participating in the study, to make the following comments:

I would hope being a participant in the research would help other women, as I felt it very interesting to listen to the tape of myself whilst being pregnant. Tina is making a great achievement for women, I hope in enlightening us all, that we are allowed to feel the way we do. Well done, Tina, and thank you.

Linda's tone is now almost zealous. Voicing her difficult experiences appears to have been cathartic. Linda comments that she has found listening to the tape of her earlier antenatal interview 'interesting' and the implication is that it may have been 'therapeutic' in some way (see chapter 7). Her perception of the research as 'enlightening us all' and enabling women 'to feel the way we do' is gratifying, and at the same time of some concern. This is because the shifts required to bring about the changes she alludes to, which are fundamentally about the ways in which motherhood is configured in many Western societies, have been at the centre of an ongoing struggle for so many years. This book can only hope to make a very small contribution to the wider, enduring debates about *how* motherhood should be socially constructed.

Conclusion

Over time, and with practice, a social self as a mother is gradually developed and eventually incorporated 'into an overall schema of self-understanding' (Lawler, 2000:57–8). Movements in and out of the practised worlds of work, less anxiety about meeting a child's needs, and coping both within and outside the home, together with interaction with an increasingly responsive child, all contribute to the development of a sense of self – a social rather than essentialist self – as a mother. Yet for some women concerns remain about their abilities to mother and their responses to their children. The trajectory of a return to normal is differently experienced, and professional practices, including monitoring and measurement, often do not fit with experiential time. This leads some to challenge once sought and accepted authoritative, expert knowledge and to reassess perceptions of risk. Becoming more practised leads to disclosure of earlier experiences previously withheld. Reflexivity is now engaged with from a position of greater ontological security in relation to being a mother. For some, this is in the context of having also regained a sense of a recognised, practised selfhood as workers outside the home. For most, a schema of self-understanding is eventually enriched through becoming mothers and managing 'good enough' mothering, but not for all. Claims made in relation to late modernity, that individuals 'are increasingly free from rules, expectations and forms of authority' (Adkins, 2002) do not hold good in relation to mothering and motherhood. This is because at the core of these relationships is an imperative to meet the needs of a dependent child and be seen to do so, responsibly. This morally circumscribed context is hard to escape in relation to making sense and performing an individualised biography through narrative construction as a new mother. Self-reflexivity and being a mother is, then, always more than playing a part and performing an individualised biography. This is because of the materiality and real fleshy bodies and conventional expectations of 'being there for others' that shape women's lives as mothers. In the following chapter we return to the arguments raised across this book, questioning and theorising dimensions of reflexivity in relation to selves, agency and mothering in late modernity. How are the contours of reflexivity constituted, gendered and (unevenly) realised?

7   Conclusions and reflections: making sense of motherhood

This chapter draws together the theoretical debates raised by the empirical data in relation to reflexivity, narratives and gendered selves in late modernity. The research and fieldwork observations collected together in this book enable us to see, close up, how mothering and motherhood are differently – and similarly – experienced, and culturally, socially, historically and politically patterned and shaped. The profound difficulties of voicing unexpected and unanticipated personal experiences of early mothering are confounded by the moral context in which women continue to mother in the West. This context is shaped in different ways and is underpinned by essentialist assumptions of women's instinctive capacities to be there for others, meeting needs and acting responsibly. So entrenched are these assumptions that women coming to motherhood are guided by reference to them and can be distressed and confused when 'natural' and 'instinctive' feelings elude them in the early days and weeks – and sometimes months – of mothering. A social self as a mother has to be developed. But letting go of essentialist expectations can be tricky, striking at the very core of a woman's sense of her self as a 'real' woman. The parameters around what can and cannot be said in relation to our dependent children can lead to normal 'difficult' experiences of early mothering remaining unvoiced; ironically, this self-silencing only serves to further perpetuate the old myths of motherhood. The lapse of time, for many women, enables them to become more practised in their mothering skills and to become experts on identifying and meeting their children's needs. Mothering, then, is hard – and often lonely, isolating and undervalued – work as it is currently configured in the West. But for all that, the positive dimensions of loving a child and unconditionally being loved back can involve a profound sense of having achieved something worthwhile, leading to a deeply meaningful, special life-long relationship. The contradictions, then, that have for many years characterised feminist and other debates in relation to mothering and women's lives show no sign of abating: the relationship is confusing, compelling, loving and ultimately confounding.

In this chapter aspects of reflexivity will be mapped in order to explore further dimensions of a reflexively constituted sense of self, and how selves are made sense of and narrated through a period of transition. This focus raises several questions. For example, in what ways is a capacity for reflexivity and narrative assumed in late modernity and do certain life events prompt periods of heightened reflexivity? How do events that are inextricably bound up with constructions of selves, especially those involving embodied change, shed light on how we make and understand our selves in late modernity? A focus on transition to first-time motherhood enables us to explore these issues, but also adds further layers of complexity, for example assumptions made in relation to needs and responsibilities and essentialist ideas about women's 'natural' capacities. Real, fleshy maternal bodies are also hard to ignore in any analysis of women becoming mothers, yet the trap of essentialism lurks at every turn. The irony of motherhood is that 'on the one hand it is an unutterably personal array of experiences' yet it is largely lived out and measured in the public sphere (Chase and Rogers, 2001). The context, then, is key as we make sense of experiences for ourselves – to maintain ontological security – and produce accounts for others; the two not necessarily being the same thing. The ways in which our understandings of mothering and motherhood in the West are powerfully shaped by bodies of expert, authoritative knowledge and associated practices and their continued grip will also be revisited. For example, what can the experiences of women living in other cultures tell us about cultural scripts in the West? The complex interplay between technology, perceptions of progress and different ways of knowing about women's (reproductive) bodies in an increasingly globalised world also requires further comment. Finally, the methodological issues arising from the work, and the ways in which a narrative approach may only serve to reproduce a modernist subject, will be considered.

Reflexivity and motherhood

What does a focus on transition to first-time motherhood tell us about reflexivity in late modernity? Theories of reflexive modernity have focused on rapid transformations leading to detraditionalisation. The certainties that once were assumed – including gender fates – can no longer be so conceived. Rather, late modernity is characterised by uncertainty, heightened perceptions of risk, a demise in trust in experts associated with a greater imperative to make our selves, reflexively (Giddens, 1991; Lupton, 1999; Adkins, 2002). Social theorists have used the term 'reflexivity' to describe both 'structural reflexivity' and 'self-reflexivity' and it is the latter which is of concern here. The question posed throughout the book has been 'how do women make sense of motherhood?' and a focus on self-reflexivity can help us to see the ways in which this is engaged with. In her critique of aspects of reflexive modernity, Adkins notes that self-reflexivity is where 'agency reflects on itself and there is increased self-monitoring' and that this takes place as a response to rapid transformations, the demise of 'structural forms of determination and the "unleashing" of agency from structure' (2002:14–15). A response to these changes has, it is argued, led to greater emphasis on individuals and their capacity to make themselves. This occurs as we are all increasingly freed from the strictures of rules and particular ways of being and behaving.

But whilst some aspects of theories of reflexive modernity are attractive and have resonance for our understanding of women's experiences of becoming mothers, others do not. This is because they do not sufficiently take account of the continuities and changes that shape women's lives. For example, mothering continues to be evaluated in morally underpinned ways, yet at the same time there have been dramatic changes in family formations. This means that in relation to childbearing and mothering, women now have much less first-hand experience than previous generations as families have fewer children and live in more geographically dispersed ways. In this context, women do not possess the experiential knowledge to enable them to confidently make individual decisions. Rather, they increasingly look to expert bodies of knowledge and expert practices to guide them through this period of uncertainty. The demise, then, of expert authoritative knowledge may 'be more apparent than real' (Lawler, 2000:19). Similarly, as noted earlier, the history of obstetrics in the West is one of separation and women have become increasingly separated from knowing their bodies (Rothman, 1992, cited in Davis-Floyd and Davis, 1997; Lupton, 1994). So in the case of reproduction, childbirth and mothering, women are 'not increasingly free from the rules, expectations, and forms of authority associated with modernity' (Adkins, 2002:16). This is because at the root of these experiences and relationships is a continued moral and cultural imperative to act responsibly towards our (even unborn) children. In relation to becoming a mother, and the contexts in which motherhood is lived out, women's agency has not been freed from structure but rather structural and material concerns continue to shape expectations and experiences, albeit patterning them in different and unequal ways. In chapter 1 it was noted that self-reflexivity is not universally experienced. This is not because individuals or some groups lack the capacity to be reflexive, but rather because of more pressing material and structural concerns in a life, for example in the case of those living a hand-to-mouth existence in extreme poverty in Bangladesh. Lash makes a similar observation and asks 'just how reflexive is it possible for a single mother in an urban ghetto to be?. . .just how much freedom from the "necessity" of "structure" and structural poverty does this ghetto mother have to construct her own "life narratives"?' (Lash, 1994:120). Yet this is not to deny certain groups agency, but once again to reiterate the need to take account of the material and structural contexts which pattern lives in different and unequal ways. The women whose journeys into motherhood we have followed across this book identified themselves predominately as 'middle class'. According to Lash's critique of the reflexive modernisation thesis, this group could be seen as 'reflexivity winners' in comparison with the single mothers in the urban ghetto he draws our attention to, who would be 'reflexivity losers'. Yet Adkins poses the more fundamental question of 'how is it that *so many women* are reflexivity losers', drawing our attention to the ways in which theories of reflexivity have largely ignored its highly gendered dimensions (2002:38, emphasis added).

My argument, then, is that in late modernity we can discern practices of self-reflexivity over and beyond intrinsic reflexivity, but that it is practised in different ways and circumstances and, importantly, may be heightened by some life events or changes. Transition to first-time motherhood is one such life event. For some this is experienced as a period of heightened and intensified reflexivity as attempts to assert or retain individuality and control in a life are made. This is because of the changes – both bodily and in terms of a shifting sense of self – that have to be accommodated as transition is experienced, and new responsibilities and identities made sense of. Indeed, it may be that self-reflexivity is more intensively practised when embodied aspects of identity and gender are challenged. Real, fleshy maternal bodies are hard to ignore, and the materiality of bodies needs to be taken account of in how we reflexively make ourselves. As noted earlier, both Giddens and Beck have been criticised in their writing on reflexivity. This is because of their failure to take account of dimensions of gendered and embodied identity and for producing masculinist and 'overly cognitive or rationalistic understanding of the late modern self and human action' (Adkins, 2002:36). So, we may reflexively make sense of our changing selves, but always from positions that are gendered and embodied, and in the context of practices that are culturally embedded and morally underpinned. We do not make sense of our selves, or exercise agency as mothers from within a vacuum, but rather from gendered positions in complex lives, shaped by material and structural circumstances.

One aspect of reflexivity which was clearly practised in the women's accounts of transition to motherhood was 'self-monitoring'. But this practice was not undertaken because rules no longer exist to guide action, although the circumstances in which we mother have changed. Rather, self-monitoring arises in response to the continued dominance of morally underpinned discourses of 'good mothering', which influence what can and cannot be said in relation to our dependent children. Although practices of self-governance shift over time 'the ideal of performing an individualised biography' – 'living ones' own life' – is in sharp conflict with the conventional expectation of 'being there for others' and this is particularly the case in relation to mothering (Adkins, 2002:45). Gendered notions of responsibilities are hard to escape and these are further compounded by perceptions of risk. Ironically, these have become heightened as scientific developments apparently offer us greater certainty, for example in relation to the viability and progress of a pregnancy, than was possible at any time previously. Perceptions of risk and acting responsibly help to explain women's engagement with hierarchical forms of expert, authoritative knowledge and medical practices, and how these have come to dominate in the West and shape available cultural scripts. Clearly, then, there are limitations in theories of reflexive modernity, not least of which is a failure by some to take sufficient account of the ways in which reflexivity is gendered, embodied and materially and structurally patterned. In her work 'Gender, Habitus and the Field', McNay (1999) has drawn attention to these particular limitations in some accounts of reflexivity, arguing that they 'reproduce the disembodied and disembedded subject of masculinist thought' (1999:95). But she also goes further to reject notions of reflexivity as arising from a generalised capacity of individuals in response to the rapid transformations of late modernity. Rather, she argues that subjects' reflexivity 'arises unevenly from their embeddedness within differing sets of power relations' (1999:110). My argument, however, is that there is a generalised capacity but that it is contingent on the material and structural conditions in which individuals live their lives. Therefore it is differently and unequally realised, and practised in different ways.

Narratives

The communicating of meanings that we give to our actions, and the ways in which these are made sense of, through some level of reflexive engagement – intrinsic or more intensive – are the constituents of the narratives that we produce about ourselves and present to others. We are, then, both the actor and the author (MacIntyre, 1981). Attention was drawn to the links between narrative construction and social identity in chapter 1. The narratives produced by the women in this book show the ways in which we can use accounts strategically to present versions of our selves, for example, as coping mothers and competent workers, and how these accounts are, over time, revised and re-edited. This again may be a heightened practice when going through and making sense of a period of personal transition, especially one which is lived out in a moral context and involves embodied changes that shape the ways in which we feel able to present particular versions of our selves. Holstein and Gubrium have noted that 'there's a persistent interplay between what is available for conveying a story and how a particular narrative unfolds in practice; it's from this interplay that both self coherence and diversity develop' (2000:107). Yet in relation to mothering this 'interplay' is circumscribed in particularly perplexing ways. These draw upon essentialist ideas of women's natural capacities to mother and a limited repertoire of possible ways of talking about experiences, which do not fit essentialist story lines. In the early postnatal interviews, for example (chapter 4), the women produced accounts of coping and meeting their children's needs. However, many of them revised these versions of their early mothering experiences in the final interviews, or the end-of-study questionnaire, saying that they had not actually felt that they were coping or feeling maternal in the ways they had expected and voiced at the time. Life events can offer new narrative opportunities, and 'the resources available for constructing identity' become enhanced as a result. However, these remain circumscribed in particular ways in relation to mothering practices and obdurate constructions of motherhood (Holstein and Gubrium, 2000:116). So, we make sense of experiences and produce and present accounts of our selves through narrative construction. Yet narratives can be reworked and selves be experienced as tenuous, and this is especially so in relation to periods of personal transition such as becoming a mother. Making sense, and producing individualised biographies of our selves as new mothers, can be a particularly confusing path to tread, as we juggle how we think we should feel – and are probably expected to feel – and how we actually feel.

Selves and bodies

What, then, can the focus on transition to first-time motherhood taken in this book contribute to debates on selves in late modernity? How are selves constituted, experienced, made sense of and presented to others through transition, anticipating and preparing for motherhood and doing mothering? Are different selves discernible and how are these incorporated into existing 'schemas of self understanding'? (Lawler, 2000:57-8). It was argued at the outset that some readings of the self did not take sufficient, or any, account of embodied, gendered and embedded dimensions of selves. Similarly, that the contexts in which selves are experienced, made sense of and presented have often been overlooked. It was also acknowledged that any discussion of selves and mothering necessarily involves engaging with 'fleshy, sensate bodies' and that this, almost unavoidably, takes us into the tricky terrain that encompasses essentialism (Jackson and Scott, 2001:9). In the discussion around selves that follows, which draws on the empirical data presented in the previous chapters, some distinctions between these contested ways of being in the world will be made. How are selves configured and understood in late modernity and what do the women's accounts of transition add to the debate?

Facets of a self – embodiment, material and fleshy bodies – in relation to motherhood can be seen to appeal to essentialist ideas of how selves are constituted, that is, as core, pre-existent and biologically given and determined. Indeed, in many ways the women in this book anticipated that they would instinctively and naturally know how to mother – clearly drawing on essentialist ideas. These ideas, then, shape professional practices and bleed into women's expectations of what their own mothering will be like. Similarly, when we talk of meeting needs and having a sense of responsibilities in relation to our dependent children, essentialism lurks close by. However, we can avoid falling into essentialist explanations because meeting needs is a gendered, conventional expectation, an expectation which is embedded in particular cultural constructions of needs and responsibilities and associated gendered practices. These are then reinforced and reproduced in different ways in different societies rather than biologically determined. For example, some of the women in the study were concerned and confused because they felt they might be thought to have borrowed or 'pinched' their children or had not 'bonded' with their child as they had expected, that is, they did not instinctively feel like mothers in the ways they had expected. These are complex and highly contested debates that will endure, particularly in relation to women and motherhood. For example, if we return to McNay's work cited earlier, she critiques aspects of theories of reflexive modernity because they fail to take account of aspects of identity which are 'pre-reflexive, unconscious and entrenched' and cites maternal feelings as an example of these (1999:103). Yet this stance appears to take us perilously close to essentialist claims in relation to women and their bodies. The sense of aspects of an identity, or self as 'entrenched', is appealing as it relates to what I refer to as practised and recognisable. But the disentangling of what is unconscious and what is socially constructed lies at the heart of these debates. For me, the idea of an entrenched and enduring self fits with the women's goal of 'getting back to normal' and regaining a sense of a pre-baby recognisable and practised self: something that for some was only felt to have been achieved once they had returned to work. Yet the idea of maternal feelings as unconscious is more complicated. Clearly a sense of love and all the associated emotions that we (usually) come to feel for a child are embedded in more than a veneer of reflexivity or a well-managed performance of mothering. However, this should not necessarily lead us into assuming unconscious or pre-reflexive maternal feelings. This is because it is the dependency of a child, and our culturally shaped expectations of meeting needs and having responsibilities to and for our children, that lead us to a relationship of love, which as a mother (or father) may be experienced immediately or only gradually acquired. But that is not to doubt or undermine the deep and all-encompassing dimensions of this relationship: we need only imagine the almost unimaginable experience of the death of a child to confirm the profound, poignant and enduring dimensions of the relationship.

For most of the women, the selves we eventually see them develop, across the accounts collected in this book, are social selves as mothers. These are constructed and understood in relation to others and contingent on past experiences, for example their old, recognisable and practised selves in the world of work. These emerge through practice and gradually making sense of initially perplexing and confusing experiences when mothering is not found to be instinctive. Eventually, a social self as a mother becomes incorporated into existing schemas of self-understanding. This ontological shift enables previous narratives, premised on essentialist versions of selfhood and constructed to satisfy what they thought they should be feeling and saying (remember the limited repertoire of available story lines that characterise this period and the risk of being labelled as not coping and, as Diana feared, having your baby taken from you), to be revoked and revised. Importantly, without the longitudinal dimensions of the research these shifts in how selves as mothers are understood, made sense of over time and narrated would have been lost. A focus just on the early postnatal interviews at six weeks after the birth of their children would have left us with a sense of the women having overcome some early difficulties and mothering now 'coming naturally'. The development of a social self as a mother is also linked to social action. Here we return to concerns expressed earlier in relation to performing a self as a mother. In chapter 1 it was noted that whilst the performative nature of self is emphasised in Goffman's work, the complexities of putting on and maintaining a performance as mothers warranted further consideration and it is to this that we now turn.

In their work, both Goffman and Giddens have been criticised for failing to take sufficient account of embodied and gendered dimensions of social action and presentation of self. Jackson and Scott have drawn attention to Goffman's social stage where 'embodied actors are ever present' but lament his lack of attention to the fleshy materiality of 'sensual, visceral' bodies (2001:11). Similarly, there is also a lack of attention to the moral context in which as pregnant women and mothers we understand and perform our selves, and the ways in which performances are shaped by wider, public expectations. This moral context also has implications for social action – where and how as new mothers we feel able to competently and confidently present our selves – to do mothering. Crucially for me, being a mother is always more than performing and playing a part. This is not because of some essentialist connection to mothering that women have. Rather it is because of a context, which as noted earlier, circumscribes a cultural and moral imperative that mothers act responsibly in relation to their children, identifying and meeting needs. Practised over time, this for most women leads to the development of a deeply felt, loving relationship. The cultural 'props', as Goffman might call them, for a performance of mothering – baby, pram, changing bag – are not enough in this moral climate because when performing or 'doing' mothering a cursory, or amateurish, performance is not sufficient, although it might initially be managed in this way. Rather doing and performing mothering requires time to master. It involves a relationship and connection to our children which is developed through practice and interaction, rather than being experienced as innate. Doing mothering in public places, then, can be particularly daunting for the new mother. Although she has the props, she has not yet become practised, and a poor performance is ultimately risky. Remember back to the profound accounts of some of the women when they ventured out in the early weeks with their babies and felt they had been 'found out' (chapter 5). Or those who confined themselves to the perceived safety of the home, where doing mothering could not be so publicly evaluated. The link between social isolation and 'postnatal depression' was highlighted earlier (Mauthner, 1995: 2002; Nicolson, 1998). Yet restricting social action in the public sphere appears a rational response to the demands that are placed on women as they try out, and come to terms with, early mothering experiences. If women knew this was a rational response and that others were feeling similarly, and could share their experiences of normal 'unnatural' feelings, we would go some way towards breaking down the old myths of motherhood (again remember in chapter 5 how friends Helen and Diana were experiencing just these feelings but felt unable to voice them to each other).

Selves, then, are interactionally and at some level reflexively experienced, narrated and practised, yet are circumscribed in particular ways. As Holstein and Gubrium have noted, 'selves don't simply "pop out" of social interaction. Nor does just anything go (and) while culture cannot specify the actual working details of the self, it does provide a broad outline for the possibilities' (2000:12–13). For example, remember back to the cultural scripts explored in chapter 2. My argument, however, is that in relation to mothering in the West, the possibilities are narrowly focused and there is a limited repertoire of story lines in which to locate unexpected and confusing experiences, and that this has implications for understanding and practising mothering and motherhood. In time, and as elements of control are regained, individual strategies of resistance can be employed. For example, women feel able to challenge expert constructions of childrearing practices and may produce counter-narratives whose plot lines are not those found in the narrowly focused 'possibilities' that equate to the 'good mothering' narrative (Garcia Coll et al., 1998). The passage of time also offers the possibility for (some) women to assert their individuality, through experiencing different dimensions of their selves, for example through a return to work; as Abigail said, 'I do like being a professional person and myself.' Selves, then, are not just performing, reflexive entities. Rather they are more complex than that, embedded in particular individual histories and cultures and inextricably bound with, and emanating from, corporeal, fleshy, sensate bodies. Yet in relation to mothering and motherhood our ideas of our selves as mothers, which are reinforced by our changing maternal bodies which have to be managed, continue to be confounded by the myths which obdurately shape our expectations and silence early experiences.

Motherhood, myths and late modernity

It is clear, then, that women continue to come to motherhood with expectations which do not match their early mothering experiences. The myths which continue to shape these expectations in many Western societies are the co-productions of health professionals, authoritative medical knowledge and other mothers. These in turn are perpetuated by new mothers themselves, as they feel unable to voice their own, sometimes difficult, experiences of early mothering which are not felt to be instinctive, and therefore are thought to be abnormal. Yet it is not the mothering per se that is the problem, although it may be initially difficult and confusing, but rather the ways in which mothering and motherhood are configured and culturally scripted in the West. This shapes what can and cannot be said about our experiences. The contradictions that women can experience on becoming mothers have been repeatedly noted over many years; for example, Oakley, writing more than twenty years ago, commented on the 'prized and necessary occupation' that mothering was, yet noting 'at the same time it is the most socially undervalued occupation of all' (1993:92). And such contradictions may have deepened as many women's lives in the West have changed, and now increasingly involve paid work outside the home. Yet other aspects of women's lives remain unchanged, for example cultural assumptions around maternal responsibilities and caring. A key factor in the configuration of motherhood continues to centre on gendered assumptions of who cares for children. As Evans has recently noted, 'science may have created new forms of reproduction, but so far it has failed to offer a form of childcare unchanged for centuries and across cultures: the primary care of children by women' (Evans, 2003:62). In the West the private responsibility for childcare is usually a solitary one, unlike other cultures where siblings and other family members are often involved. Indeed, is mothering a more lonely and isolating experience than in previous times? Have changes in family size, more complicated living arrangements and greater geographical mobility translated into women caring in more solitary ways than women in previous generations? Certainly, many of the women found the doing of mothering lonely, and seeking support from other mothers outside the home only served to confirm them in their decisions to return to work: mothering was not enough for them. As Clare, a teacher, said, 'I still sort of want to get a part of my life back and not just talk nappies . . . it wasn't really me going to parent–toddler groups all the time . . . I mean when I'm at work I'm more my old self.' Again, it is important to note that 'choices', particularly in relation to work outside the home, do not exist in the same way for all women who are mothers and 'that women's choices about fertility and participation in the labour market are often very far from free' (Evans, 2003:65; Segura, 1994; Duncan and Edwards, 1999). Similarly, individual experiences are diverse and women who are able to 'choose' not to work but opt for intensive, full-time mothering construct their experiences in different ways, where mothering is accepted as a primary role. For example, in an earlier chapter, Sheila drew on such discourses to justify her decision not to work outside the home, saying, 'I really want to be there for them, the old-fashioned style isn't it?"

The debates which have occupied feminists and others over many years around 'the uniqueness of women's embodied experience and the desire to deny that any such uniqueness exists' continue, and progress can feel slow (Lupton, 1994:131). Key to these debates have been attempts to delineate what it is that mothers do, what represents meeting children's needs and how maternal responsibilities are constructed and played out. The ways in which 'conceptualisations of children's needs' feed into powerful and dominant constructions of maternal responsibilities and mother–child relationships and good mothering in late modernity has provided a particular focus in recent research (Duncan and Edwards, 1999:126). Clearly, the often taken for granted association between children's needs and maternal responsibilities, emanating from essentialist ideas about women's natural capacities to nurture and care for others, provides a difficult context in which to make sense of early mothering experiences: a context that in late modernity is morally inscribed and closely bound up with risk and responsibility. Being responsible for a new baby, and finding that you do not instinctively know what to do, is a daunting situation and the women in this book looked to others to share the responsibility. In this climate it is little surprise that women feel unable to risk talking about these early experiences and may only voice them – and in so doing challenge constructions of maternal responsibilities – once they have developed mothering skills through practice.

In an earlier chapter, Rothman eloquently drew our attention to 'the history of Western obstetrics' being a 'history of technologies of separation', noting that 'it is very very hard to conceptually put back together that which medicine has rendered asunder' (Rothman, 1992 cited in Davis-Floyd and Davis, 1997:315). This theme of separation highlighted through the processes of medicalisation, characterises contemporary, Western constructions of mothering and motherhood at many levels. It inscribes individual experiences and dominant discourses, and it is difficult to see how we go back, how we repair and make good the connections once again: indeed, how far would women even regard this as desirable? In many ways, as noted earlier in chapter 2, this would involve moving to a more consensual model of authoritative knowledge. But this again raises the question of how willing women would be to relinquish, or change, the relationships they have with those they perceive to be experts. The focus on cultural scripts and associated practises explored in chapter 2 illuminated the differences, and indeed some similarities, in women's expectations and corresponding experiences. In the West, women come to mothering knowing less about their bodies and usually with little or no first-hand experience, because of the changing patterns in how we now live. The average family size in the UK, for example, is predicted to be 1.74 children per woman born in, or after, 1985 (*Social Trends*, 2003). This trend is echoed across other Western countries. Women have become further separated from knowing their bodies or the practices associated with childbirth because experts have managed preparation and birth occurs for most in hospitals, a practice now largely accepted as 'normal' and 'natural'. Heightened perceptions of risk further separate women from feeling able to take decisions without recourse to the experts who they look to – either to share or take – responsibility. As Peggy commented in an earlier chapter, 'don't keep giving me decisions to make, I don't know, I've not done this before.' Many women have greater possibilities in their lives in comparison with previous generations, for example in relation to education and employment. However, these serve to emphasise their non-expert status in relation to mothering and mother-hood, which they tend to come to – if at all – later in life, adding a further dimension to experiences of separation. So, in many ways heightened perceptions of risk, and not being skilled in mothering, can be seen to explain 'rational' behaviours of seeking out professional expert advice, of colluding with expert, authoritative knowledge. Yet ironically the prac-tices and procedures that characterise Western hierarchical forms of authoritative knowledge further separate us from knowing our bodies. Does this context make it harder to reveal difficult experiences in the early postnatal period when the expectation – previously shared by the women and the experts – that women will instinctively know how to mother is found to be misplaced? Certainly it can lead to confusion and a reassess-ment of what has gone before. But again, how far are such concerns shared with other women who may not have experienced control in their lives, for example through having similar educational opportunities and career choices, or experienced individuality in the same ways? Whatever the differences in life experiences – and clearly these are inscribed by class, gender and cultural location – the overriding concern here is with the ways in which motherhood is currently configured in the West. Although individual responses to its configuration will differ within and between different groups of women, this should not preclude us from continuing to challenge its more oppressive dimensions.

So, in the early twenty-first century, changes in the ways we live have led to new challenges to conceptualisations of motherhood, maternal bodies, women and selves: and some dominant themes persist. For example, obdurate constructions of children's needs and mother's responsibilities in many Western cultures remain. These continue to be reinforced through the processes of medicalisation, policy initiatives and legal statute; see for example the 'Unborn Victims of Violence Act' recently passed in the USA (March 2004). Yet as much research has now indicated, medicalisation and hierarchical forms of authoritative knowledge are accepted and widely engaged with by most women in the West as they become mothers, although they may later come to challenge aspects of them. Indeed, 'unlearning deeply ingrained beliefs, skilfully implanted, is never a quick or painless process' (Tew, 1998:384). So, what can we learn from the ways in which reproduction, childbirth and motherhood are currently constructed in the West when we turn our gaze to women's reproductive rights and experiences in other parts of the world? Earlier, in chapter 2, the contours of cultural scripts and different ways of knowing in relation to reproduction and childbirth were explored. This provided an important backdrop against which to compare Western practices and experiences, to see how we have got to where we are. We now turn to consider how perceptions of development and progress, in the context of an increasingly globalised world, are played out in relation to reproduction and childbirth in other parts of the world. Once again, just as in the debates around essentialism, this requires us to negotiate a sensitive and tricky path.

Progress, authoritative knowledge and women's lives

Earlier in this book the question of how we can move towards a more collaborative, consensual model of authoritative knowledge, in which different types of knowledge can be accommodated and shared, was posed. This question arose in chapter 2 in the context of mapping different cultural practices in relation to childbearing and motherhood. According to Jordan this was, and remains, 'the challenge for the future of childbirth in the technologized western world, as well as in the developing countries of the third world' (1997:73). As noted at the time, this quest is particularly challenging because of the complex interplay between technology, perceptions of progress and different ways of knowing, all of which are set within an increasingly globalised world, where boundaries are more fluid than at any time before. It requires us to discern between liberating and oppressive dimensions of what constitutes progress, and importantly, whose voices are heard and/or count in the discussions. It also requires us to once again note the problems explored earlier in this chapter in relation to reflexivity and priorities in lives, to take account of how lives are differently affected by material and structural circumstances, and intersected by class and caste position and gendered inequalities. In many ways here the discussions do not hinge on constructions of maternal responsibilities and good mothering but on the more profound concerns of maternal and child mortality rates and supporting women's reproductive (and human) rights. But there are huge challenges in trying to achieve this, not least assuming that Western notions of individuality, selfhood and personhood – the Western modernist subject – can be translated, or have relevance to the lives of others in different parts of the world. Similarly, there are dangers inherent in translating 'basic rights across society and culture, even when as seemingly blameless as promoting the citizenship rights of women and children' and clearly reproductive rights and associated practices are equally difficult terrain (Scheper-Hughes and Sargent, 1998:7). Yet many developing countries aspire to patterns of development and progress they discern in the West. To return to a section from much earlier in the book, where I described the birth of my first daughter and interpreting for the 'bewildered' Bangladeshi woman in the next bed (chapter 2), what to me seemed culturally baffling and bewildering for her, might for her have been regarded as progress, although still bewildering and far removed from the very different experiences she would have had giving birth in Bangladesh. For her husband and family, a hospital birth would almost certainly have been regarded as progress, largely because it would be perceived to be safe. Yet in the West wholesale hospitalisation for childbirth has mostly led to increased interventions, including rapidly increasing caesarean rates and a 'mistaken hypothesis' that caesarean rates are responsible for a decrease in perinatal mortality rates (Tew, 1998:171).

Clearly we need to be 'suspicious of a simple universal solution' in relation to improving the lives of women and their children in developing countries. It is important to caution against development in terms of reproductive rights and childbirth being unquestioningly equated with increasing numbers of hospital births (Scheper-Hughes and Sargent, 1998:4). But the question remains of how we move to more consensual forms of authoritative knowledge in relation to reproduction and childbirth, how we avoid the medicalisation and pathologising of childbirth and motherhood and provide all women with real choices in relation to their reproductive health. Certainly in those societies characterised by more horizontal forms of authoritative knowledge, and where technology has not largely replaced more embodied, experiential ways of knowing, there remains the opportunity to build more collaborative and inclusive models of authoritative knowledge. But, ironically, whilst we question how we can 'conceptually put back together that which medicine has rendered asunder' in the West, in other parts of the world, much more fundamental concerns exist for many women related to survival. Which is not to say our quest in the West is wrong or misplaced, but both to point to the differences in concerns between developing countries and those in the West, and to highlight the difficulties of translating concerns from, and between, countries (see chapter 2). In many ways there has never been a more urgent need to try to tread a pathway between such polarised positions, to seek more consensual models of authoritative knowledge that relate to women's lives in meaningful, culturally and locally relevant ways. Certainly, it is not the case that the West has all the answers, indeed far from it; we only need look to patterns of Western behaviours and their associated problems now adopted and discernible in many developing countries to confirm this. For example, reproductive health problems recently documented in the Solomon Islands note an increasing incidence of sexually transmitted diseases, teenage pregnancies and problems of HIV/AIDS. They also note an increase in unprotected sexual activity among young people together with more alcohol and substance abuse and the emergence of organised prostitution rings. Is this the price of progress? When I lived in the Solomon Islands more than twenty years ago betel nut was the locally grown and harvested 'narcotic' of choice, resulting in red and numb lips and teeth but not organised prostitution rings. In particular, the emergence of organised prostitution rings implies oppression in some form, or at the very least a lack of choices in women's lives. For me it invokes a view, long held amongst feminists in the West, that 'patriarchal (and racist and classist) societies have devalued, controlled, or appropriated women's reproductive capacities', which is not a description I would have used to describe the Solomon Islands when I lived there all those years ago (Chase and Rogers, 2001:11). Indeed, as noted earlier in chapter 2, at that time patriarchy was not a dominant, organising feature in the society. In contrast, patriarchy was identified as, and continues to be, a defining feature of society in Bangladesh.

In the intervening years since I lived and worked in Bangladesh, 'making motherhood safer' has been a declared aim of many aid organisations. Yet maternal mortality continues to be high. According to recent UN figures three women die every hour due to pregnancy-related complications. These figures provide a sobering indicator and reminder of the continued inequity in women's lives in Bangladesh. And indeed, figures may actually be higher, as not all incidences of maternal mortality are reported. For example, the families of unmarried teenage girls who might die as a result of an abortion are unlikely to report the death because of the associated shame. Clearly, these untimely deaths are not just a consequence of a lack of available health care, but rather the result of the coming together of social, cultural and economic factors. As we saw in chapter 2, childbearing has been one area in the lives of Bangladeshi women from which men are largely excluded and in which women have 'control'. But 'control' is always limited by the conditions and circumstances in which it is experienced. In this highly patriarchal society, deeply ingrained religious and cultural ideas of male and female difference circumscribe women's lives and 'choices' in particularly unequal ways. An example of this is the poor levels of literacy that continue amongst women. Only one third of school-age girls attend school, and it is estimated that half of all girls will marry and begin having children before they reach the age of eighteen years. For Bangladeshi women, then, choices remain very limited and stand in stark contrast to those we have seen utilised by the women in the previous three chapters. Yet mapping the different cultural terrains of reproduction, childbirth and motherhood enables us to see the cultural differences and sometimes the similarities. It has become even more important as the processes of globalisation increasingly influence individual lives and spread across and between cultures and countries. Such work enables us to learn from the practices in other cultures, for example, in relation to the ways in which childrearing practices are differently organised, and maternal responsibilities differently conceived. The scripts and discourses drawn upon by the women in the previous chapters stand in contrast to those available to Bangladeshi women. There is also a need to urge caution in relation to the ways in which legitimacy can be given to particular practices, which then become accepted as 'natural'. That is, we need to learn from our own experiences of medicalisation in the West to reflect on how particular practices have come to be unquestioningly accepted whilst others have been relinquished. Moving on from these important global concerns, it is now to the lives of individuals in the West we return, focusing on the debates around narratives and subjectivity.

Narratives and the modernist subject

A key concern in this book has been to explore the ways in which reflexivity is a feature of changing lives, heightened through particular life events in late modernity and more discernible amongst certain groups in the West. Linked to this, the narrative approach taken has sought to explore how individuals actively construct and reconstruct narratives reflexively in the process of making sense and presenting their selves. Yet, ironically, one of the threads that runs across the chapters of this book relates to what can and cannot be said about mothering and motherhood. There is some irony, then, that what I have attempted to do is capture women's accounts of transition, through a focus on narratives, in the knowledge that only particular versions of experiences will, or indeed apparently can be voiced (see for example the exchange with Abigail in chapter 6, page 124). But of course all research is circumscribed in various ways. The empirical data in this book illustrates the ways in which women draw upon the limited repertoire of story lines available to them in the West in the context of late modernity. Further, it shows how these are strategically used to present versions of a changing, and sometimes tenuous, sense of self as transition to motherhood is experienced and made sense of. It also shows how eventually the repertoire of narrowly focused story lines can be challenged and counter-narratives produced. And of course it is not just the limited story lines that shape the types of individual narratives that can be constructed in an interview, even a relatively unstructured one. The interview is a social interaction, the questions asked will in some ways shape the responses given, and the materials gathered are a co-production. The interpretation of those materials continues to rest with the researcher, although more recently alternative research practises have been advocated in relation to the greater involvement of participants in aspects of the interpretation process (Birch and Miller, 2002). Clearly, as researchers we have a responsibility to give credible and trustworthy accounts of our research, especially when it involves us in narrating 'the narrations of others' as is the case in this book (Andrews, 2000:3). Indeed, I 'tried out' my developing ideas as the research unfolded on the women participating in the study. I have also used lengthy extracts so that their voices can be seen and heard; nevertheless, the final product rests on my interpretations, for which I am accountable.

This leads us to consider how far qualitative research methods in general, and the sort of narrative approach taken here, serve only to reproduce the modernist subject. It has recently been argued that the 'interaction in the research interview tends to elicit presentations of self which largely conform to dominant cultural forms because of the implicit expectations that shape the interview process' (Alldred and Gillies, 2002:146). In the West this presupposes and reproduces a model of the individual as 'bounded, rational and autonomous' (*ibid.*, 2002:146). These arguments are of course closely bound up with those discussed earlier in relation to reflexivity, and how far a generalised capacity for reflexivity exists and is experienced and embedded in (un) equal ways. Taking a narrative approach of course assumes some capacity for reflexivity, as does all qualitative, interview-based, research. It assumes that as individuals we have stories to tell, but clearly the enterprise of gathering materials in such circumstances is more complex than this statement might suggest. As we have seen across the chapters of this book, reflexively making sense and producing culturally recognisable, and socially acceptable, narratives of becoming a mother initially involves drawing on a limited repertoire of possible story lines and is further shaped by women increasingly having little or no first-hand experience of mothering or motherhood against which to weigh these up. Clearly, then, the qualitative, or in-depth interview, invites constructions of selves that are recognisable, and in turn participants (mostly) produce accounts that draw on what they perceive to be culturally and socially acceptable ways of talking about their experiences. It is clear that as researchers 'we elicit performances of self in which radical difference is suppressed by virtue of contemporary understandings of research' (Alldred and Gillies, 2002:147). Yet to break out of this culturally configured way of exploring personal experiences requires more than just a rethinking of the research process. It necessitates a fundamental re-evaluation of Western models of selfhood and reflexivity, well beyond the scope of the work in this book, but certainly food for thought. Working with a Western model of selfhood, the research focus taken here has shown how participants have expectations of the interview encounter (not always met – remember Faye's surprise that I did not produce a questionnaire? chapter 4, page 67), how they initially present what they perceive to be appropriate accounts of mothering, only retrospectively disclosing different versions of their experiences. Strategies of self-governance in the interview encounter (and beyond) also shape how, and what, and when, experiences of transition to motherhood and mothering are voiced.

Other factors clearly influence the interview encounter. The fact that I was a researcher who had intimate experience of the topic under study – I am the biological mother of three children – will also have shaped the ways in which women presented their experiences to me. This was especially so during the early antenatal interviews. Recall, for example, how in chapter 5 Felicity talks of feeling let down because I had not told her exactly what giving birth could be like. As a mother I must surely have known – and of course I did. In fact, I side-stepped this question from the women in all the antenatal interviews, saying that it was different for everyone, which it would be. Ironically, by doing this, I was contributing to the conspiracy of silence that so often exists around the pain of labour and childbirth. For others my experience as a mother was regarded as having a positive affect on the research design; for example in the end-of-study questionnaire, Diana wrote:

I thought the interviews were timed to perfection, possibly because the researcher was a mother herself and therefore understood the amazing swing of emotions during that very short period . . . in relation to life before baby, once you have accepted that the life you are now living is yours – not someone else's, and that the baby is here to stay. (end-of-study questionnaire)

Qualitative research methods in general, and research focusing on narrative construction in particular, assume, then, a modernist subject with a capacity for reflexivity. I am aware that by inviting individuals to narrate their experiences this may lead them to reflect in ways that they may otherwise not have done: to engage in heightened reflexivity, even to experience the research encounter as 'therapeutic' (Birch and Miller, 2000). Also, as I have earlier argued, periods of personal transition such as becoming a mother may in any case heighten reflexive practice as we make sense of our changing maternal bodies and selves and associated experiences. Some extracts taken from interview transcripts and the end-of-study questionnaires demonstrate this and once again reinforce ideas of reproducing the reflexive, modernist subject:

I'll think about all these questions and I'll think, you know, God, I haven't asked myself that, and you know, how is life going to change, and . . . I have, I've thought about it, but not really asked myself, you know. (Lillian: interview transcript)

The interviews themselves were extremely adept at making me consider certain issues and feelings which I might otherwise have dismissed. It was also fascinating to look back at the way in which I had responded in previous interviews and then to consider my changing views and feelings. It also helped me to rationalise my otherwise irrational thought processes. (Diana: end-of-study questionnaire)

I found the interviews very thought provoking and good for myself because it gave me time to sit and reflect on my life and also to see how my views changed once babies arrived. (Sheila: end-of-study questionnaire)

At the third interview I didn't recognise any of my answers to the second one . . . I always thought of lots of things I'd wanted to say after the interview was finished, but of course had forgotten them completely by the next interview. (Peggy: end-of-study questionnaire)

I remember when, you know, I was in hospital and things, I thought, oh, I'll have to tell Tina this, I'll have to tell Tina that. (Philippa: interview transcript)

Clearly the interviews – or anticipation of subsequent interviews – were a catalyst for the women, provoking some to be (more) sensitive to the processes in which they were caught up, to reflect in ways they might otherwise not have done about their experiences of transition. The timing of interviews was also a clear factor in how accounts were constructed and presented. As Sarah informed me in one interview, I had got her on a 'good day':

SARAH: And you have caught me on a good day.
TINA: Oh right, and that, so what is a bad day like?
SARAH: I just wander round moping.

Similarly, in the following extract, Felicity's comment on the timing of the interviews again illuminates the tenuous dimensions of the modernist subject:

I mean, it would have been really different because, I remember thinking after I'd had Harry in subsequent days and I thought if Tina came and spoke to me and asked me these questions now about how the birth was, it would have just been so awful. (early postnatal interview)

A further important dimension of the research that provides the empirical data for much of this book was that it was longitudinal, following women through a year in their lives. This meant that over time, I had the opportunity to develop relationships with the women, to receive news about their babies and to be a small part of this significant period in their lives. This will almost certainly have contributed to the ways in which the women felt able to voice their experiences to me in the later interviews. Interestingly, though, it was the cold, objective research tool that was the end-of-study questionnaire, posted out to the women after the final interview, that elicited some of the most heartfelt comments about how they had really felt at times during the interviews.

It is clear, then, that taking a narrative approach in order to research individual experience implicitly and/or explicitly presumes a modernist subject. The interview does not just 'look in upon but actively serve(s) to produce modern subjects' through inviting and assuming reflexivity (Alldred and Gillies, 2002:146). But if this approach is applied longitudinally, it can illuminate the ways in which Western assumptions or understandings of individuals as 'bounded, rational and autonomous' are misplaced as the tenuous (and entrenched) dimensions of schemas of self-understanding are played out. Rather than such an approach 'reinforce the centrality and superiority of this Western model of the self' (Alldred and Gillies, 2002:147), it can challenge such assumptions and contribute to debates on how selves are constituted, understood and maintained in late modernity. Similarly, reflection on the research encounter and any awkward lapses experienced in the interview can be illuminating and challenge our assumptions as researchers. Remember, for example, Faye saying to me in her first interview 'I'm not very good on words and things like that' (chapter 4). At the outset, then, my intention was to create a space, through informal and friendly interviews, in which women would (hopefully) feel able to talk about any, or all, of their feelings and experiences, as they journeyed into motherhood. Yet this space, the interview, was already circumscribed by the limited cultural story lines or scripts which shape expectations and experiences of childbearing in the West. For example, in her end-of-study questionnaire, Helen reflects back on the early postnatal interview and talks of my (unintentional) concentration on her emotional state,

In the second interview it was one of the first times anyone had taken so much time in concentrating on my emotional state (even more than the health visitor) – but I now realise that I was not being 100 per cent honest with my answers and was too eager to attempt to create a feeling of control, relaxation and total happiness and contentment. In fact I was feeling quite disorientated and out of control.

Of course Helen could not have risked revealing how she had been really feeling at that time, and I was naïve to presume that I could create a space in which such things could be voiced – at that time. Yet this again serves to reinforce the moral climate that exists around mothering and motherhood. It confirms how hard it is to reveal what are felt to be difficult 'unnatural' – but actually quite widely shared – experiences of early mothering. Certainly, later interviews offered the possibility of producing counter-narratives encompassing more challenging story lines.

All research involves ethical considerations and there have been many in my work. One I am most acutely aware of and feel responsibility for is that of the ethics of raising expectations, in some ways 'conscious-ness-raising'. In the end-of-study questionnaire, Sarah wrote, 'I hope my input will be able to help others', and Linda also hoped that her input (and bravery in voicing her very difficult experiences, see chapter 6) would help 'in enlightening us all, that we are allowed to feel the way we do'. My concerns arising from this are twofold. The first is that I am aware of the difficulty of enabling women's voices to be heard, and that this research can only make a small, albeit timely, contribution to much needed debates that prioritise women's voices. Arendell has recently drawn attention to the need for 'more attention to...mothers' own voices' (2000:1202) and Brook has also noted that 'discourses of preg-nancy and childbirth from the perspectives of pregnant women them-selves are limited and usually invisible' (1999:41). The approach taken in this book goes some way to addressing their concerns. However, one research project will not in and of itself allow women more generally to 'feel the way they do' – and more importantly feel able to openly talk about their feelings. But it might in a very small way help, for example by changing the practices of a midwife or other health professional who reads the book. My second concern is that the women's accounts be dismissed as relativist and therefore of little consequence in certain arenas within the social sciences. Although I will not rehearse here the ways in which a 'relativist despair' is avoided (see for example Edwards and Ribbens, 1998), my response to this, and noted earlier, is that 'somewhere behind all this story telling there are real active, embodied, impassioned lives' (Plummer, 1995:170). These lives are worthy of our scrutiny as social scientists and help us in theorising the connections and dissonances between individual lives and experiences and wider social and cultural contexts.

Conclusion

Making sense of motherhood is both complicated and at some level intrinsic, and practised in different ways, in different material and structural circumstances by different women. A focus on transition to motherhood requires us to engage with essentialist ideas of a core, biologically determined self. Yet this focus illuminates the ways in which selves are gendered and embodied, enduring and tenuous. When instinctive knowledge about mothering is found to be absent, it is a social self as mother which women gradually acquire, through practise and meeting the needs of their child. But difficult experiences may be concealed whilst this is achieved. The time taken to feel competent in the practices and skills of mothering vary, and by focusing on maternal practices as a dimension of making sense of motherhood the intention is not to universalise women's experiences, although clearly there are some common threads. In the West the backdrop against which women make sense of their transition to motherhood continues to circumscribe the mothering relationship in particular cultural, social and moral ways. The conventional and gendered expectation of being there for others continues to be hard to escape. This can make disclosure of what are felt to be unnatural difficulties as early mothering experiences unfold, too risky to voice. Yet concealing experiences helps to perpetuate the old myths of motherhood, and so the cycle goes on and women continue to come to motherhood with unrealistic expectations. It is not, then, the mothering per se that is the problem, although it may be initially difficult and confusing. Rather, the problem emanates from the ways in which mothering and motherhood are configured in the West, which in turn shapes what can and cannot be said about our experiences. It is, then, the narrowly focused and limited repertoire of possible story lines that exist around mothering that we urgently need to challenge.

Sample characteristics of women in 'transition to motherhood' study

Name	Age at first interview	Educational qualifications	Occupation	Class (self-defined as specified on end-of-study questionnaire)	Partnership status
Angela	30	'O' levels	Secretary	Middle class	Married
Gillian	33	'O' levels	Nurse	Middle class	Married
Wendy	33	'O' levels	Civil servant	Middle class	Married
Linda	29	'O' levels	Office manager	Middle class	Married
Rebecca	32	Degree	Teacher	Middle class	Married
Clare	26	Degree	Teacher	Middle class	Living with partner
Lillian	29	'O' levels	Technician	Did not specify	Married
Philippa	29	Degree	Sales manager	Middle class/professional	Married
Kathryn	32	Degree	Estate secretary	Upper-middle class	Married
Sarah	19	'O' level equivalents	Sandwich maker	In between working and middle class	Non-resident boyfriend
Abigail	28	Did not specify	Computer programmer	Middle class	Married
Sheila	32	'A' level	Secretary	Middle/working class	Married
Felicity	32	Degree	University lecturer	Did not specify	Married
Diana	34	Law degree	Lawyer	Working class	Married
Helen	30	Did not specify	Recruitment manager	Working/middle class	Married
Faye	31	'O' levels	Local government officer	Working/professional class	Married
Peggy	29	Degree	Teacher	Professional?	Married

All names have been changed.
'O' level school examinations were taken by sixteen-year-olds prior to either leaving school to work or staying on to study for 'A' level exams. These have since been replaced by GCSE exams.

References

Abbott, P. and Wallace, C. (1990). *An Introduction to Sociology: Feminist Perspectives.* London: Routledge.

ACC News Online (9 March 2004). http://abc.net.au/news/

Adams, B. (1995). *Timewatch. The Social Analysis of Time.* Cambridge: Polity Press.

Adkins, L. (2002). *Revisions: Gender and Sexuality in Late Modernity.* Buckingham: Open University Press.

Alldred, P. and Gillies, V. (2002). 'Eliciting research accounts: re/producing modern subjects?', in M. Mauthner, M. Birch, J. Jessop and T. Miller (eds.), *Ethics in Qualitative Research.* London: Sage.

Almond, B. (1988). 'Women's rights: reflections on ethics and gender', in M. Griffiths and M. Whitford (eds.), *Feminist Perspectives in Philosophy.* London: Macmillan.

Andrews, M. (2000). 'Introduction', in M. Andrews, S.D. Sclater, C. Squire and A. Teacher (eds.), *Lines of Narrative.* London: Routledge.

Annandale, E. (1998). *The Sociology of Health and Medicine: A Critical Introduction.* Cambridge: Polity Press.

Annandale, E. and Clark, J. (1997). 'A reply to Rona Campbell and Sam Porter', *Sociology of Health and Illness,* 19: 521–32.

Anthias, F. (2002). 'Where do I belong ? Narrating collective identity and trans-locational positionality', *Ethnicities.* London: Sage.

Arendell, T. (2000). 'Conceiving and investigating motherhood: the decade's scholarship', *Journal of Marriage and the Family,* 62: 1192–207.

Atkinson, P. (1997). 'Narrative turn or blind alley ?', *Qualitative Health Research,* 7.3: 325–44.

Atkinson, R. (1998). *The Life Story Interview.* (Qualitative Research Methods Series 44) London: Sage.

Bailey, L. (1999). 'Refracted selves? A study of changes in self-identity in the transition to motherhood', *Sociology,* 33.2: 335–52.

(2001). 'Gender shows: first time mothers and embodied selves', *Gender and Society,* 15.1: 110–29.

Barbour, R. (1990). 'Fathers: the emergence of a new consumer group', in J. Garcia, R. Kilpatrick and M. Richards (eds.), *The Politics of Maternity Care*. Oxford: Clarendon Press.

Barclay, L., Everitt, L., Rogan, F., Schmied, V. and Wyllie, A. (1997). 'Becoming a mother – an analysis of women's experience of early motherhood', *Journal of Advanced Nursing*, 23: 719–28.

Barker, W. (1998). 'Open space. Let's trust our instincts', *Community Practitioner*, 71.9: 305.

Barthes, R. (1977). *Image, Music and Text*. New York: Hill and Wang.

Beck, U. (1992). *Risk Society: Towards a New Modernity*. London: Sage.

    (1994). 'The reinvention of politics: towards a theory of reflexive modernisation', in U. Beck, A. Giddens and S. Lash, *Reflexive Modernization: Politics, Tradition and Aesthetics in the Modern Social Order*. Cambridge: Polity Press.

Beck, U. and Beck-Gernsheim, E. (1995). *The Normal Chaos of Love*. Cambridge: Polity Press.

Belenky, M.F., Clinchy, B.M., Goldberger, N.R., Tarule, J.M. (1986). *Women's Ways of Knowing: The Development of Self, Voice and Mind*. New York: Basic Books.

Benhabib, S. (1992). *Situating the Self: Gender, Community and Postmodernism in Contemporary Ethics*. Cambridge: Polity Press.

Birch, M. and Miller, T. (2000). 'Inviting intimacy: the interview as "therapeutic opportunity"', *Social Research Methodology, Theory and Practice*, 3: 189–202.

    (2002). 'Encouraging participation: ethics and responsibilities', in M. Mauthner, M. Birch, J. Jessop and T. Miller (eds.), *Ethics in Qualitative Research*. London: Sage.

Birch, M., Miller, T., Mauthner, M. and Jessop, J. (2002). Introduction, in M. Mauthner, M. Birch, J. Jessop and T. Miller (eds.), *Ethics in Qualitative Research*. London: Sage.

Blanchet, T. (1984). *Women, Pollution and Marginality in Rural Bangladesh*. Dhaka: Dhaka University Press.

Blaxter, M. (1990). *Health and Lifestyles Survey*. London: Routledge.

Blum, L.M. (1993). 'Mothers, babies and breastfeeding in late capitalist America: the shifting contexts of feminist theory', *Feminist Studies*, 19.2: 291–311.

Boston Women's Health Book Collective (1978). *Our Bodies, Ourselves*. Harmondsworth: Penguin.

Boulton, M. G. (1983). *On Being a Mother: A Study of Women and Pre-School Children*. London: Tavistock.

Bowler, I. (1993). 'Stereotypes of women of Asian descent in midwifery: some evidence', *Midwifery*, 9: 7–16.

Branaman, A. (1997). 'Goffman's social theory', in C. Lemert and A. Branaman (eds.), *The Goffman Reader*. Oxford: Blackwell.

Brannen, J. and Moss, P. (1988). *New Mothers at Work. Employment and Childcare*. London: Unwin Hyman Limited.

Brook, B. (1999). *Feminist Perspectives on the Body*. London: Longman.

Browner, C. H. and Press, N. (1997). 'The production of authoritative knowledge in American prenatal care', in R.E. Davis-Floyd and C. Sargent (eds.),

Childbirth and Authoritative Knowledge: Cross-Cultural Perspectives. Berkeley: University of California Press.

Bury, M. (1982). 'Chronic illness as biographical disruption', *Sociology of Health and Illness*, 4: 167–82.

Butler, J. (1990). *Gender Trouble: Feminism and the Subversion of Identity*. London: Routledge.

—— (1993). *Bodies that Matter*. New York: Routledge.

Callaway, H. (1983). '"The most essentially female function of all": giving birth', in S. Ardener (ed.), *Defining Females. The Nature of Women in Society*. Oxford: Berg.

Campbell, R. and MacFarlane, A. (1990). 'Recent debate on the place of birth', in J. Garcia, R. Kilpatrick and M. Richards (eds.), *The Politics of Maternity Care*. Oxford: Clarendon Press.

Chase, S.E. (1995). 'Taking narrative seriously: consequences for method and theory in interview studies', in R. Josselson and A. Lieblich (eds.), *The Narrative Study of Lives*, vol.III. Newbury Park, CA: Sage.

—— (2001). 'Mothers and feminism', in S. Chase and M. F. Rogers, *Mothers and Children: Feminist Analyses and Personal Narratives*. New Brunswick, NJ: Rutgers University Press.

—— (2001). 'Pregnancy and childbirth', in S. Chase and M. F. Rogers, *Mothers and Children: Feminist Analyses and Personal Narratives*. New Brunswick, NJ: Rutgers University Press.

Chase, S. E. and Rogers, M.F. (2001). *Mothers and Children: Feminist Analyses and Personal Narratives*. New Brunswick, NJ: Rutgers University Press.

Chodorow, N. (1978). *The Reproduction of Mothering: Psychoanalysis and the Sociology of Gender*. London: University of California Press.

Collins, P.H. (1994). 'Shifting the center: race, class and feminist theorising about motherhood', in E. Nakano Glenn, G. Chang and L. Rennie Forcey (eds.), *Mothering, Ideology, Experience and Agency*. London: Routledge.

Coole, D. (1995). 'The gendered self', in D. Bakhurst and C. Sypnowich (eds.), *The Social Self*. London: Sage.

Cornwell, J. (1984). *Hard Earned Lives*. London: Tavistock.

Corradi, C. (1991). 'Text, context and individual meaning: rethinking life stories in a hermeneutic framework', *Discourse and Society*, 2.1: 105–18.

Cresswell, J. (1999). *Qualitative Enquiry and Research Design: Choosing Among Five Traditions*. London: Sage.

Daly, M. (1973). *Beyond God the Father: Towards a Philosophy of Women's Liberation*. Boston: Beacon Press.

Davis-Floyd, R.E. (1992). *Birth as an American Rite of Passage*. Berkeley: University of California Press.

Davis-Floyd, R.E. and Davis, E. (1997). 'Intuition as authoritative knowledge in midwifery and home birth', in R.E. Davis-Floyd and C. Sargent (eds.), *Childbirth and Authoritative Knowledge: Cross-Cultural Perspectives*. Berkeley: University of California Press.

Davis-Floyd, R.E. and Sargent, C. (1997). *Childbirth and Authoritative Knowledge: Cross-Cultural Perspectives*. Berkeley: University of California Press.

Delphy, C. (1992). 'Mother's union?' *Trouble and Strife*, 24: 12–19.

Denny, E. (1996). 'New reproductive technologies: the views of women under-going treatment', in S. Williams and M. Calnan (eds.), *Modern Medicine: Lay Perspectives and Experiences*. London: UCL Press.

Denzin, N. K. (1991). *Images of Postmodern Society*. London: Sage.

De Vries, R., Benoit, C., van Teijlingen, E. and Wrede, S. (eds.) (2001). *Birth by Design*. London: Routledge.

Dixon-Woods, M., Shaw, R.L., Agarwal, S. and Smith, J.A. (2004). 'The problem of appraising qualitative research', *Quality and Safety in Health Care*, 13: 223–5.

Douglas, M. (1966). *Purity and Danger: An Analysis of Concepts of Pollution and Taboo*. London: Routledge and Kegan Paul.

Duncan, S. and Edwards, R. (1999). *Lone Mothers, Paid Work and Gendered Moral Rationalities*. Basingstoke: Macmillan.

Edwards, R. and Ribbens, J. (eds.) (1998). *Feminist Dilemmas in Qualitative Research*. London: Sage.

Elliott, A. (2001). *Concepts of the Self*. Cambridge: Polity Press.

Eurostats (2000). http//www.europa.eu.int

Evans, M. (2003). *Gender and Social Theory*. Buckingham: Open University Press.

Firestone, S. (1971). *The Dialectic of Sex*. London: Jonathan Cape.

Forcey, L.R. (1999). Book reviews, *Signs*, 25: 301–4.

Foster, P. (1995). *Women and the Health Care Industry*. Buckingham: Open University Press.

Fox, B. and Worts, D. (1999). 'Revisiting the critique of medicalised childbirth', *Gender and Society*, 13.3: 326–46.

Frank, A. (1995). *The Wounded Storyteller*. Chicago: University of Chicago Press.
(2002). 'Why study people's stories? The dialogical ethics of narrative analysis', *International Journal of Qualitative Methods*, 1.1: 1–20.

Garcia, J. and Marchant, S. (1996). 'The potential of postnatal care', in D. Kroll (ed.), *Midwifery Care for the Future*. London: Balliere Tindall.

Garcia, J., Kilpatrick, R. and Richards, M., (1990). *The Politics of Maternity Care: Services for Childbearing Women in Twentieth Century Britain*. Oxford: Clarendon Press.

Garcia Coll, C., Surrey, J.L. and Weingarten, K. (1998). *Mothering Against the Odds. Diverse Voices of Contemporary Mothers*. New York: The Guliford Press.

Georges, E. (1997). 'Fetal ultrasound and the production of authoritative knowledge in Greece', in R.E. Davis-Floyd and C. Sargent (eds.), *Childbirth and Authoritative Knowledge: Cross-Cultural Perspectives*. Berkeley: University of California Press.

Giddens, A. (1990). *The Consequences of Modernity*. Cambridge: Polity Press.
(1991). *Modernity and Self-Identity*. Cambridge: Polity Press.
(1994). 'Institutional reflexivity and modernity', in *The Polity Reader in Social Theory*. Cambridge: Polity Press.

Gieve, K. (1987). 'Rethinking feminist attitudes towards motherhood', *Feminist Review*, 25: 38–45.

Gilligan, C. (1982). *In a Different Voice: Psychological Theory and Women's Development*. Cambridge, MA: Harvard University Press.

Glazener, C.M.A., MacArthur, C. and Garcia, J. (1993). 'Postnatal care: time for a change', *Contemporary Review of Obstetrics and Gynaecology*, 5: 130–6.

Glenn, E.N. (1994). 'Social constructions of mothering: a thematic overview', in E.N. Glenn, G. Chang and L.R. Forcey (eds.), *Mothering, Ideology, Experience and Agency*. London: Routledge.

Goffman, E. (1969). *The Presentation of Self in Everyday Life*. Harmondsworth: Penguin.

Graham, H. and Oakley, A. (1986). 'Competing ideologies of reproduction: medical and maternal perspectives on pregnancy', in C. Currer and M. Stacey (eds.), *Concepts of Health, Illness and Disease*. Leamington Spa: Berg.

Griffiths, M. (1995). *Feminisms and the Self. The Web of Identity*. London: Routledge.

Guba, E.G. and Lincoln, Y.S. (1994). 'Competing paradigms in qualitative research', in N.K. Denzin and Y.S. Lincoln (eds.), *Handbook of Qualitative Research*. Thousand Oaks, CA: Sage.

Helman, C. (2001). *Culture, Health and Illness*. London: Arnold.

Hill Collins, P. (1994). 'Shifting the center: Race, class and Feminist theorizing about motherhood', in E.N. Elenn, E. Chang and L.R. Forcey (eds.), *Mothering, Ideology, Experience and Agency*. London: Routledge.

Holstein, J.A. and Gubrium, J.F. (2000). *The Self We Live By: Narrative Identity in a Post-Modern World*. Oxford: Oxford University Press.

Home Office (1998). *Supporting Families: a Consultative Document*. London: Home Office.

Hochschild, A.R. (1983). *The Managed Heart: The Commercialization of Human Feeling*. Berkeley, CA: University of California Press.

Hyden, L.C. (1997). 'Illness and narrative', *Sociology of Health and Illness*, 19: 48–69.

Illich, I. (1976). *Limits to Medicine*. London: Marion Boyars.

Ireland, M.S. (1993). *Postmodern Motherhood*. New York: The Guilford Press.

Islam, M. (1980). *Folk Medicine and Rural Women in Bangladesh*. Dhaka: Women for Research Group.

Jackson, S. and Scott, S. (2001). 'Putting the body's feet on the ground:towards a sociological reconceptualisation of gendered and sexual embodiment', in K. Backett-Milburn and L. McKie (eds.), *Constructing Gendered Bodies*. London: Palgrave.

Jain, C. (1985). 'Attitudes of pregnant Asian women to antenatal care'. West Midlands Regional Health Authority Report.

Jenkins, R. (1996). *Social Identity*. London: Routledge.

Jessop, J. (2001). 'Pyscho-social dynamics of post-divorce parenting. Unpublished PhD dissertation. Cambridge University.

Jordan, B. (1993). *Birth in Four Cultures*. 4th edition. Illinois: Waveland Press. 'Authoritative knowledge and its construction', in R.E. Davis-Floyd and C. Sargent (eds.), *Childbirth and Authoritative Knowledge: Cross-Cultural Perspectives*. Berkeley: University of California Press.

Kleinman, A. (1988). *The Illness Narrative*. New York: Basic Books.

Laqueur, T. (1992). 'The facts of fatherhood', in B. Thorne and M. Yalom (eds.), *Rethinking the Family: Some Feminist Questions*. Boston: Northeastern University Press.

Lash, S. (1994). 'Reflexivity and its doubles: structure, aesthetics, community', in U. Beck, A. Giddens and S. Lash, *Reflexive Modernization: Politics, Tradition and Aesthetics in the Modern Social Order*. Cambridge: Polity Press.

Lawler, S. (2000). *Mothering the Self. Mother, Daughter, Subjects*. London: Routledge.

Lazarus, E. (1997). 'What do women want? Issues of choice, control, and class in American pregnancy and childbirth', in R.E. Davis-Floyd, and C. Sargent (eds.) *Childbirth and Authoritative Knowledge: Cross-Cultural Perspectives*. Berkeley: University of California Press.

Leavitt, J.W. (1986). *Brought to Bed: Childbearing in America 1750–1950*. New York: Oxford University Press.

Letherby, G. (1994). 'Mother or not, mother or what? Problems of definition and identity', *Women's Studies International Forum*, 17.5: 525–32.

Lewis, J. (1990). 'Mothers and maternity policies in the twentieth century', in J. Garcia, R. Kilpatrick and M. Richards (eds.), *The Politics of Maternity Care: Services for Childbearing Women in Twentieth Century Britain*. Oxford: Clarendon Press.

Lieblich, A., Tuval-Mashiach, R. and Zilber, T. (1998). *Narrative Research*. London: Sage.

Lincoln, Y.S. and Guba, E.G. (1985). *Naturalistic Inquiry*. Beverly Hills, CA: Sage.

Lupton, D. (1994). *Medicine as Culture*. London: Sage.

——— (1999). *Risk*. London: Routledge.

MacIntyre, A. (1981). *After Virtue*. London: Duckworth.

Martin, E. (1990). 'Science and women's bodies: forms of anthropological knowledge', in Jacobus *et al.* (eds.), *Body/Politics: Women and the Discourse of Science*. London: Routledge.

Mathieson, C.M. and Stam, H.J. (1995). 'Renegotiating identity: cancer narratives', *Sociology of Health and Illness*, 17: 283–306.

Mattingly, C., Garro, C. (1994). Introduction, *Social Science and Medicine*, 38.6, 771–4.

Mauthner, N. (1995). 'Postnatal depression. The significance of social contacts between mothers', *Women's Studies International Forum*, 18: 311–23.

——— (1998). 'Bringing silent voices into a public discourse', in R. Edwards and J. Ribbens (eds.), *Feminist Dilemmas in Qualitative Research*. London: Sage.

——— (2002). *The Darkest Days of My Life: Stories of Postpartum Depression*. Cambridge, MA: Harvard University Press.

McConville, F. (1988). 'The birth attendant in Bangladesh', in S. Kitzinger (ed.), *The Midwife Challenge*. London: Pandora Press.

McLead, J. (1997). *Narrative and Psychotherapy*. London: Sage.

McNay, L. (1999). 'Gender, habitus and the field. Pierre Bourdieu and the limits of reflexivity', *Theory, Culture and Society*, 16.1: 95–117.

McRae, S. (ed.) (1999). *Changing Britain: Families and Households in the 1990s*. Oxford: Oxford University Press.

Mead, G.H. (1934). *Mind, Self and Society*. Chicago: University of Chicago Press.

Miller, T. (1995). 'Shifting boundaries: exploring the influence of cultural trad-
    itions and religious beliefs of Bangladeshi women on antenatal interactions',
    Women's Studies International Forum, 18.3: 299–309.
    (1998). 'Shifting layers of professional, lay and personal narratives: longitu-
    dinal childbirth research', in R. Edwards and J. Ribbens (eds.), *Feminist
    Dilemmas in Qualitative Research*. London: Sage.
    (2000). 'Losing the plot: narrative construction and longitudinal childbirth
    research', *Qualitative Health Research*, 10.3: 309–23.
    (2002). 'Adapting to motherhood: care in the postnatal period', *Community
    Practitioner*, 75.1: 16–18.
    (2003). Shifting perceptions of expert knowledge: transition to motherhood,
    Human Fertility, 6: 142–6.
Miller, T., Kabir, N. and Isherwood, D. (1983). 'Report on follow-up study of
    patients discharged after rehabilitation from severe malnutrition'. Save the
    Children Fund, Dhaka, Bangladesh.
Mishler, E. (1986). 'The analysis of interview-narratives', in T.R. Sarbin (ed.),
    Narrative Psychology. The Storied Nature of Human Conduct. Praeger: New
    York.
Mitchell, J. and Goody, J. (1997). 'Feminism, fatherhood and the family in
    Britain', in A. Oakley and J. Mitchell (eds.), *Who's Afraid of Feminism?*
    London: Hamish Hamilton.
Munro, J. (1988). 'Parentcraft classes with Bengali mothers', *Health Visitor*,
    61: 48.
Murphy, E. (1999). '"Breast is best": infant feeding decisions and maternal
    deviance', *Sociology of Health and Illness*, 21.2: 187–208.
National Center for Health Statistics (2004). http:www.cdc.gov.nchs
National Vital Statistics Reports (2000): 48.3.
Nettleton, S. (1995). *The Sociology of Health and Illness*. Cambridge: Polity Press.
Nicolson, P. (1998). *Post-Natal Depression*. London: Routledge.
Norris, C. (2000). 'Postmodernism: a guide for the perplexed', in G. Browning,
    A. Halcli and F. Webster (eds.), *Understanding Contemporary Society*.
    London: Sage.
Oakley, A. (1979). *Becoming a Mother*. Oxford: Martin Robertson.
    (1980). *Women Confined: Towards a Sociology of Childbirth*. Oxford: Martin
    Robertson.
    (1993). *Essays on Women, Medicine and Health*. Edinburgh: Edinburgh
    University Press.
Page, L. and Sandall, J. (2000). 'The third way: A realistic plan to reinvent the
    profession', *British Journal of Midwifery*, 8.11: 696–700.
Phoenix, A. and Woollett, A. (eds.) (1991). *Motherhood, Meanings, Practices and
    Ideologies*. London: Sage.
Plummer, K. (1995). *Telling Sexual Stories*. London: Routledge.
Polkinghorne, D.E. (1995). 'Narrative configuration in qualitative analysis',
    International Journal of Qualitative Studies in Education, 8.1: 5–23.
Rajan, L. (1996). 'Pain and pain relief in labour', in S.J.Williams and M. Calnan
    (eds.), *Modern Medicine: Lay Perspectives and Experiences*. London: UCL
    Press.

Rapp, R. (2000). *Testing Women, Testing the Fetus*. New York: Routledge.

Reid, M. (1990). 'Pre-natal diagnosis and screening: a review', in J. Garcia, R. Kilpatrick and M. Richards (eds.), *The Politics of Maternity Care: Services for Childbearing Women in Twentieth Century Britain*. Oxford: Clarendon Press.

Reissman, C.K. (1983). 'Women and medicalisation: a new perspective', *Social Policy*, 14: 3–18.

—— (1989). 'Life events, meaning and narrative: the case of infidelity and divorce', *Social Science and Medicine*, 29: 743–51.

—— (1990). 'Strategic uses of narrative in the presentation of self and illness: A research note', *Social Science and Medicine*, 30 11: 1195–200.

Ribbens, J. (1994). *Mothers and their Children: A Feminist Sociology of Childrearing*. London: Sage.

—— (1998).'Hearing my feeling voice ? An autobiographical discussion of motherhood', in R. Edwards and J. Ribbens (eds.), *Feminist Dilemmas in Qualitative Research*. London: Sage.

Ribbens McCarthy, J., Edwards, R. and Eillies, V. (2000). 'Parenting and step-parenting. Contemporary moral tales'. Occasional paper 4, Centre for Family and Household Research, Oxford Brookes University.

Ribbens McCarthy, J. and Edwards, R. (2001). 'The individual in public and private: the significance of mothers and children', in A. Carling, S. Duncan and R. Edwards (eds.), *Analysing Families: Morality and Rationality in Policy and Practice*. London: Routledge.

Rich, A. (1977). *Of Woman Born*. London: Virago.

Richardson, D. (1993). *Women, Motherhood and Childrearing*. London: Macmillan.

Ricoeur, P. (1981). 'The narrative function', in J. Thompson (ed.), *Hermeneutics and the Human Sciences*. Cambridge: Cambridge University Press.

Robinson, S. (1990). 'Maintaining the independence of the midwifery profession: a continuing struggle', in J. Earcia, R. Kilpatrick and M. Richards (eds.), *The Politics of Maternity Care: Services for Childbearing Women in Twentieth-Century Britain*. Oxford: Clarendon Press.

Romito, P. (1997). '"Damned if you do and damned if you don't": psychological and social constraints on motherhood in contemporary Europe', in A. Oakley and J. Mitchell (eds.), *Who's Afraid of Feminism?* London: Hamish Hamilton.

Ross, E. (1995). 'New thoughts on "the oldest vocation": mothers and motherhood in recent feminist scholarship', *Signs*, 20: 397–413.

Rothman, B.K. (1989). *Recreating Motherhood*. New York: Norton Press.

—— (1992). Plenary address, Midwives Alliance of North America Conference, New York, cited in R.E. Davis-Floyd and E. Davis (1997), 'Intuition as authoritative knowledge in midwifery and home birth', in R.E. Davis-Floyd and C. Sargent (eds.), *Childbirth and Authoritative Knowledge: Cross-Cultural Perspectives*. Berkeley: University of California Press.

Ruddick, S. (1980). 'Maternal thinking', *Feminist Studies*, 6.2: 342–67.

—— (1992). 'Thinking about fathers', in B. Thorne and M. Yalom (eds.), *Rethinking the Family*. Boston: Northeastern University Press.

Sargent, C.F. and Bascope, G. (1997). 'Ways of knowing about birth in three cultures', in R.E. Davis-Floyd and C. Sargent (eds.), *Childbirth and Authoritative Knowledge: Cross-Cultural Perspectives*. Berkeley: University of California Press.

Scheper-Hughes, N. and Sargent, C. (eds.) (1998). *Small Wars. The Cultural Politics of Childhood*. Berkeley: University of California Press.

Segura, D.A. (1994). 'Working at motherhood: Chicana and Mexican immigrant mothers and employment', in E.N. Glenn, G. Chang, and L.R. Forcey (eds.), *Mothering, Ideology, Experience and Agency*. London: Routledge.

Shaw, M., Dorling, D., Gordon, D. and Davey Smith, G. (1999). *The Widening Gap: Health Inequalities and Policy in Britain*. Bristol: The Policy Press.

Social Trends, 28 (1999). Office for National Statistics, London.

Social Trends, 31 (2001). Office for National Statistics, London.

Social Trends, 33 (2003). Office for National Statistics, London.

Somers, M.R. (1994). 'The narrative constitution of identity: a relational and network approach', *Theory and Society* 23: 605–49.

Spencer, L., Ritchie, J., Lewis, J. and Dillon, L. (2003). *Quality in Qualitative Evaluation: A Framework for Assessing Research Evidence*. London: Government Chief Social Researcher's Office.

Stacey, J. (1996). *In the Name of The Family: Rethinking Family Values in a Postmodern Age*. Boston: Beacon Press.

Stanley, L. (1993). 'The knowing because experiencing subject: narratives, lives and autobiography', *Women's Studies International Forum*, 16.3: 205–15.

Stanley, I. and Wise, S. (1990). 'Method, methodology and epistemology in feminist research processes', in *Feminist Praxis: Research Theory and Epistemology in Feminist Sociology*. London: Routledge.

Stanworth, M. (ed.) (1987). *Reproductive Technologies: Gender, Motherhood and Medicine*. Cambridge: Polity Press.

Stephenson, S. (1999). 'Narrative', in G. Browning, A. Halcli and F. Webster (eds.), *Understanding Contemporary Society: Theories of the Present*. London: Sage.

Szurek, J. (1997). 'Resistance to technology-enhanced childbirth in Tuscany', in R.E. Davis-Floyd and C. Sargent (eds.), *Childbirth and Authoritative Knowledge: Cross-Cultural Perspectives*. Berkeley: University of California Press.

Tew, M. (1990; second edition, 1998). *Safer Childbirth: A Critical History of Maternity Care*. London: Chapman Hall.

The New Deal, (Miscellaneous Provisions) Order 1998, London: HMSO. http://www.hmso.gov.uk

The Personal Narratives Group (eds.) (1989). *Interpreting Women's Lives. Feminist Theory and Personal Narratives*. Indianapolis: Indiana University Press.

The Winterton Report (1992). *Report of the Social Services Select Committee on Maternity Services*. London: HMSO.

Treichler, P.A. (1990). 'Feminism, medicine and the meaning of childbirth', in M. Jacobus, E. Fox Keller and S. Shuttleworth (eds.), *Body/Politics. Women and the Discourse of Science*. London: Routledge.

Tudor Hart, J. (1971). 'The inverse care law', *Lancet*, 1: 405–12.

Unicef, 1997. http://www.unicef.org/infobycountry/bangladeshstatistics.html

Urwin, C. (1985). 'Constructing motherhood: the persuasion of normal development', in C. Steedman, C. Urwin and V. Walkerdine (eds.), *Language, Gender and Childhood*. London: Routledge & Kegan Paul.

Ussher, J.M. (1992). 'Reproductive rhetoric and the blaming of the body', in P. Nicolson and J.M. Ussher (eds.), *The Psychology of Women's Health and Health Care*. London: Macmillan.

Valdes, M.J. (ed.) (1991). *A Ricoeur Reader: Reflection and Imagination*. Toronto: Harvester Wheatsheaf.

Webster-Stratton, C. (1997). 'From parent training to community building', *The Journal of Contemporary Human Services*, 78: 156–71.

Willard, A. (1988). 'Cultural scripts for mothering', in C. Gilligan and J.V. Ward (eds.), *Mapping the Moral Domain: A Contribution of Women's Thinking to Psychological Theory and Education*. London: Harvard University Press.

Williams, G. (1984). 'The genesis of chronic illness: narrative reconstruction', *Sociology of Health and Illness*, 6: 175–200.

Yasmin, S., Osrin, D., Paul, E. and Costello, A. (2001). 'Neonatal mortality of low-birth-weight infants in Bangladesh', *Bulletin of the World Health Organisation*, 79.7: 608–14.

Index